SO GREAT A LIGHT, SO GREAT A SMOKE

A volume in the series
Conjunctions of Religion and Power in the Medieval Past
edited by Barbara H. Rosenwein

A list of titles in the series is available at
www.cornellpress.cornell.edu.

SO GREAT A LIGHT,
SO GREAT A SMOKE

THE BEGUIN HERETICS
OF LANGUEDOC

LOUISA A. BURNHAM

Cornell University Press
Ithaca and London

Copyright © 2008 by Cornell University

All rights reserved. Except for brief quotations in a review, this book, or parts thereof, must not be reproduced in any form without permission in writing from the publisher. For information, address Cornell University Press, Sage House, 512 East State Street, Ithaca, New York 14850.

First published 2008 by Cornell University Press

Printed in the United States of America

Library of Congress Cataloging-in-Publication Data
Burnham, Louisa A. (Louisa Anne), 1964–
    So great a light, so great a smoke : the Beguin heretics
of Languedoc / Louisa A. Burnham.
        p. cm — (Conjunctions of religion and power in
the medieval past)
    Includes bibliographical references and index.
    ISBN 978-0-8014-4131-8 (cloth : alk. paper)
    1.   Olivi, Pierre Jean, 1248 or 9-1298. 2.   Franciscan
Spirituals—France—Languedoc. 3.   Third orders—France—
Languedoc. 4.   Languedoc (France)—Church history.   I.
Title.   II. Series: Conjuctions of religion & power in the
medieval past.

    BX3632.L3B87 2008
    282'.4480902—dc22

                        2007031126

Cornell University Press strives to use environmentally responsible suppliers and materials to the fullest extent possible in the publishing of its books. Such materials include vegetable-based, low-VOC inks and acid-free papers that are recycled, totally chlorine-free, or partly composed of nonwood fibers. For further information, visit our website at www.cornellpress.cornell.edu.

Cloth printing   10 9 8 7 6 5 4 3 2 1

Beguinis combustis
Narbone, Bitteris,
et Montispessulani
mcccxviii–mcccliiii

✠

Requiescant in pace

Quando audivit eorum condemnationem cor suum incepit admirari qualiter tam magnum lumen quam magnum ostendebant esset ita cito conversum in tam magnum fumum.

When she first heard of their condemnation, her heart began to marvel at how so great a light as the great light that they revealed could be changed so quickly into so great a smoke.

—Jacma Sobirana, Beguine heretic

✠

CONTENTS

LIST OF MAPS

ACKNOWLEDGMENTS

I am very grateful for the financial support I have received for the research and writing of this book. A year of archival research in Paris and Montpellier was sponsored by a Fulbright grant, and several months of idyllic research and writing in Cassis were supported by a residential fellowship from the Camargo Foundation. The Northwestern Alumnae Association also supported me for a year of writing. A summer in Italy studying Franciscan sources (and visiting manuscripts) was made possible by an NEH Seminar led by the incomparable William C. Cook. At Middlebury College, I have benefited from grants from the Faculty Professional Development Fund and the C. V. Starr Schools Abroad, in addition to a year's leave from teaching responsibilities, all of which helped with last-minute manuscript questions as well as time to think and write.

But debts are accrued through means other than financial, and I have racked up my share. So many scholars, medieval and not, have been of tremendous help bringing this project to completion, and I am grateful to them all, but especially to John Ackerman, Christina Caldwell Ames, John Arnold, Marco Bartoli and the team at Capestrano, Jacques Berlioz, John Bollweg, Alain Boureau, David Burr, David Collins, Sean Field, David Flood, Holly Grieco, Kathe Hartnett, Tom Head, Sandra Hindman, Karen Hwa, William Jordan, Richard Kieckhefer, Paul Lachance, Elsa Marmursztejn, Lynn Mollenauer, Edward Muir, Piroska Nagy, Barbara Newman, Alexander Patschovsky, Sylvain Piron, Marie-Anne Polo de Beaulieu, Licia Porcedda, Michael Pretina, Nina Rowe, Kay Scheuer, Monique Zerner, Pat Zupan, and my enthusiastic fellow members of Heretics Without Borders and WiFIT (Women in the Franciscan Intellectual Tradition).

The staff in a number of libraries and archives have been of enormous help, but I would like to single out especially Guilhem Boussaguet of the Archives Municipales of Montpellier, Liberto Valls of the Archives Départementales de l'Hérault, Padre Marino Bigaroni of the Biblioteca Storico-Francescana at the Chiesa Nuova in Assisi, and the Interlibrary Loan staff at the libraries of both Northwestern University and Middlebury College. I am also grateful to Dott. Osvaldo Avallone, Direttore and Dott.ssa Maria Jacini, Ufficio fotoriproduzioni of the Biblioteca nazionale Vittorio Emanuele, Roma, and Sig. Gloria Donati of the GAP s.r.l. for their assistance in procuring the reproduction of MS Vitt. Em. 1167, fol. 75r, that appears on the jacket, as well as the permission to use it.

I would also like to express my gratitude to all my former students, who have ever been willing and eager to share in the fruits of the archives and the many pleasures of the historical endeavor.

Family and friends including Marie-Thérèse Perron, Molly Bidwell, Ruthie Gelfarb, Ellen Kennelly, Meg Miller, John Filan, and a mad group of dear British friends too numerous to mention by name have all expressed boundless enthusiasm and kept up my spirits when the slog seemed too long. I thank you all from the bottom of my heart.

And then there are my fellow founding editors of *Spatulum*, without whose friendship, camaraderie, and medieval expertise I would surely never have written a dissertation, a book, or a silly bit of detective fiction set in fourteenth-century Montpellier at all. To Michael Bailey, Jennifer Kolpacoff Deane, and Samantha Kelly, I thank you and salute you: *Unus pro omnibus, omnes pro uno!*

I am especially grateful for the help and guidance of my esteemed *Doktorvater*, Robert E. Lerner. Not only did he first point me in the direction of Na Prous Boneta and Olivi, but over the years he has been unstintingly generous with his time, his books, the contents of his file drawers, his praise, his gentle criticism, and even his vegetables.

My gratitude runs particularly deep in the case of two thoughtful readers of this manuscript, James Given and Barbara Rosenwein. Professor Given first encouraged me as a college freshman, and indeed, read my very first paper based on inquisitorial sources back in 1983. Professor Rosenwein has known me nearly as long, and has forgiven me many things, not the least for never having responded to her kind and encouraging letter back in 1986. Both have attentively read drafts of this work and have helped shape its final form in countless ways.

Portions of chapters 3 and 4 have been previously published as "Reliques et résistance chez les Béguins de Languedoc" in *Annales du Midi* 108 (2006): 352–368, and as "The Visionary Authority of Na Prous Boneta" in *Pierre de Jean Olivi (1248–1298): Pensée scolastique, dissidence spirituelle et société*, ed. Alain Boureau and Sylvain Piron (Paris, 1999), 319–339.

Last but not least come my boys. Astrolabe and his silky beagle ears have slept peacefully and encouragingly beside me through so much of the writing of this book. And to Stefano Mula, husband, friend, cheerleader, and proofreader par excellence, and most beloved companion through it all, *grazie*.

This book is dedicated with respect to those who lost their liberty and their lives in passionate pursuit of their religious aspirations, the Beguins of Languedoc.

ABBREVIATIONS

ADH   Archives Départementales de l'Hérault, Montpellier

AFH   *Archivum Franciscanum Historicum*

ALKG   *Archiv für Literatur- und Kirchengeschichte des Mittelalters*

AMM   Archives Municipales de Montpellier

Baluze-Mansi   Giovanni Mansi, *Stephani Baluzii Tutelensis Miscellanea*, 4 vols. (Paris, 1761–1764).

BF   Conrad Eubel, ed., *Bullarium Franciscanum*, vols. 5–6 (Rome, 1898–1904).

BnF   Bibliothèque nationale de France, Paris

CF   *Cahiers de Fanjeaux*

Doat   Collection Doat, Bibliothèque Nationale de France

Hist. Litt.   *Histoire Littéraire de la France*

Liber sententiarum   Bernard Gui, *Le Livre des sentences de l'inquisiteur Bernard Gui (1308–1323)*, ed. Annette Palès-Gobilliard, 2 vols. (Paris, 2002).

Manuel   Bernard Gui, *Le Manuel de l'Inquisiteur*, ed. G. Mollat, 2 vols. (Paris, 1926).

PdJO   Alain Boureau and Sylvain Piron, eds., *Pierre de Jean Olivi (1248–1298): Pensée scolastique, dissidence spirituelle et société* (Paris, 1999).

Registre   *Le Registre de Jacques Fournier (1318–1325)*, ed. Jean Duvernoy, 3 vols. (Toulouse, 1965).

Thalamus parvus   Société archéologique de Montpellier, ed., *Thalamus parvus: Le petit thalamus de Montpellier* (Montpellier, 1840).

WM   Wolfenbüttel Martyrology, in Louisa Burnham, "So Great a Light, So Great a Smoke: The Heresy and Resistance of the Beguins of Languedoc (1318–1330)" (Ph.D. diss., Northwestern University, 2000), appendix A, 315–320.

NOTE ON BEGUIN NAMES

A thorny problem for medievalists is what to call individuals whose names are given to us in Latin. For those whose names are well known to the historical record (such as Peter Olivi, Jacques Fournier, or Michael of Cesena), there is little question: I use the form most commonly encountered in English-language literature, and when there is a doubt, I use the form of the individual's name which reflects his or her geographical origins (such as Arnau de Vilanova, a Catalan). For those individuals whose origin cannot be determined, or whose careers were particularly international, I have sometimes chosen to leave their names in Latin.

The little-known heretics of Languedoc remained problematic, however. At this beginning of the twenty-first century Languedoc is decidedly French, but over the turn of the fourteenth the language its population spoke was Occitan, not French at all. It seemed oddly dismissive, therefore, to call these individuals by French names, per French academic practice (and frequently English-language practice as well). Catalan was hardly more appropriate, and English seemed very awkward. Luckily, there exist a number of documents in the medieval vernacular of Languedoc that I have been able to use as a crib; in particular the lists of consuls and *obriers* of the Commune Clôture of Montpellier. *Franciscus*, for example, is consistently *Frances* in fourteenth-century Occitan. Thus, I have plumbed the Christian names (and where possible, the surnames) of the individuals who appear in these pages from these documents. Occitan equivalents for trade name-based surnames (such as *Verrerii*) were taken from the lists of such trades found in the *Petit Thalamus* of Montpellier (Veyrier). Where my sources were inconsistent (giving Guilhem, Guillelm, and Guillem, for instance), I simply chose what seemed simplest or most mellifluous, or had some basis in later naming patterns: Guilhem has remained a peculiarity of the region, for instance, as seen in the monastery Saint-Guilhem-le-Désert.

The names of women were an even more intractable problem since they do not appear in the lists of *obriers* or consuls. Some names were also held by famous women whose names appear in Montpellier's "Chronique Romane," such as Johanna. Many other women's names, however, do not seem to have had a simple Latin equivalent, and so the scribes probably wrote them down as they sounded (Alisseta, for instance, or Prous). Unless I had firm evidence that an Occitan equivalent to a name existed, therefore, I chose to leave women's names in the form encountered in the Latin literature.

SO GREAT A LIGHT,
SO GREAT A SMOKE

Languedoc and Provence

INTRODUCTION

When you drive across the Midi, you are swiftly made to understand that the important heretics of Languedoc are the Cathars. The département of the Aude calls itself the "Pays Cathare," as it is home to Carcassonne, Fanjeaux, and several of the exceedingly popular "Châteaux Cathares." While the historian may quibble about the "catharicity" of some of the monuments promoted by the departmental commission on tourism, there is no question in the mind of the tourist: the Midi is Cathar Country. There is also little question in the minds of local governmental officials. When plans were in the works in 1998 for an international conference in Narbonne to commemorate the seven-hundredth anniversary of the death of the Franciscan Peter Olivi, representatives of the local mayor wondered aloud if there might not be a way to work some Cathars into it, since that way they would be sure to be able to get money out of the département. Cathars are indeed fascinating, and Cathars are wildly popular. Cathars are even big business, with a huge local industry catering to those who swarm southern France in search of them.

There is no need for us here to debunk either the current popularity of the Cathars or their dominance of the heretical scene during the late twelfth and early thirteenth centuries. But there is also no need to dwell on it. Events such as the Albigensian Crusade and the justly famous massacres of Béziers in 1209 and of Montségur in 1244 will always hold the popular imagination. But the present is not the past, and a hard look at the evidence compels us to admit that by the beginning of the fourteenth century, what was dominating the popular religious imagination of Languedoc was no longer the played-out martyrs' shrines of Béziers or Montségur, but the grave of a now somewhat obscure Franciscan friar named Peter Olivi in Narbonne. This friar, a prominent, though controversial theologian during his lifetime, had become in death the most popular "saint" of Languedoc, and believers came to ask his intercession from all over the region, despite the fact that his cult was never approved by the ecclesiastical hierarchy, and he was never officially made a saint. This "uncanonized saint" (as so many called him) was widely venerated, and the sheer numbers of his followers made them a force to be reckoned with. These followers were generally known as "Beguins," a term that was used throughout the Middle Ages to refer to the members of many different religious groups, especially more informal groups whose orthodoxy was in question. From the time of Olivi's death in 1298, the Beguins of Languedoc were regarded with growing suspicion, and official efforts to repress them as schismatic heretics began in 1314. From then until the late 1320s, the papacy and the inquisitors of Carcassonne and Toulouse led a campaign against them that sent over 100 to the stake and forced many others into hiding or apostasy.

Too often, the Beguins of Languedoc are confused with their homonymic cousins in northern Europe, the beguines of Flanders and Germany, pious women whose lives, while occasionally controversial, generally stayed within the bounds of orthodoxy, and who ultimately remained in the bosom of the Church. The origins of their common name are obscure, but in Languedoc, unlike Flanders, the term *Beguin* could refer to both men and women.[1] It commonly meant members of the Franciscan Third Order, lay men and women who were the most outspoken of the followers of Peter Olivi. Olivi himself once jokingly referred to his tendency to "beguinize" those who associated or corresponded with him. Becoming beguinized meant following Olivi's radical interpretation of Franciscan poverty (which got him into trouble even during his own lifetime), but most problematically, it meant adhering to his apocalyptic take on contemporary history, which he most fully expounded in a commentary on the book of Revelation finished not

---

[1] The best recent discussion of the origins of the word *beguine* can be found in Walter Simons, *Cities of Ladies: Beguine Communities in the Medieval Low Countries, 1200–1565* (Philadelphia, 2001).

long before his death. According to Olivi and to the Beguins, the last days were virtually upon them, and the apocalyptic battles of good and evil were to begin any day. As early as 1299, Beguins could be heard in the streets of Languedoc proclaiming that "Antichrist is upon us! (or almost)." The transfer of the papacy to nearby Avignon in 1305 could only have served to reinforce the Beguins' expectation that the battle would begin in their own back yard, with the minions of Antichrist to be found in and around the papacy itself.

It is perhaps not surprising, then, that ecclesiastical authorities saw these men and women as threatening, indeed, as considerably beyond the orthodox pale. But the Beguins were firmly ensconced in their urban environments in Languedoc, protected by the many friars of the Franciscan convents in southern France who were also sympathetic to Olivi and to his ideas. The friars of Narbonne and Béziers were the most outspoken, and preached to capacity crowds with Olivian themes and inflammatory rhetoric. Censuring the so-called Spiritual friars was no easier after Olivi's death than it had been before—especially since his followers soon proclaimed him to be an uncanonized saint, and successfully promoted pilgrimages to his grave in Narbonne. When the overt attempts at suppression of the Spiritual Franciscan friars and of the Beguins began, they provoked an uproar in Languedoc, an uproar that is the subject of this book.

To follow these fifteen tumultuous years in Languedoc and to understand the significance of the Beguins for both the history of southern France and the history of heresy requires us to look in a variety of directions. There is Peter Olivi himself and the movement of the Franciscan Spirituals which he inspired—a story itself inspired by Saint Francis and his radical devotion to Lady Poverty and transformed by Olivi's apocalyptic conception of contemporary history. There are the Beguins of Narbonne, Béziers, and Montpellier, men and women who first found in the company of those same Spiritual Franciscans a spiritual home and a loosely institutional identity, and who later labored to keep the apocalyptic flame alive under persecution. There are the larger numbers of men and women who declined to associate themselves publicly with the movement, but who nonetheless contributed money and other resources to help their friends and fellows escape the ever-tightening inquisitorial dragnet. There are their tactics of resistance: the evasions, the network of safe houses and secret helpers, the money they raised, their propaganda. There is the unprecedented participation of women in the resistance movement, including the remarkable case of a woman, Na Prous Boneta, whose authority as a Beguin leader was given her by her apocalyptic visions. By looking at each of these subjects in turn, and by examining sources as diverse as the sometimes dramatic testimony of accused heretics before the inquisitors of Toulouse and Carcassonne, the seemingly mundane (but nonetheless strikingly informative) registers of the notaries of the city of Montpellier, and a hitherto unpublished Beguin martyrology, this book will endeavor to illuminate the history of the Beguins, their convictions, their lives, their resistance, and even their deaths.

One of the first books I read on the subject of medieval heresy was Emmanuel Le Roy Ladurie's *Montaillou*, which I perused on the beach at the age of seventeen.[2] As so many others have been before and after me, I was captivated by its vivid detail and rich texture, made possible by the thoroughness of Le Roy Ladurie's principal source, the inquisitorial register of Bishop Jacques Fournier. Though critics have justly assailed Le Roy Ladurie for his unquestioning acceptance of the stories that the men and women of Montaillou told the inquisitor who questioned them, Le Roy Ladurie's vivid evocation of early fourteenth-century life in the uplands of the Ariège makes *Montaillou* uniquely satisfying, and has been the source of its enduring popularity.

Not every inquisitor was as thorough or kept such good records as Jacques Fournier, alas, and not even examination of the notarial records of Montpellier can fully pierce the veil that shields from us the lives of the Beguins of Languedoc. By choosing to tell the story of their heresy and resistance from the point of view of the Beguins themselves, however, I have tried to evoke for the reader the texture of their world, to personalize their struggle, and to make their choices, their sacrifices, and their resistance come to life. After a preliminary chapter that will explore the conflicts in which they were embroiled, this book consists almost entirely of their stories.

Chapter 2, "The Weapons of the Truly Weak," explores the world and resistance of the Beguins by looking at four individuals found in the inquisitorial depositions preserved from the Beguin conflict. Raimon and Bernarda d'Antusan, a Beguin couple from the small town of Cintegabelle, allow us to see how ordinarily pious men and women could come to be part of a network of secret conspirators, a stop on an "underground railway" that attempted to lead fugitives to safety. The story of Esclarmonda Durban, one of the most celebrated and venerated of the martyrs created by the inquisitors of Languedoc, shows us the importance of persecution and martyrdom to the Beguins' understanding of themselves, and one of the most telling ways in

---

[2] Emmanuel Le Roy Ladurie, *Montaillou: The Promised Land of Error*, trans. and abridged by Barbara Bray (New York, 1978). The original, *Montaillou: Village occitan de 1294–1324*, was published in Paris in 1975.

which they transformed orthodox pious practice into heretical propaganda. By examining the story of a priest from Narbonne named Bernard Maury as he fled from his hometown to Provence, we also follow the Beguins into the exile that so many of them chose as the only alternative to martyrdom.

As the networks of resistance were tried and the success of the inquisitors increased, many Beguins took refuge in the south's largest city, Montpellier, which is the subject of chapter 3, "An Urban Underground: Heresy in Montpellier." Peire de Tornamira, a Beguin priest from one of the city's wealthiest and most prestigious families, used his familial influence not only to escape prosecution himself for an extended time, but also to help his fellow believers. Though Peire's story has a brutal and tragic ending that evokes all the cruelty for which the inquisitions of the Middle Ages are famous, the story of the widow Sibillia Cazelas will remind us that the inquisitors did not always achieve everything they sought. Currents of underground resistance can sometimes, as in this case, lie hidden for centuries, only to be uncovered by a tell-tale document lying in a dusty archive.

Finally, in chapter 4, "Heretics, Heresiarchs, and Leaders," the stories of the extraordinarily bold Beguine Na Prous Boneta and the repeatedly elusive Peire Trencavel open up for us the world of those who led the Beguins in these years of resistance. Leadership in such a time of crisis necessarily ran the gamut from practical to inspirational, and it was often the unlikeliest of individuals who stepped in when the vacuum of other authority brought them to the fore. The story of Peire Trencavel, whose heretical and fugitive career stretched across southern France and northern Italy and spanned the full length of the decade of Beguin resistance, serves also as an opportunity to stand back and look at the movement as a whole.

Such an evocation of the world of the Beguin heretics of Languedoc does not come without its hazards, and the use of inquisitorial sources is chief among them. Inquisitors were not anthropologists, as one of Le Roy Ladurie's critics has reminded us, and neither were they narrative storytellers.[3] Those who testified before the inquisitors did so in peril of their lives, and the stories they told were frequently carefully crafted simply in order to satisfy the inquisitor, and not in order to tell the truth, the whole truth, and nothing but the truth. Nor are the documents that record their testimony anything close to the

---

[3] Renato Rosaldo, "From the Door of His Tent: The Fieldworker and the Inquisitor," in *Writing Culture: The Poetics and Politics of Ethnography*, ed. James Clifford and George E. Marcus (Berkeley, 1986), 77–97. But see also Carlo Ginzburg, "The Inquisitor as Anthropologist," in his *Clues, Myths, and the Historical Method*, trans. John and Anne C. Tedeschi (Baltimore, 1989).

transcripts of a modern court stenographer. The notaries who transcribed and translated them, abridged them, and ultimately shaped their current form had purposes of their own that are not those of the modern historian. We must use these sources with circumspection and respect.

One of the most exciting discoveries in recent heretical scholarship has been that of a source precious to the Beguins themselves, a martyrology that they created to honor those of their faith who perished on the stake. By using this martyrology, as well as the records of the inquisitors, I have created the most complete list of Beguins who died at the stake that is currently possible. Those who wish to follow the course of the Beguin persecution as it unfolded chronologically will find the appendix an invaluable resource.

The title of this book comes from the deposition of Jacma Sobirana of Carcassonne, a thoughtful and faithful supporter of the Spiritual friars of Languedoc and their Beguin followers. She remarked that when she heard of the condemnation of the first friars, "her heart began to marvel at how so great a light as the great light that they revealed could be changed so quickly into so great a smoke."[4]

---

[4] "Quando audivit eorum condemnationem cor suum incepit admirari qualiter tam magnum lumen quam magnum ostendebant esset ita cito conversum in tam magnum fumum." Doat 28, fol. 212v.

CHAPTER ONE
POVERTY AND APOCALYPSE
Their Patron "Saint" and His Cult

Against the will of the lax brothers, the feast of brother Peter of John was celebrated in Narbonne so solemnly by the clerics and by all the people, that never in these parts in these days was a feast so solemnly celebrated. For the people of the whole province came together to his tomb; no fewer, as they say, than come to the feast of Saint Mary of the Portiuncula.

—ANGELO CLARENO, *Epistole*

In April of the year 1313, Angelo Clareno, an Italian Franciscan friar of radical tendencies, was in Avignon, having just returned from a midwinter voyage to Majorca.[1] When he wrote a letter to some of his equally radical confrères, he told them about a celebration he had attended in Narbonne only three weeks before: the feast of a locally venerated Franciscan, Peter Olivi, celebrated on March 14. The memory was clearly still fresh and vivid. The people of Narbonne, and the entire region in fact, had come in droves to visit the site of Olivi's tomb. Doubtless, the church of the Franciscans outside the walls of Narbonne was full to bursting—a situation that reminded Angelo of the feast of Saint Mary of the Portiuncula in Assisi, where the even tinier chapel was also overrun with pilgrims annually on August 2. The comparison is even more telling if we realize that pilgrims to the feast at the Portiuncula had benefited from a

---

[1] April 3, 1313. Angelo Clareno, *Angeli Clareni Opera*, bk. I, *Epistole*, ed. Lydia Von Auw (Rome, 1980), 174–175. Angelo wrote a letter from Montpellier at Epiphany and apparently went directly to Majorca, where he spent fifty days. Allowing a generous week for each sea voyage, that places him back on the mainland just in time to spend March 14 in Narbonne. See also Von Auw, *Angelo Clareno et les spirituels italiens* (Rome, 1979), 111–112. The letter was addressed to a number of Franciscans, variously in the March of Ancona, near the city of Rome, and in the kingdom of Naples.

general indulgence since the time of Saint Francis, whereas Peter Olivi, as we shall see, was a figure of considerable controversy.[2] But Peter Olivi's followers nonetheless felt that they had something important to celebrate: the Church Council of Vienne, which had ended in May of the previous year, had not condemned their patron by name, and in his bull *Exivi de Paradiso*, Clement V gave qualified approval to certain customs of Olivi's followers. Not only that, but as Angelo also pointed out in his letter, Celestine V, the short-lived pope of 1294 who had embodied many of the hopes of these Spiritual Franciscans, was imminently to be canonized.[3] Though Angelo did not mention it, we also know that only the previous summer, Clement V had reprimanded quite a number of Franciscan superiors of the Midi hostile to the Spirituals.[4] The hierarchy seemed to be on their side, and the convents were no longer warring within themselves. While the news was not all good, neither was it all bad, and a celebration was clearly in order.[5] Angelo's letter attests to the "Olivi fever" that appears to have taken over Languedoc, making for quite a feast for Olivi, the people of Narbonne, and all those who came from across Languedoc to participate.

Nor was Narbonne the only center of this "Olivi fever." Nearby Béziers was also affected. When a Dominican friar named Raimon Barrau later

[2] John Moorman, *A History of the Franciscan Order from Its Origins to the Year 1517* (Oxford, 1968), 30n4 and 155.

[3] The canonization came on May 5, 1313. Celestine was pope from July 5 to December 13, 1294. Among the few acts of his brief pontificate, brought to an end by his abdication, was the creation of a new order, the Poor Hermits of Pope Celestine, which was composed of radical Spirituals (including Angelo Clareno) who had been suffering in the Order of Friars Minor. Unsurprisingly, many of the Franciscan rigorists revered Celestine as an "angel pope." See Robert E. Lerner, "On the Origins of the Earliest Latin Pope Prophecies: A Reconsideration," *Fälschungen im Mittelalter,* Monumenta Germaniae historica, Schriften 33, vol. 5 (Hannover, 1988), 611–635.

[4] The bull summoning them, dated July 23, 1312, can be found in *Archiv für Literatur- und Kirchengeschichte des Mittelalters* (hereafter abbreviated *ALKG*), 2:158–159, and also in *Bullarium Franciscanum* (hereafter *BF*) 5:89.

[5] The two bulls dealing with Olivi and the Spirituals, *Fidei catholicae fundamento* and *Exivi de Paradiso*, are dated 1312 (May 6 and November 20), but Clement V did not approve their formal publication until the spring of 1314—and this was interrupted by his death in April. It was not until October 25, 1317, that the letters were sent out by John XXII. Evidently, their contents were well known by at least some (see Clareno, *Angeli Clareni Opera*, bk. 1, *Epistle,* 110n2 and 174n4). Malcolm Lambert seems to think that the Conventuals had "come out ahead" with these two bulls (*Franciscan Poverty* [London, 1961], 199), but Angelo's letter to his brethren implies that some of the Spirituals, at least, saw the decisions as favorable to their cause. Angelo wrote: "Now, or so we hope, Celestine will be canonized, and the constitutions from Vienne will be published. There are many things in these constitutions that are useful for the servants of God, and will help to hold back perverse men."

remembered his years in Béziers, the year 1313 stuck out in his memory because it was in that very year that his friendship with the bishop of Béziers, Guilhem Frédol, came to an end. As he wrote, "the lord Bishop, his officials, the entire curia and the canons supported the Beguins and Spirituals... unto death, considering them to be saints of God and fundaments of the Church of God, sent by God as if they were apostles, and the entire city of Béziers followed them."[6] Since Barrau was hostile to Olivi and his followers, his intimate friendship with the bishop necessarily ended. And from 1313 on, Raimon Barrau complained, Béziers, like Narbonne, was afire with enthusiasm for Olivi, for his cult, and for the Spiritual Franciscan friars who followed his teachings and venerated his memory.

Who was this "uncanonized saint" whom they venerated, this Peter Olivi, that his grave should attract such crowds, not to mention so much hostility? What were these communities of Spiritual Franciscan friars who kept his memory alive? What were the issues that they held so sacred and that brought them into such conflict with other groups in the Church? Who were the laypeople who both flocked to Olivi's grave and supported the convent in Béziers with such enthusiasm and devotion? To learn the answers, which set the stage for this entire book, we need first to make a foray into the charged and frequently hostile world of thirteenth-century Franciscan politics and the debate over Franciscan poverty that dominated them. We will then discuss one of the most controversial figures of the poverty controversy, Peter Olivi, whose death in 1298 did not close that debate, but sharpened it. Then we will return to Languedoc and its struggles over heresy and orthodoxy and, finally, to the crowds gathered around Olivi's grave, the penitents known as the Beguins.

---

[6] P. Botineau, ed., "Les tribulations de Raimond Barrau, O.P. (1295–1338)," *Mélanges d'Archéologie et d'Histoire, École Française de Rome* 76 (1965): 475–528 at 505. I am grateful to Robert Lerner for calling this document to my attention. See also: Alan Friedlander, *The Hammer of the Inquisitors: Brother Bernard Délicieux and the Struggle against the Inquisition in Fourteenth-Century France* (Leiden, 2000), 233; and *Processus Bernardi Delitiosi: The Trial of Fr. Bernard Délicieux, 3 September–8 December 1319*, ed. Friedlander (Philadelphia, 1996), 135. Raimon Barrau places the beginning of the split at the arrival of Bernard Délicieux in Béziers, an event that took place in 1313. Bernard Délicieux, a Franciscan friar from Montpellier who was originally part of the convent of Carcassonne, was a virtually professional rabble-rouser against the inquisitors of Languedoc, first on behalf of the Cathars, and later on behalf of the Spirituals. The precise date of Bernard's arrival in Béziers is not known, though it was probably in the late summer or fall. It was certainly after the election of Alexander of Alessandria as Franciscan minister general, an event that took place at the General Chapter of Barcelona, held at Pentecost (June 3, 1313). I thank Alan Friedlander for taking the time to discuss the timing of Barrau's arrival in Béziers with me.

Because the Order of Saint Francis was founded by Francis the *poverello* (the "little poor man"), it was perhaps destined to struggle over poverty. The image of Saint Francis stripping himself naked before the bishop of Assisi is one of the most striking of the Middle Ages and has captured the imagination of centuries of inquirers and artists. How could poverty get any more radical than that: "naked, following a naked Christ"?[7] According to his biographers, Francis even insisted that the habit, breeches, and hood he wore on his deathbed be loaned to him by someone else so that he could leave this world with no more than he had brought into it. Thomas of Celano wrote:

> Meanwhile, as their sobs somewhat subsided, his guardian, who by divine inspiration better understood the saint's wish, quickly got up, took the tunic, underwear and sackcloth hood, and said to the father: "I command you under holy obedience to acknowledge that I am lending you this tunic, underwear and hood. And so that you know that they in no way belong to you, I take away all your authority to give them to anyone." The saint rejoiced, and his heart leaped for joy seeing that he had kept faith until the end with Lady Poverty.[8]

Here was the crux of the matter. The thirteenth-century Franciscan Order as a whole held that Francis's accustomed poverty was in imitation of Christ and the apostles, who, they maintained, had owned nothing, either individually or in common.[9] In their understanding of this absolute poverty, they claimed that while Christ and the apostles may have *used* certain things (as

[7] This phrase, originally written by Saint Jerome, was most memorably borrowed by Walter Map to describe Waldensian heretics, not Saint Francis. Francis and Waldo had many things in common, however, including their commitment to apostolic poverty. Lambert considers it a central image in the thought of Francis himself. Lambert, *Franciscan Poverty*, 61–62; Walter Wakefield and Austin P. Evans, *Heresies of the High Middle Ages* (New York, 1991), 204.

[8] He absolutely required the head gear because of the eye cauterization he had recently suffered in Rieti: "He had been wearing a sackcloth cap on his head to cover the scars he had received in the treatment of his eyes; what was really needed for this was a smooth cap of the softest and most expensive wool." 2 Celano, in *Francis of Assisi: Early Documents* 2, trans. Regis J. Armstrong et al. (New York, 2000), 386. A very similar story is in Bonaventure's *Legenda Maior*, ibid., 642. See also Moorman, *History*, 76.

[9] This was also to be the sticking point of the separate poverty controversy of the 1320s. In a series of bulls ending with *Cum inter nonnullos* in 1323, John XXII repudiated this belief, causing a break with the Franciscan Minister General Michael of Cesena, who had been hostile to the Spirituals, and a further split in the order itself. For a recent

Saint Francis used the habit, breeches, and hood on his deathbed), they did not *own* them. Franciscans believed that it was their particular calling to imitate Christ and the apostles in this regard in a manner that was unique among medieval religious orders. Such a high standard of poverty may well have worked for an individual like Saint Francis (especially one with a "guardian" who was able so tactfully to balance the dying man's need for bodily protection and his equally pressing spiritual need to be absolutely poor), but it was a challenge for an entire order to follow to the letter.[10]

In his bull *Quo elongati* (September 28, 1230) Pope Gregory IX, a personal friend of Saint Francis, created the definition of Franciscan poverty which was to govern the order throughout the rest of the thirteenth century: though the Rule declared that Franciscans were to live "without property," such a declaration was impossible to take literally, and so long as the pope or the cardinal-protector of the order legally owned them, houses, books, furniture, and all other goods were acceptable for Franciscans to use. But while Pope Gregory no doubt thought that he was settling the question once and for all, *Quo elongati* consistently failed to satisfy the more radical members of the order and thus simply fueled the debate.

During much of the next thirty or forty years, Franciscans wrangled over these questions. Pope Innocent IV (no particular advocate of Franciscan poverty) issued two bulls further relaxing the regime of the Franciscan Rule in the 1240s.[11] Shortly thereafter, however, beginning in 1247, a new

---

discussion of these events more focused than that of Lambert, *Franciscan Poverty*, 208–246, see Andrea Tabarroni, *Paupertas Christi et Apostolorum: L'ideale francescano in discussione (1322–1324)* (Rome, 1990). Also, "The Franciscan Crisis under John XXII," *Franciscan Studies* 32 (1972): 123–143, and Thomas Turley, "John XXII and the Franciscans: A Reappraisal," in *Popes, Teachers, and Canon Law in the Middle Ages*, ed. James Ross Sweeney and Stanley Chodorow (Ithaca, 1989), 74–88.

[10] Debate over the "true" character of Franciscan poverty (and especially Francis's poverty) still rages. The first chapter of Lambert's survey of Franciscan poverty is devoted to a review of the literature and its various camps: *Franciscan Poverty*, 1–30. Some scholars, notably Kajetan Esser and Lambert with him, have argued that it was not Francis himself who was seeking a greater degree of compliance with poverty, but the radical friars around him in his last moments by whom he was strongly influenced at a time when he was most vulnerable. In any event, the successors to those radical friars took it as Francis's last word. Even the most pro-poverty historians, however, have had to be realistic about the difficulties of its radical practice by an entire order.

[11] *Ordinem vestrum* (1245) and *Quanto studiosius* (1247). *Ordinem vestrum* broadened the conception of the occasions when Franciscans (through an intermediary) might use money to procure commodities, simplified the way in which this might occur, and officially named the papacy as the legal owner of all the Franciscans' property. *Quanto studiosius* made it easier for Franciscans to arrange for agents to handle their goods. Lambert, *Franciscan Poverty*, 101.

minister general named John of Parma sought to return the order to a more primitive style of both rule and poverty. His stance was not merely a political or bureaucratic one; as he tirelessly walked from convent to convent across Europe with a single habit and a single companion, he appeared the very embodiment of Francis's ideals. Though it is premature to speak of the order splitting into "parties" at this stage, clearly it was polarizing into two groups: those friars who welcomed relaxations of the Rule and a moderate lifestyle, and those whose conception of poverty was anything but moderate, echoing Saint Francis himself. Later these two groups would coalesce into openly hostile factions known as the Conventuals (or the Community) and the Spirituals.[12]

With the person of John of Parma, we are plunged directly into another one of the most contested topics among scholars of the Franciscans: Joachim of Fiore. This twelfth-century Calabrian abbot, monastic founder, exegete, and prophet sought out by Richard the Lion-Hearted among others, was either a saint or a devil, depending on whom you ask. But certain of Joachim's ideas—and contemporary interpretations of them—were very widely accepted. At the end of the twelfth century, Joachim had written that the world was "trembling on the brink of the third age"[13] and had prophesied the emergence of a new monastic order. When Franciscans read his words, they interpreted this new order as themselves. Not only did Francis found the order that was to lead the new Age of the Spirit, but they went on to claim that the Angel of the Sixth Seal (Revelation 7:2) was Francis himself. Thus three important elements of radical Franciscan thought were extrapolated from Joachim: the idea that history was about to change in a tremendous upheaval, the idea that the Franciscan Order was to play a crucial role in this crisis, and the idea that, in this time of trouble, the order was likely to come into direct conflict with the ecclesiastical hierarchy.[14]

Nor was it only the most radical of the friars who saw the order this way: John of Parma's more moderate successor, Saint Bonaventure, identified Francis as the Angel of the Sixth Seal in the prologue of his *Legenda Maior* in

[12] According to David Burr, it is only after 1279 and *Exiit qui seminat* that this split gradually begins to occur. David Burr, *Olivi and Franciscan Poverty: The Origins of the Usus Pauper Controversy* (Philadelphia, 1989), 29. The first use of the term "spiritual" as referring to rigorists on poverty, however, appears to have been by Hugh of Digne in Provence in the middle of the thirteenth century in his *Dispute between a Zealot for Poverty and His Domestic Enemy*: Burr, *Olivi and Franciscan Poverty*, 20, 37n114.

[13] David Burr, *The Persecution of Peter Olivi* (Philadelphia, 1976), 10.

[14] Marjorie Reeves, *The Influence of Prophecy in the Later Middle Ages: A Study in Joachimism*, rev. ed. (South Bend, IN, 1993), 175.

1263, thus placing this apocalyptic claim squarely in the mainstream of the order.[15] The reliance of Bonaventure's theology of history on Joachim has even been trumpeted by no less a rigorist theologian than Joseph Ratzinger, now Pope Benedict XVI.[16] Devotion to Joachite ideas and interpretations was certainly strongest among the most radical advocates for Franciscan poverty, however, and in many cases the two went together.

Under Bonaventure's aegis, another attempt was made to codify and define the poverty of Francis and the order, an attempt that would set the scene for the conflicts of the following century. Toward the end of his life in 1269, Bonaventure wrote his widely read *Apologia pauperum*, which became not merely the official doctrine of the order on poverty, but was accepted as such by the papacy.[17] We can best explain Bonaventure's solution by returning to the anecdote of Francis and the habit that he "borrowed" so shortly before his death. Under the Seraphic Doctor's scholarly pen the concept that had made Francis so joyful was enshrined in scholastic prose, and bolstered with arguments from scripture. On his deathbed, Francis had been content to have the "use" (*usus*) of the habit and underwear supplied for him, but he refused to have "dominion" (*dominium*) over them, a distinction which his guardian so carefully preserved in his "loan" of the habit to the dying man. Francis was unable to give the habit away to anyone else because it was not his to give. According to Bonaventure, it was specifically this renunciation of dominion which was at the foundation of Christ's own perfection of poverty: "This standard of poverty, perfect as by special prerogative, Christ observed in himself, and gave to the apostles to observe and gave as a counsel to those who desired to follow their steps."[18] By following in Francis's path (and Christ's) and renouncing dominion, the Franciscans thus believed that they were able to achieve a higher standard of poverty than any other order.

This Bonaventuran doctrine of the absolute poverty of Christ and the apostles became not only a Franciscan rallying cry, but also a convenient target for nay-sayers. Pope Nicholas III (who before becoming pope had been cardinal-protector of the Franciscan Order) sought to put an end to the

[15] *Francis of Assisi: Early Documents* 2, 527. The *Legenda Maior* was soon declared to be the only official life of Saint Francis, and all other lives were declared to have been superseded by this one, and ordered to be burned. See Moorman, *History*, 286–287.

[16] Joseph Ratzinger, *The Theology of History in St. Bonaventure*, trans. from the German by Zachary Hayes (Chicago, 1971). Prior to his election to the papacy in April 2005, Ratzinger was head of the Vatican Congregation for the Defense of the Faith (successor to the early modern Roman Inquisition) and a respected theologian.

[17] In *The Works of Bonaventure*, trans. José de Vinck (Paterson, NJ, 1966), vol. 4.

[18] In Lambert, *Franciscan Poverty*, 129.

struggles both inside and outside the order with a bull meant to be definitive, *Exiit qui seminat*, promulgated in 1279. The bull's substance (and frequently its wording) was borrowed from Bonaventure, though Nicholas and the committee that helped him to draft it sought an even greater precision in the legalistic terminology of property and poverty. "Use" and "dominion" were to remain fighting words, but they were joined by "property" (*proprietas*), "possession" (*possessio*), "usufruct" (*ususfructus*), "the right to use" (*ius utendi*), and "pure use" (*simplex usus facti*). This last was the one held by the Franciscans for temporal goods, "a license to use certain goods, revocable at the will of the conceder," as one scholar has defined it.[19] This, presumably, was what Francis had held in his habit, underwear, and hood.

Exiit qui seminat was only moderately successful in quieting the debate, however. In the last two decades of the thirteenth century, polarization between rigorists and moderates in the order increased dramatically, and it was a friar from the south of France, Peter Olivi, whose ideas and writings served as the primary propaganda for those insisting on a yet more radical interpretation of Franciscan poverty. It is at this stage that we may begin to speak comfortably of Spirituals and Conventuals.[20] Olivi formulated a concept known as the *usus pauper*, or "poor use," to describe the way in which Franciscans were to use goods they did not own (or have dominion over). "Poor use" called for a limited use of goods and declared that violations of such a restricted and moderate use constituted an essential breach of the Franciscan vow of poverty. For Olivi, poor use was the real issue, not controversies over dominion and pure use. He based this on common sense and popular opinion as much as on anything else. Who can deny that "the man in the street" would consider the friars hypocrites if they professed "absolute poverty" by not owning (or having dominion over) anything, but dressed in sumptuous clothes and ate like kings? The figure of fat and bibulous Friar Tuck, surely a parody of actual friars, comes swiftly to mind. Poverty, for those unversed in scholastic distinctions (and here we may undoubtedly include Francis himself), really ought to be about making do with less.

Though poor use was interpreted in many ways, one example, which was to become emblematic for the Spirituals in southern France, will serve to make the point. The question of what the friars were to wear had long been controversial. In his Testament, Francis waxed nostalgic about the habit "patched inside and outside" that he and the early friars had worn—and in

---

[19] Ibid., 144.
[20] Though Burr (*Persecution*, 7) rejects the claim that there was ever a "party": "Least of all is there any evidence of a 'spiritual party' which Olivi could join and later head."

fact, the various relics of his habit preserved in Assisi and at La Verna are quite evocative.[21] The Spirituals did their best to imitate Francis, and a later pope described the resulting habits as "short, tight, unusual, and squalid."[22] The habits were presumably short and tight in order not to waste cloth, and the friars wore them and patched them until they wore out entirely, thus making them squalid. That they were unusual (or distinctive) is made clear by the fact that lay observers often referred to the Spirituals simply as "the friars of the short habits."[23]

While there were groups of Spirituals to be found in Italy,[24] they were especially numerous in the south of France. They formed a majority in the convents of Narbonne, Béziers, and Carcassonne, and were also certainly present in the convents of Marseille, Sisteron, Avignon, Arles, and Orange on the Provençal side of the Rhône, in Montpellier in Languedoc, and also in certain convents in the Franciscan province of Aquitaine, which began in Toulouse.[25]

PETER OLIVI, THE "UNCANONIZED SAINT"

Since the Franciscan Spirituals revered Peter Olivi as their teacher and prophet in matters of both poverty and apocalyptic, it would behoove us to

---

[21] A photograph of the Assisi habit is in Malcolm Lambert, *Medieval Heresy: Popular Movements from the Gregorian Reform to the Reformation*, 2nd ed. (Oxford, 1992), 191.

[22] "Curtos, strictos, inusitatos et squalidos," in *Quorumdam exigit, BF* 5:128b.

[23] These habits, torn, patched, and also short had appeared as early as the 1240s in the March of Ancona. This was under the generalship of Crescentius of Iesi (1244–1247), who reportedly encountered "a sect of brothers who,...despising the institutions of the order and thinking themselves better than others, wanted to live as they wished and attributed all to the spirit, wearing cloaks so short that they came up to their buttocks." (The anecdote was reported many years later, by Pelegrino da Bologna.) Burr (*Olivi and Franciscan Poverty*, 17) notes our lack of understanding of what was really going on in the March: "Pelegrino's story is intriguing but not very informative. What did these scantily attired Franciscans want? What did they complain against?" The only answer comes from Angelo Clareno, who naturally turns them into proto-partisans of the fourteenth-century Italian Spirituals, though this cannot be proven.

[24] Though there were certainly points of connection between the Spirituals in Italy (often referred to as the *fraticelli de paupere vita*) and the Spirituals in Languedoc, this book is primarily concerned with those in the south of France. For information on the Spirituals in Italy, see Von Auw, *Angelo Clareno*; Decima Douie, *The Nature and Effect of the Heresy of the Fraticelli* (Manchester, 1932); Gian Luca Potestà, *Angelo Clareno dai poveri eremiti ai fraticelli* (Rome, 1990); and idem, *Storia ed escatologia in Ubertino da Casale* (Milan, 1980).

[25] In 1312, Clement V summoned the *custodes* of the convents of Narbonne, Marseille, Sisteron, Avignon, Arles, Montpellier, and Alès, the guardians of Montpellier, Narbonne, Orange, and Avignon, and three others, to reproach them for their persecution of the Spirituals. Pierre Péano, "Ministres provinciaux de Provence et les Spirituels," *Cahiers*

say a little more about him. Who was Peter Olivi? His life, works, trials, and posthumous persecution have all received more full descriptions elsewhere.[26] Only the briefest summary is possible here. Born in the town of Sérignan, near Béziers, in 1248, Petrus Johannis Olivi entered the Franciscan convent of Béziers at the age of twelve.[27] Though his name is best translated literally as "Peter of John Olivi," most English-language scholars refer to him simply as Peter Olivi or brother Peter of John.[28] By the late 1260s, he was a student in Paris, where he heard Bonaventure lecture. In subsequent years he lived and taught at Narbonne (probably 1278–79) as well as other convents of the Midi, at Santa Croce in Florence (1287–1289), Montpellier (1283, and 1289

---

de Fanjeaux (hereafter *CF*) 10 (1975): 41–65, at 57. The papal letter ordering them to appear is found in *BF* 5:89, and *ALKG* 2:158–159. The presence of friars in the province of Aquitaine is attested to in Livarius Oliger, "*Fr. Bertrandi de Turre processus contra spiri-tuales Aquitaniae* (1315) *et Card. Iacobi de Columna litterae defensoriae spiritualium Provinciae* (1316)," *Archivum Franciscanum Historicum* (hereafter *AFH*) 16 (1923): 323–355.

[26] The best introduction to the subject of Peter Olivi remains Burr, *Persecution*, supplemented especially by his two other books, *Olivi and Franciscan Poverty* and *Olivi's Peaceable Kingdom* (Philadelphia, 1993). The published proceedings of two recent conferences (Grottaferrata, 1997, and Narbonne, 1998) are indispensable complements (*AFH* 91 [1998], and Alain Boureau and Sylvain Piron, eds., *Pierre de Jean Olivi (1248–1298): Pensée scolastique, dissidence spirituelle et société* [Paris, 1999], hereafter *PdJO*). Additionally, the as-yet-unpublished thesis of Sylvain Piron is invaluable for its chronology of Olivi's works. "Parcours, d'un intellectuel franciscain. D'une théologie vers une pensée sociale: L'œuvre de Pierre de Jean Olivi (ca. 1248–1298) et son traité *De contractibus*" (Ph.D. diss., L'École des hautes études en sciences sociales, Paris, 1999), especially in the first part, chaps. 3 and 4. The online "micro-révue" *Oliviana: Mouvements et dissidences spirituels xiiie-xive siècles*, directed by Alain Boureau and Sylvain Piron, presents new work on Olivi and those inspired by him (http://www.oliviana.org). See, for example, Robert E. Lerner, Sylvain Piron, and Gian Luca Potestà, "Notes bibliographiques (2002–2003)," *Oliviana* 1 (2003), http://www.oliviana.org/document23.html.

[27] Though the word "convent" may evoke a community of nuns to many readers, male Franciscans even today use the term to describe the communities in which they live and study. In the Middle Ages (in sharp contrast to present practice), a convent was generally a more open community than a monastery. Franciscans were not cloistered, as they considered themselves to be an order of preaching friars, and were thus frequently out in their communities.

[28] His Latin name is often shortened simply to Petrus Johannis in the sources. French scholars frequently write his name as Pierre Déjean Olieu, which is no doubt closer to being correct than Pierre Jean, or Pierre Jean d'Olieu. French, however, was not Olivi's native language; he spoke a language more akin to modern Occitan. This leaves us with Peire de Johan Olieu, which would be the most correct of all. In any event, English-language convention has settled on Peter Olivi, and to avoid linguistic squabbles and the unnecessary unwieldiness of Peter of John Olivi (or Peire de Johan Olieu), so shall I. See Burr, *Persecution*, 6, and *PdJO*, 9n1.

to no later than 1292),[29] and again in Narbonne until his death in 1298. His writings on subjects other than evangelical poverty have earned him the accolades of both theologians and philosophers, and in recent years there has been a considerable efflorescence of interest in Olivi studies. As we look at the Beguins of Languedoc, however, we are more interested in Peter Olivi as an inspirational figure than as a theologian. For this, it was primarily his writings on "poor use," adopted by the Spirituals as a way of life, and his apocalyptic exegesis that are most important. In Olivi's own mind, the two were indissolubly linked.

Though events like the siege of Waco and Y2K have brought apocalypticism into common currency, they have also given it a bad name. But as David Burr has pointed out, in the thirteenth century there was nothing "inherently ridiculous" about the present applicability of apocalyptic. Even the most cautious of theologians would have agreed that "a careful examination of Daniel 7 or Revelation 6 might enable the Christian to construct a theology of history which would explain the past, illuminate the present and even predict the future."[30]

Yet, while the genre of apocalyptic exegesis may have been thoroughly respectable, not all apocalyptic commentary was accepted by the whole Church, and Olivi's 1297 commentary on the Apocalypse was controversial from the beginning.[31] To Olivi's followers it was equal to the Gospels, while to his detractors it was dangerously full of heretical statements. It was ultimately condemned as heretical, but not until 1326, twenty-eight years after Olivi's death.[32] Opinions differ widely as to the justice of that judgment: the Franciscan scholar David Flood has called the commentary "bold yet orthodox," while Warren Lewis has described Olivi as "a thirteenth-century Moonie" with a load of heretical ideas.[33]

[29] Sylvain Piron, "Marchands et confesseurs. Le *Traité des contrats* d'Olivi dans son contexte (Narbonne, fin XIIIe-début XIVe siècle)," in Congrès des médiévistes de l'enseignement supérieur, *L'argent au Moyen Âge* (Paris, 1998), 289–308.

[30] Burr, *Persecution*, 9.

[31] Ibid., 17.

[32] The statement of the fugitive friars, originally published by Baluze, has been recently republished in Guido Terreni, Bertrand de la Tour, Guillaume de Laudun, Nicolas de Saint-Just, Laurentius Anglicus, Simon Anglicus, Arnaud Royard et Pierre de la Palud, "Littera magistrorum," *Oliviana* 2 (2006), http://www.oliviana.org/document179.html.

[33] Raoul Manselli also places Olivi on the orthodox end of the spectrum. See Burr, *Olivi's Peaceable Kingdom*, x; David Flood, "Poverty as Virtue, Poverty as Warning, and Peter of John Olivi," *PdJO*, 157–172, esp. 171; and Warren Lewis, "Peter John Olivi, Author of the *Lectura super Apocalipsim*: Was He Heretical?" *PdJO*, 135–156.

Fourteenth-century critics went nearly as far as Lewis. Gui Terré, the Carmelite bishop of Elne, and a well-informed opponent of Olivi's ideas, wrote a *Summa* on heresy which attacked Olivi (and Joachim along with him) in considerable detail and with considerable venom: "These two [*isti duo*], Joachim and Peter of John, have said and written many fatuous and fictitious, reckless, blasphemous, and heretical things."[34] Primarily, he accuses the two (whom he appears to view as essentially one and the same, Olivi simply taking his master a little farther down the slippery slope) of misconstruing the course of history, with their definition of the third age coming under particular fire. The commission whose report helped to condemn Olivi in 1326 was more polite and refrained from *ad hominem* attacks, but nonetheless characterized a vast array of Olivi's positions as heretical.[35]

All polemics aside, the most balanced view of Olivi's apocalypticism comes from David Burr, who has scoured the libraries for other mendicant commentaries on the Apocalypse and thus placed Olivi in the context of other similar works of his time and milieu. According to Burr, Olivi was indeed simultaneously temerarious and conservative, wishing to preserve both an understanding of poverty sanctified by Francis himself and the apocalyptic interpretation of the role of both Francis and his order. Though he shared certain characteristics with other commentators, Olivi differed widely from his contemporaries in his perception of the immediacy of the events he predicted. While other commentators may have used Joachim as an authority to be mined selectively, for Olivi Joachim was a prophet whose revelations had been both accurate and timely.

The characteristic elements of Olivi's apocalypticism emerge from both friendly and hostile accounts. His view of the progression of history was borrowed from Joachim and modified. Like Joachim, he subscribed to the notion of history as a double pattern of sevens, with the times of the Old Testament and the New each divided into seven periods. Also like Joachim, he superimposed a second, Trinitarian pattern (three ages, one each of the Father, Son, and Holy Spirit) upon the pattern of sevens, and as Burr has described it, "the two patterns fit together in such a way that the seventh period of church history corresponds with the third age in the threefold

---

[34] Gui Terré, *Summa de haeresibus* (Paris, 1528), fol. 94v. Gui Terré was both a member of the commission which condemned Olivi's Apocalypse commentary in 1326 and one of the two bishops who investigated the Catalan pamphlet which translated (or rather adapted) it (José Pou y Marti, *Visionarios, Beguinos y Fraticelos Catalanes [Siglos XIII–XV]*, rev. ed. [Madrid, 1991], 483–512). The *Summa* was written in 1342.

[35] Giovanni Mansi, *Stephani Baluzii Tutelensis Miscellanea* (Paris, 1761–1764; hereafter Baluze-Mansi), 2:258–270. See also Lewis, "Peter John Olivi," 138–146.

pattern, although the third age can also be said to begin in the sixth period."[36] For Olivi, these various periods could overlap, even significantly, and he saw mankind poised on the lengthy cusp between the fifth and the sixth periods. The fifth period was a time of the progressively increasing corruption of the Church: by the end, "practically the whole church from head to foot is corrupted and thrown into disorder and turned, as it were, into a new Babylon."[37] He is speaking of his own day. Of all the crimes of which he accuses the Church, the worst is that of the rejection of poverty, in particular the Franciscan interpretation of poverty of which he himself was the foremost promoter: poor use. This understanding of the apocalyptic significance of Francis's poverty is central to Olivi's thought.[38] For Olivi, rejection of it placed the Church as not merely "starting down a long slide," but as being uncomfortably close to the bottom.[39]

For Olivi, there was simply no question that Francis was the Angel of the Sixth Seal (Revelation 7:2): he had himself heard Bonaventure declare it in Paris. In fact, he worked carefully through the entire equation in his own writings, declaring that Francis was "the renewer of the evangelical life and rule to be propagated and glorified in the sixth and seventh periods, and its greatest observer after Christ and his mother."[40] The sixth period had begun with Francis and was "the hinge on which all of later church history turns," as Burr has put it.[41] In the sixth period, spiritual understanding (including the understanding of evangelical poverty) would begin to increase and "spiritual men," modeled after Francis himself, would begin to defend their ideals against those set against them, the so-called carnal church. Their illumination would rival and in time surpass even the understanding of the apostles.[42] It was not only Francis's stigmata that marked him as an *alter Christus*, another Christ, but also his poverty. Thus, the various assaults on Franciscan poverty of the thirteenth century were far more than just an attack on a religious order: they were an essential part of the apocalyptic crisis.[43]

[36] Burr, *Olivi's Peaceable Kingdom*, 1.
[37] Quoted ibid., 76.
[38] Ibid., 87–88.
[39] Ibid., 91.
[40] Ibid., 119.
[41] Ibid., 77.
[42] Terré, *Summa de haeresibus*, fol. 99r. "They say that the Gospel was not preached by the Apostles except according to the word, and not according to the spiritual understanding. They also say that the Holy Spirit will more perfectly exercise dominion in the conversion of the gentiles through the preachers of their order in the third age than through the Apostles, or the preachers of the second age."
[43] Burr, *Olivi's Peaceable Kingdom*, 88, 110.

It was Olivi's interpretation of the imminence and the dimensions of that crisis—though his timetable is a bit vague, he certainly expected it to begin within twenty-five years—that set him apart from the mainstream of commentators on the Apocalypse and won for himself the especial wrath of critics like Gui Terré. Olivi saw the world trembling on the brink of crisis, with the advent of Antichrist virtually upon it and the overthrow of the established order through violence not far behind. The Church around him was little better than a "carnal Church" in perpetual apocalyptic struggle with the "spiritual Church," whose eventual triumph would usher in the sweet refreshment of the third age and the seventh period. Olivi declared that the third age would be characterized by a new *intellectus spiritualis*, or spiritual intelligence, where the meaning of scripture (especially the book of Revelation) and of apostolic poverty would become clearer and would be spread to those who lived holy lives and delighted in "chaste and sweet contemplation," instead of to those who approached it through scholarship.[44] The progress of spiritual illumination was inevitable with the approach of the third age, and as Robert E. Lerner has pointed out, most believed that "the gift was showered most copiously on the humble."[45] However just some scholars may be about the essential orthodoxy of Olivi's positions on Franciscan poverty, his critics were right to fear his endowing them with such apocalyptic significance. They were indeed revolutionary and proceeded rather quickly to spark a revolution.[46]

Peter Olivi died on March 14, 1298, not long after completing this commentary. His death was noted by his brothers as the passing of a particularly saintly man. They composed a short text celebrating it, which, in the absence of a real *vita*, was frequently read aloud by those who soon began venerating him as a saint. It briefly documents his life and death, highlights his learning, and also reveals his mystical inspiration. It is worth quoting in full, since it was so central in the way Olivi's followers understood him:

In the name of our Lord Jesus Christ who is eternally blessed, in the year of his incarnation 1297, on Friday, March 14, at the sixth hour, in the city

---

[44] Burr, "Olivi, Apocalyptic Expectation, and Visionary Experience," *Traditio* 41 (1985): 273–288, at 280.

[45] Robert E. Lerner, "Ecstatic Dissent," *Speculum* 67 (1992): 33–57, at 54.

[46] As Burr observes, "apocalyptic interpretation of the *usus pauper* controversy often functioned as a self-fulfilling prophecy. It not only encouraged dissenters to take a strong stand, but provided a context in which punishment of dissent functioned as evidence that the dissenters were righteous and the persecutors minions of Antichrist. Thus such punishment was more likely to corroborate the dissenters' views than to alter them." Burr, *Olivi's Peaceable Kingdom*, 71.

of Narbonne, the most holy father and distinguished doctor Peter John Olivi migrated from this world in the fiftieth year of his life and the thirtieth since his entry into the order of Brothers Minor. He was born in the castle of Sérignan, which lies a thousand paces from the sea in the diocese of Béziers, and his most holy body rests in sanctity in the church of the Brothers Minor at Narbonne, in the middle of the choir. The most admirable and perfect progress of this holy man's conversion and the glorious end of his sojourn are more fittingly venerated in holy silence than exposed to the baying attack of vicious dogs. There is one thing, however, that I think should not be passed over. The venerable father, toward the end of his passing, after he had received holy unction and with the entire convent of Brothers Minor of Narbonne standing about, said all of his knowledge had been infused in him by God, and that in the church at Paris at the third hour he had suddenly been illumined by the Lord Jesus Christ.[47]

At the time of his death, Peter Olivi was clearly thought to be far more than just a philosopher or a theologian, far more than a writer on the subject of poverty, and even far more than merely an inspirational master of apocalyptic. To the brothers he was closest to in his own convent of Narbonne, and soon to many others outside that convent in Languedoc, Olivi was quite simply a saint—uncanonized so far, to be sure, but nevertheless venerated as such. The brothers buried him in a place of honor at the very center of

---

[47] Bernard Gui, *Le Manuel de l'Inquisiteur*, ed. G. Mollat, 2 vols. (Paris, 1926; hereafter *Manuel*), 1:190–193. The translation is from "Bernard Gui: The Inquisitor's Manual" by David Burr, http://www.history.vt.edu/Burr/heresy/beguins/Gui_beguins.html. The precise author of the text is unknown. Another version of the text exists in two manuscripts, both of which contain a summary of Olivi's ideas on the *usus pauper* in the form of a "confession." In this other version, Olivi also submits all his works to the papacy for approval. In one manuscript, the pope's name is left blank, while in another, the pope is named Martin (Martin IV, 1281–1285). This would seem to indicate that the "confession" was a separate document, drafted at least fourteen years before Olivi's death, which was then grafted on to some manuscripts of the memorial. Ubertino da Casale also records a somewhat different and much shorter version of the confession, including the name of Pope Martin IV (*ALKG* 2:411–412). The fact that Gui records the shorter version would lead us to conclude that it was this version that was circulating among the Beguins of Languedoc. Heysse, "Descriptio codicis bibliothecae Laurentianae Florentinae, S. Crucis, plut. 31 sin. cod. 3," *AFH* 11 (1918): 251–269. The other manuscript is Pistoia, Fort. D298, fols. 253v–255v. Wadding also supplies a version, in which the pope named is Boniface. *Annales Minorum*, ann. 1297, n. 33. See the discussion and comparison of these various texts in Burr, *Persecution*, 73. Though the text reads "year of his incarnation 1297," due to the use of the dating style of the Annunciation, the year was actually 1298 by our reckoning. A new translation of portions of Bernard Gui's manual has recently been released: *The Inquisitor's Guide: A Medieval Manual on Heretics*, trans. Janet Shirley (Welwyn Garden City, UK, 2006).

their choir, where his earthly remains would be safest and easiest to revere.[48] The composition of this short text, widely disseminated in Languedoc twenty years after Olivi's death, is another tribute to their perception of his sanctity.

Another text, this one probably written in 1317 after the cult had come under attack, made an attempt to explain the widespread veneration for Olivi and to make it sound less suspicious, but, in the process, the text reveals both an extensive cult and particularly the fact that the brothers of the convent of Narbonne were hoping that their saint would still manage to be canonized officially.

> For if such things [cultic activities] had been prohibited for the saints most recently canonized—Francis, Dominic, Anthony, and Louis—holy mother church would not have had such clear motives, which along with their holy lives, have led the church to celebrate them on earth, whom the Lord glorifies in heaven.

The author goes on to elaborate on the prestige of this cult of a saint not yet canonized:

> For who would dare to reprove the pious devotion of other reverend fathers and of lord cardinals and bishops and other prelates of the Church, who in the merits of the aforesaid father have sensed holiness, and have sent their solemn benedictions to his tomb?[49]

If cardinals and bishops were persuaded of the merit of Olivi's cult, the author opined, why should anyone else be troubled by it? His disingenuous-

---

[48] Such precautions appear to have been usual for those whose saintliness was suspected at the time of their demise. The vigilance over the earthly remains of Saint Francis is particularly well known (Moorman, *History*, 77, 88), but the monks of Fossanova took similar precautions with the body of Saint Thomas Aquinas (André Vauchez, *La Sainteté en occident aux derniers siècles du moyen âge*, 2nd ed. [Rome, 1988], 504). The body of the blessed Douceline of Digne, who died in Marseille in 1274, was assaulted many times on its way to its resting place in the Franciscan convent. *The Life of Saint Douceline, Beguine of Provence*, trans. Kathleen Garay and Madeleine Jeay (Cambridge, 2001), 92–93. That Olivi's remains were indeed valuable and needed protection was further proved by their confiscation in 1318, alluded to by Bernard Gui, a subject to which we will return (*Manuel* 1:193).

[49] The text is anonymous, and is published by Ehrle, *ALKG* 3:443. Ehrle dates it to 1316, but since the Louis to whom the author doubtless refers, Louis of Toulouse, was not canonized until April 7, 1317, it must be after that date.

ness about a "saint" who rejected the entire Church as infected by Antichrist may have found a receptive audience in Narbonne, but it was to prove ineffective at the curia.

Nor was it only the friars of Narbonne and their supporters at the curia who flocked to Olivi's grave. Extensive evidence exists regarding the cult's popularity among the lay people of Languedoc.[50] One particularly vivid example comes from the deposition of the Montpellierain Beguine Prous Boneta. At the age of ten, on March 14, 1306, Olivi's "feast," she visited his tomb and had experiences there that clearly indicate that she considered him a saint. As she prayed over the tomb, she reported that God gave her three gifts: abundant tears, the sweetest aroma she had ever smelled, and a feeling of warmth as though someone had placed a cloak on her shoulders.[51] While Prous's imagery of the cloak on her shoulders is particularly vivid, all of these "signs" are classic popular indicators of sanctity.[52] Many others also expressed their confidence in Olivi as a saint. Brother Peter of John was holy, they said, an uncanonized saint, and his relics brought healing.[53] Some of them cast his sanctity in apocalyptic terms borrowed from Olivi's own works. While Francis was the angel with the sign of the living God, Olivi was the angel whose face shone like the sun.[54]

Once active persecution of the Spirituals began, Olivi's cult seemed even more dangerous to the papacy. Bernard Gui noted in his inquisitorial manual that Olivi's bones had mysteriously vanished in 1318: "but where they may

[50] Though Jean-Louis Biget and I are primarily working from the same sources, he draws rather different conclusions from them than do I. He believes that the cult was never a "popular" one, and was merely promoted by the Spiritual friars. Biget, "Culte et rayonnement de Pierre Déjean Olieu en Languedoc au début du XIVe siècle," in *PdJO*, 277–308, esp. 305–306.

[51] W. H. May, "The Confession of Prous Boneta, Heretic and Heresiarch," in *Essays in Medieval Life and Thought*, ed. A. P. Evans (New York, 1955), 3–30, at 11. Prous had vowed virginity nine months before this.

[52] See Vauchez, *La Sainteté*, 499–514. Aviad Kleinberg points out that though they were popular, they were never canonical. *Prophets in Their Own Country* (Chicago, 1992), 35.

[53] For witnesses to the relics' thaumaturgic power, see the testimony of Johan Orlach and Sibillia Cazelas. Both believed that their sick children were cured at Olivi's tomb. Doat 27, fols. 16r–18v, 25r.

[54] Revelation 7:2 and 10:1–2. See, for instance, the report by Gui Terré and Pierre de la Palud on the Catalan pamphlet containing material based on Olivi's Apocalypse commentary: "quod credit fratrem Petrum Iohannis esse illum angelum fortem descendentem de celo, Apoc. X, quia inter omnes alios doctores singulariter est sibi aperta ueritas scripture et notitia ac intelligentia Apocalypsis." Pou y Marti, *Visionarios*, 501. Examples in the inquisitorial material are myriad.

be is questioned by many, and different people say different things."[55] Some have suggested the culprits were the Conventuals.[56] Angelo Clareno did not indict anyone in particular, but certainly suspected foul play, angrily protesting that "they exhumed his bones, and insultingly and furiously destroyed his tomb, the offerings of his sanctity and of the devotion of the faithful to him, and with all their strength they extinguished the operation of the spirit in all the faithful."[57] In fact, the late fourteenth-century inquisitor Nicolau Eymeric confirmed Angelo's suspicions and attributed responsibility to John XXII himself, who commanded the exhumation of Olivi's remains and the public burning of them along with the offerings brought to Olivi's tomb. After being burned in Narbonne, the remains were brought secretly by night to Avignon and thrown into the Rhône, lest even Olivi's ashes become sought-after relics.[58] Olivi's cult had assumed so much importance by this time that its eradication was imperative.

Languedoc and Heresy

Even today, Languedoc's best-known products—besides wine—are heretics, and dominant in both contemporary and historical accounts are the Cathars. Though the story of the Cathars in Languedoc is only marginally related to the story of the Spiritual Franciscans and the Beguins, there are certain factors worth recalling as they shed light on how other heresies were both received by laypeople and prosecuted by the Church.[59] Catharism, the great heresy of Europe in the twelfth century, was a dualist faith related in a

[55] *Manuel* 1:192–193. "Fuit autem corpus ejus inde extractum et alibi portatum et absconditum sub anno Domini M°CCC°XVIII°; set ubi sit a pluribus dubitatur et diversi diversa circa hoc locuntur et dicunt."

[56] In particular, Ehrle in *ALKG* 2:443, an opinion which was adopted by Gui's editor, G. Mollat (*Manuel* 1:193n1).

[57] *ALKG* 2:293. "Exhumaverunt ossa eius et contumeliose et furibunde exterminaverunt sepulcrum et sanctitatis eius et devocionis fidelium ad ipsum oblata signa et totis viribus spiritus operacionem in fidelibus extinxerunt."

[58] Biget, "Culte et rayonnement," 296. The original citation is found in Eymeric, *Directorium Inquisitorum* (Rome, 1578), 2:77.

[59] There is a vast literature on Catharism. There are two recent general scholarly works in English, Malcolm Lambert's *The Cathars* (Oxford, 1998), and Malcolm Barber's *The Cathars: Dualist Heretics in Languedoc in the High Middle Ages* (Harrow, England, 2001). They are still usefully supplemented by Walter Wakefield, *Heresy, Crusade, and Inquisition* (London, 1974). Anne Brenon's *Le vrai visage du catharisme* (Loubatières, [1989]), and *Les femmes cathares* (Paris, 1992) are useful for summaries of the inquisitorial sources and for identification and analysis of the spread of Catharism among the cities, towns, and villages of Languedoc. Another recent book on Catharism is written for a more general public and

tenuous manner to Bogomilism in Bulgaria, and perhaps from there to the Manichaeism of the early Church.[60] Though there were Cathars throughout much of Europe, the greatest surviving documentation is for the communities in northern Italy and Languedoc, where they flourished to a remarkable degree. It is surely an exaggeration to say that the majority of Languedocians were Cathars, but nonetheless true that the alternative theology of the Cathars was popular and well ensconced in the society. There is no proof of any substantial involvement of the southern French political élite in Catharism directly, but Cathars do not appear to have been significantly persecuted in Languedoc before the turn of the thirteenth century, a fact that Malcolm Lambert considers a reflection of a certain "meridional toleration" of religious difference.[61] As a Catholic knight countered an episcopal request to expel Cathars from his lands: "We cannot. We have been reared in their midst. We have relatives among them and we see them living lives of perfection."[62] In the thirteenth century, the bulk of the region's Cathars were concentrated primarily in Upper Languedoc, that is to say roughly in the areas surrounding the cities of Albi, Toulouse, and Carcassonne. The center of gravity, as it were, was located in the Lauragais, the plain between these last two cities.[63]

The repression of Catharism in Languedoc is rather more relevant to our story than is the heresy itself. After the murder of the Cistercian papal legate Peter of Castelnau in 1208, the response from the papacy was swift and violent. The Albigensian Crusade (1209–1229) was the well-known result.[64] In the spring of 1209, a crusading army summoned by Innocent III

---

is less satisfactory: Stephen O'Shea, *The Perfect Heresy: The Revolutionary Life and Death of the Medieval Cathars* (New York, 2000).

[60] As James Given so aptly put it, "The question of the origins of the Cathar sect is a vexed and obscure matter and need not detain us here." Given, *Inquisition and Medieval Society: Power, Discipline, and Resistance in Languedoc* (Ithaca, 1997), 9n28.

[61] Lambert, *The Cathars*, 68, 135.

[62] From Guillaume de Puylaurens, quoted in Wakefield, *Heresy, Crusade, and Inquisition*, 75. The region's tolerance for religious difference was also reflected in its attitudes toward the Jews, who in most cities lived not in ghettoes, but in and among the rest of the population. Carol Iancu, ed., *Les juifs à Montpellier et dans le Languedoc à l'époque médiévale* (Montpellier, 1988), and Danièle Iancu-Agou, "Topographie des quartiers juifs en Provence médiévale," *Revue des études juives* 133 (1974): 11–156.

[63] The maps in Brenon, *Le vrai visage du catharisme*, 119, and in Wakefield, *Heresy, Crusade, and Inquisition*, 69, are instructive.

[64] The best introduction to the events of the Crusade in English remains Joseph R. Strayer, *The Albigensian Crusades* (New York, 1971), reprinted with an epilogue by Carol Lansing (Ann Arbor, 1992). A more recent short and vivid summary is in Mark Gregory Pegg, *The Corruption of Angels* (Princeton, 2001), 4–19.

from the north, and composed of many with ties to the French crown, came down the Rhône and headed west into the regions "tainted" by Catharism. Though the precise events of these years need not concern us here, it is important to note the devastating effect the campaigns had on all the inhabitants of Languedoc. The infamous siege of Béziers appears to have been especially vividly remembered. According to legend, the crusading abbot of Cîteaux, Arnaud Amaury, refused to try to distinguish between heretics and the orthodox when the walls were stormed, commanding "Kill them all, God will know his own."[65] His words may be legendary, but his report to the pope, which boasted of 20,000 dead, is not. There is no question that the massacre was of unprecedented ferocity and savagery, and the Crusaders spared no one they encountered.[66] It was a shattering event for the entire Midi, Cathar or Catholic. For Peter Olivi, nearly ninety years later, it may have been a veritable earthquake. In his commentary on the Apocalypse, he wrote, "moreover, at the beginning of the Order of Saint Francis, an earthquake was seen in many parts, as in the county of Toulouse shattered in that time by the crusaders; whence, the city of Béziers, where I was raised, was destroyed by them in the third or fourth year of that Order."[67] There is no evidence of an actual earthquake in Languedoc in 1209 or any other year until 1224.[68] For Olivi, the tragic event was to be interpreted as the earthquake of Revelation 6:12–17 that announced the

[65] For the authoritative debunking of this persistent myth, see Jacques Berlioz, 'Tuez-les tous, Dieu reconnaîtra les siens': La croisade contre les Albigeois vue par Césaire de Heisterbach (Portet-sur-Garonne, 1994).

[66] Strayer, The Albigensian Crusades, 62–63.

[67] "Preterea in initio ordinis Francisci factus est terremotus in pluribus partibus, puta in comitatu tolosano tunc temporis per cruce signatos dissipato; unde et urbs Biterris, in qua fui nutritus, fuit vel tertio vel quarto anno huius ordinis diruta [or destructa] per eosdem." Warren Lewis, "Peter John Olivi: Prophet of the Year 2000," Ph.D. diss., Tübingen University, 1972, 399–400. In fact, Olivi was off by about four years, since Béziers fell in the first campaign of the Crusade in July 1209, and was not attacked again. See also Burr, Olivi's Peaceable Kingdom, 109.

[68] There is no municipal chronicle for Béziers or Narbonne, where Olivi was writing, but the municipal chronicle of Montpellier, which frequently mentions natural catastrophes or events (e.g., solar eclipses in 1157, 1239, and 1333, floods in 1220, 1308, and 1331, an earthquake in 1224, "vint lo crotle a Montpellier egal hora nona, e tenc tant quant hom poiria dire tres ves Pater noster," and another in 1309, which lasted the space of only 1 Pater noster, eclipses of the moon in 1225, 1290, 1301, 1309, and 1321, famines in 1285 and especially 1333, a comet in 1297, and another in 1301, and droughts in 1313, 1323, and 1330), includes no such thing. Montpellier is only 60 kilometers from Béziers and 80 kilometers from Narbonne. Société Archéologique de Montpellier, ed., Thalamus parvus: Le petit thalamus de Montpellier (Montpellier, 1840; hereafter Thalamus parvus), 330–347.

beginning of the sixth period of history in the time of Saint Francis.[69] This "earthquake" was a sign: "For the great day of His wrath has come, and who is able to stand?" (Revelation 6:17).

Other Cathar strongholds fell soon afterwards. Though many of the perfects or "good men" (Cathar believers who had been "consoled" in a kind of ordination) were burned to death in a series of autos-da-fé in the region, the overwhelming violence of the Crusade did not encourage believers to convert, and may have hardened many in heresy. A vast underground movement of clandestine good men and supporting believers continued to exist across Languedoc throughout much of the century. The second stage of repression, therefore, was the implantation of inquisitors in the region. Where the Crusade had been primarily directed by Cistercian monks, the inquisitions of Languedoc were a Dominican phenomenon.[70] Dominic, after all, had practically cut his eyeteeth preaching against the Cathars of Fanjeaux in the Lauragais, and it was only a few kilometers away that he established the very first Dominican foundation: the convent of Prouille, intended as a haven for converted Cathar "good women," who henceforth lived as nuns.

It was in 1233 that Pope Gregory IX appointed Dominican inquisitors to several dioceses in the south of France—the beginning of a virtually permanent tribunal against heresy.[71] The friars soon developed a system: first,

[69] Lewis, "Peter John Olivi," 399–400. See also Burr, *Olivi's Peaceable Kingdom*, 109. It should not be assumed that Olivi's bitter characterization of the massacre meant that he was soft on the Cathar heresy. Even more than Joachim, Olivi considered the Cathar heresy to be untenable, one of the enemies of the fifth period, which was nearly extinguished. As he wrote, it "contains so many stupid and patently absurd errors that the wise can in no way be seduced by it": Lewis, "Peter John Olivi," 86.

[70] The notable exception, of course, is the inquisition led by the Cistercian bishop Jacques Fournier of Pamiers. Fournier, however, conducted his inquisitions in his capacity as bishop, not as any kind of representative of the Cistercian order.

[71] Richard Kieckhefer has successfully argued for the inappropriateness of the term "the Inquisition" when speaking of medieval inquisitors and their individual inquisitorial processes and campaigns, in both *The Repression of Heresy in Medieval Germany* (Philadelphia, 1979) and "The Office of Inquisition and Medieval Heresy: The Transition from Personal to Institutional Jurisdiction," *Journal of Ecclesiastical History* 46 (1995): 36–61. He points out, however, that "institutional development" was clearly taking place with the inquisitors of Toulouse and Carcassonne in the thirteenth and fourteenth centuries. While the activities of inquisition were undertaken by "individually commissioned inquisitors," the significant stores of registers and other documents and the tendency for Languedocian inquisitors to act in concert on public occasions gave expression to "a sense of ecclesiastical and judicial solidarity": ibid., 53–54, 60. In this work, I will avoid the use of the term "inquisition" as a collective noun describing the acts of individual inquisitors. It is difficult to avoid entirely, however. As Alan Friedlander has observed (*Hammer of the Inquisitors*, 7), eliminating "inquisition" entirely leaves protestors and resisters like Bernard Délicieux "like a desolate Don Quixote, bereft even of a windmill against which

a public sermon and a call for confessions, then the inquisition proper, where suspects were summoned and examined, and finally, the public sentencing known as the General Sermon.[72] Only obdurate or relapsed heretics were handed over to the secular arm for burning; others were sentenced to perpetual imprisonment in inquisitorial prisons known as "the Wall," to pilgrimages, or to the wearing of yellow crosses sewn onto their clothing. Frequently, the bodies of the heretical dead were ordered to be exhumed and burned.[73] It was not long before the inquisitors began to collect in registers the confessions of those who appeared before them, and to use those registers as tools in prosecution: indexing and cross-referencing became weapons far more dangerous to those with something to hide than the rack or the wheel.[74]

The effective resistance of the Cathars came to an end in March 1244, when the Cathar fortress of Montségur fell after a long siege. Some 220 of the perfect and believers were burned. Though inquisitions continued against the stragglers for decades, and though the last so-called Cathar fortress (Quéribus; it was held by noblemen rebelling against the crown known as *faidits*, not by Cathar perfects) did not fall until 1269, Catharism was definitively in retreat. A brief revival around the year 1300, largely in the Pays de Foix, a mountainous region now in the département of the Ariège, was not enough to rekindle the flame.[75]

---

to tilt." The individuals fighting against the inquisitors were not always as subtle in their distinctions as are we, and simply sought to resist prosecution for heresy by any inquisitor, whether the Dominican inquisitor of Carcassonne or Toulouse, or the Cistercian bishop of Pamiers. Given (*Inquisition*, 15), provides a useful and concise description of inquisitorial tribunals and their similarities across distance.

[72] Wakefield, *Heresy, Crusade, and Inquisition*, 140–142. See also Given, *Inquisition*, especially chap. 3. The best source for contemporary descriptions of the inquisitorial process is Bernard Gui's inquisitorial manual. Gui, a Dominican, was himself inquisitor of Toulouse between 1307 and 1324.

[73] The "secular arm" also confiscated the goods of those burned alive or dead, a significant source of conflict and agitation. One year of accounts balancing the expenses and profits of such an exchange has been published in *Comptes royaux (1314–1328)*, ed. François Maillard (Paris, 1953), vol. 1.

[74] Given, *Inquisition*, 25–50.

[75] Because of the extraordinary richness of the documentation, this revival is very well known. The records from the inquisitions of 1308–1309 and 1318–1325 in Carcassonne and Pamiers have generated a significant amount of scholarship, beginning with Le Roy Ladurie's *Montaillou*. Matthias Benad, *Domus und Religion in Montaillou* (Tübingen, 1990), is based on the same records, as is the more recent popular book by René Weis, *The Yellow Cross: The Story of the Last Cathars' Rebellion against the Inquisition (1290–1329)* (New York, 2002).

Opposition to the inquisitors, all drawn from the Dominican Order, was still fierce, however.[76] Moreover, most of them were from northern France—the only inquisitor whose native language was any variant on the *langue d'oc* was Bernard Gui, from the Limousin. Jean Favier has emphasized the association between opposition to the Dominican inquisitors and opposition to the king of France, Philip the Fair. As he wrote: "By their shady deals with secular authority—necessary in order for them to be effective—the Dominican inquisition took sides with the agents of the king, with the forces of centralization, and with a royalty that frequently looked more like the taxman."[77] This association was real, in that the secular authority carried out the sentences of the inquisitors (to be "relaxed to the secular arm" after all, was official shorthand for death at the stake) and confiscated the goods of the condemned to the benefit of the central government,[78] but, perhaps more important, it was enshrined in the popular imagination. Philip the Fair did the inquisitors no favor by eliminating the royal court of appeals in Languedoc in 1291, thereby forcing those who wished to appeal decisions of royal judges to undergo the expense of correspondence and journeys to Paris.[79] Even more unpopular were the heavy taxes Philip attempted to levy on Languedoc. As Joseph Strayer has observed, "the dominant feature of Philip's reign is the financial embarrassment of the government," and tax after tax (in 1294, 1295, 1297, and 1298) was demanded of an increasingly uncooperative population, particularly in the south.[80] Though each of these levies was accompanied by promises of future lenience, each promise was broken. And after Philip's disastrous defeat in the Flanders war at Courtrai in 1302, the exactions increased. The fact that Philip deemed it expedient to travel through Languedoc in 1303–1304 (the only such voyage in his reign, during his period of greatest financial distress)[81] distributing expanded privileges to the inhabitants of many areas is testimony to the particular antagonism of the south to the new taxes, and to Philip's very real fear of a southern rebellion.[82] As Favier so rightly observed, "the old *pays Cathare* was

[76] Given, *Inquisition*, 93–139, provides many examples of resistance (both individual and collective) to the inquisitors in Languedoc.

[77] Jean Favier, *Philippe le Bel* (Paris, 1978), 131.

[78] The accounts of the inquisition of Carcassonne in 1322–1323 ran considerably in the black to the tune of the "£1,050 16s. 6d. and pittance" that was sent to the royal treasury. Doat 34, fol. 231r.

[79] Favier, *Philippe le Bel*, 68.

[80] Joseph R. Strayer, "Consent to Taxation under Philip the Fair," in *Studies in Early French Taxation*, ed. Strayer and Charles H. Taylor (Cambridge, MA, 1939), 45–53.

[81] Favier, *Philippe le Bel*, 179.

[82] Strayer, "Consent," 66.

a good listener to anyone talking independence, respect for its rights, and the retreat of the inquisition."[83]

In the city of Carcassonne at this time, opposition to this villainous association took a particularly activist vein. Under the leadership of a charismatic Franciscan friar from Montpellier, Bernard Délicieux, the people of Carcassonne rose up in 1300 to defend the reputations (and property) of their ancestors, who had been condemned by a particularly diligent inquisitor. The struggle dragged on for years, with protests to the papacy and to King Philip, and reached a dramatic climax with the storming of the inquisitorial Wall of Carcassonne in 1303, following an inspirational sermon by Bernard Délicieux.[84] In the end, however, it was the inquisitors who won: Bernard Délicieux was charged with a long list of offenses against the inquisitors and ecclesiastical authority and sent to die in the Wall at Carcassonne in 1319, while the inquisitors were able to maintain their tight grip on the people of the city. We may assume, however, that during the first quarter of the fourteenth century, tensions between inquisitors and the flocks whose orthodoxy they were responsible for were at an all-time high.

THE POOR BROTHERS AND SISTERS OF PENITENCE AND THEIR BEGUINIZATION

The Cathars were not the only objects of the inquisitors' interest. Who were those laypeople that flocked to Olivi's grave? For Bernard Gui and other hostile observers in Languedoc at the beginning of the fourteenth century, they were all Beguins, a pejorative term then commonly in use for the members of the Franciscan Third Order. The Beguins referred to themselves, however, as "the poor brothers and sisters of penitence."[85] The Third Order had its origins in the lay penitents who flocked around Francis himself and the earliest Franciscans.[86] The meaning of the word "penitence" for Saint Francis and those who followed him is of considerable importance. These were not the kind of flagellants seen so often in popular depictions of the Middle Ages, whipping themselves into a seemingly penitential frenzy. Nor did penitence refer exclusively to the sacrament of confession, though that was certainly a part of the penitents' practice. *Penitentia* is the word that

---

[83] Favier, *Philippe le Bel*, 317,
[84] Friedlander, *Hammer of the Inquisitors*, 122–150.
[85] *Manuel* 1:108–111.
[86] Raffaelle Pazzelli, *Saint Francis and the Third Order: The Franciscan and pre-Franciscan Penitential Movement*, trans. from the Italian (Chicago, 1989), 100.

the Vulgate Bible used to translate the Greek *metanoia*, or conversion (the act of turning one's life to God), and it is in this sense that we can best understand these Franciscans' penitence.[87] Recent scholarship has concluded that Saint Francis acknowledged a group of lay penitents associated with the Franciscan brothers and wrote his *Letter to the Faithful* explicitly for them.[88] In time, the exhortations he expressed in the *Letter* were codified into a first Rule in the 1220s, which governed the Third Order for sixty years.

In 1289, a "General Chapter" of Italian Penitents requested a definitive Rule from the Franciscan Pope Nicholas IV, which he granted in his bull *Supra montem* (August 19, 1289).[89] In most of its essentials, this Rule is a reorganization of the material already contained in the earlier Rule of the 1220s, and *Supra montem* became the real Rule for the Third Order. Chief among its tenets were indications about the way the penitents ought to dress (humbly, modestly, and in inexpensive cloth), what they were to eat (with temperance, and considerable fasting), and the canonical hours they were to

[87] A useful discussion of the meaning of this word is found in Théophile Desbonnets, "La lettre à tous les fidèles de François d'Assise," *I Frati Minori e il Terzo ordine, problemi e discussioni storiografiche. Convegni del centro di studi sulla spiritualità medievale (17–20 ottobre 1982)* (Todi, 1985), 51–76, esp. 70–72. Pazzelli sums up the biblical meaning of *metanoia* or *penitentia*, as "a constant yet developing idea; it is a conversion that is theocentric (turn to God), ethical (flee evil and do good), and affective (love God)": *St. Francis and the Third Order*, 4. Pazzelli traces the history of the penitence movement from the third to the thirteenth century: ibid., 7–66. See also Robert M. Stewart, *"De illis qui faciunt penitentiam." The Rule of the Secular Franciscan Order: Origins, Development, Interpretation* (Rome, 1991), chap. 2.

[88] Stewart, *"De illis qui faciunt penitentiam,"* especially chaps. 1 and 3. His side-by-side comparisons of the various "rules" for the Third Order (a *recensio prima* vs. the *Letter to the Faithful*, the *Letter to the Faithful* vs. the *Memoriale propositi* of 1228, and the *Memoriale propositi* vs. the Rule of 1289) are particularly valuable. Before Stewart's publication (which provides a useful and nonpolemic summary), the debate was carried on primarily in a series of conferences on the subject of the Third Order: O. Schmucki, ed., *L'Ordine della Penitenza di san Francesco d'Assisi nel sec. XIII* (Rome, 1973); M. d'Alatri, ed., *I Frati Penitenti di san Francesco nella società del Due e Trecento* (Rome, 1977); idem, ed., *Il movimento francescano della Penitenza nella società medioevale* (Rome, 1980); R. Pazzelli and L. Temperini, eds., *Prime manifestazioni di vita comunitaria, maschile e femminile, nel movimento francescano della Penitenza (1215–1447)* (Rome, 1982); and Pazzelli and Temperini, eds., *La 'Supra montem' di Niccolò IV (1289): Genesi e diffusione di una regola* (Roma, 1988). Editions of most of the early documents can be found in G. G. Meerseman, *Dossier de l'Ordre de la Pénitence au xiiie siècle* (Fribourg, 1961; 2nd ed., 1982).

[89] The most accessible edition of this bull is found in *Bullarii Franciscani Epitome*, ed. Conrad Eubel (Quaracchi, 1908), 302–306. A version taken directly from the Vatican Register, with minor variations and no divisions (which were evidently added by Eubel) can be found in Edith Pasztor, "La 'Supra montem' e la cancelleria pontificia al tempo di Niccolò IV," *La 'Supra montem' di Niccolò IV (1289)*, 65–83, appendix, 84–90. Pasztor also provides information regarding a recently discovered original of the bull, 91–92.

observe. The Psalms they were to recite for the hours were extensive, but the unlettered were given the option of saying the *Our Father* instead of the Psalms if they did not know them. They were to "refrain from formal oaths, unless where necessity compels...that is, for peace, for the Faith, under calumny, and in bearing witness." They were to hear mass daily, confess and take communion regularly three times a year, avoid the use of arms, and keep peace among themselves.

Their corporate life was also given a shape: there were to be ministers for each local congregation who organized the penitents to meet at least once a month in a given church for services, and also gathered them together for exhortations by "some religious who is informed in the words of God." A "visitor" was to have final authority over the Brothers and Sisters. They were encouraged to succor each other when sick, attend each others' funerals, and pray for the dead. A procedure was laid out for those who wished to join the order: after a year's probation, and having reconciled any debts and obligations, a candidate could be received. At that time, she was to promise in writing to obey the Rule and to have her promise registered by a public notary. Her promise was irrevocable, except in the case of her deciding to join a religious order or her being expelled for bad conduct.[90]

The 1289 Rule was more explicitly "Franciscan" in character than the earlier versions, particularly in its specification of the visitors and overseers of the tertiaries as Franciscan friars, appointed by the leaders of a nearby convent. Many believe that Nicholas IV felt obliged to specify this because the friars had "neglected" their "obligations" toward the tertiaries. In fact, since at least the middle of the century, relations between the two groups had been strained. In his *Answers to Questions about the Order of Friars Minor*, Bonaventure commented rather trenchantly about the friars' reluctance to get too involved with the penitents for a number of reasons he considered quite valid. Principally, the friars were concerned with their own reputation and did not want to take the risk of being tarred with the same brush as wayward brothers and sisters of penitence. What if a tertiary were to get into debt, or worse, into prison? And would it not then be blamed on the friars if one of the sisters (whom he also calls *beghine*) were to go astray, and barefoot, bring forth barefoot little children?[91] It is certainly possible that this wariness reflects the voice of experience: the very first injunction of *Supra montem* is an

---

[90] *Bullarii Franciscani Epitome*, 302–305.

[91] Bonaventure, *Opera Omnia*, 8:367–368. "Si aliqua ipsarum de aliquo crimine infamaretur fornicationis vel adulterii, statim qui nos forte non diligerent divulgarent istud in nostram infamiam, dicentes: ecce sorores nudipedissae parvulos nudipedes procreant eis;

admonition against harboring heretics within the Third Order, witness to the fear of the Church about such potentially undisciplined brethren.[92]

When they are not actually thinking of Cole Porter and "Begin the Beguine," most people who hear the word "beguine" think of the groups of holy women of northern Europe who lived in communal residences known as *béguinages* (as in Bruges). In Languedoc in the fourteenth century, however, "Beguin" or "Beguine" came to mean members of the Franciscan Third Order, male and female respectively. How did this come to be? In the 1250s, Bonaventure called the sisters of the Order of Penitence "beghine." In 1282, the members of the Franciscan Third Order in Bologna were known as "Pizocari."[93] The term "bizzochi" also seems to have been common.[94] By the end of 1317, John XXII was using the words "beghini" and "bizzochi" to describe certain members of the Third Order, variously in Italy, Sicily, and Provence, who "bustle about concealed under the veil of such a name."[95] His implication was hardly friendly. Increasingly, *Beguin* came to mean not merely a Franciscan tertiary, but particularly one who was a devotee of Peter Olivi, imbued with Olivi's ideas on poverty and its apocalyptic significance.[96]

This is made very clear by a document dating from 1295. When Peter Olivi wrote a letter to the three sons of Charles II of Naples (the future Saint Louis of Toulouse, the future King Robert the Wise of Naples, and another brother, Raymond-Béranger), he was writing to three princes held hostage in Catalonia. Their chaplain, the Franciscan Pierre Scarrier, had suggested they write to him for solace, and he wished that he could help them. However, he knew that their father feared that he might "beguinize

---

sed a quo illos concipiunt, nisi ab eis qui toto die occupantur cum ipsis?" It is evident that "barefoot and pregnant" is not merely a modern turn of phrase. The text is also found in Meerseman, *Dossier,* 123–125.

[92] *Bullarii Franciscani Epitome,* 302.

[93] Michael Bihl, "Elenchi Bononienses Fratrum de Poenitentia," *AFH* 7 (1914): 232.

[94] See Mario Sensi, *Storie di bizzoche tra Umbria e Marche* (Rome, 1995).

[95] "Sub velamine talis nominis satagunt palliare." *Sancta Romana, BF* 5:134–135.

[96] Exactly how to *use* the appellation "Beguin" is also a problem. Is a person who sympathized with the Franciscan tertiaries under persecution a Beguin, or does the term apply only to the tertiaries themselves? Not many scholars have made this distinction. For the purposes of this book, I have chosen to use the term "Beguin" narrowly in the period before the beginning of persecution (that is, applying it only to members of the Franciscan Third Order) and more broadly thereafter, considering anyone who confessed to the heretical Beguin ideas of the sanctity of Peter Olivi, the imminence of the coming of Antichrist, and the identification of the Church as the carnal church, to be a Beguin. I have often also used the term "Beguin sympathizer" to apply to the latter group when it seemed desirable to make a distinction.

them" (that is, indoctrinate them with Beguin ideas), and thus he was afraid to be too bold.[97]

Only a year after Olivi's death, the acts of a provincial council of October 30, 1299, held in Béziers make it clear that the ecclesiastical hierarchy was becoming suspicious of people "commonly called Beguins." They were known for several things: their practice of novel forms of *penitentia*, their distinctive clothing (worn by both sexes), and especially their preaching to many that the end of the world was at hand and that the time of Antichrist was here, "or almost." Though the name of Olivi was never mentioned, it is not difficult to recognize followers of Olivi's ideas on poverty and the imminence of the apocalyptic crisis in the description. The council further complained that the Beguins gathered by night (that is, secretly) to preach the word of God, but when rebuked for this practice, they claimed that they were not preaching, but merely "talking about God." The council took a stand against them: "we forbid the further observation of the cult of this superstition, since it is inimical to the holy canons." They did not go so far as to call the Beguins heretics; that dubious honor was reserved for the Cathars, who had been rebuked in another act of the council. But it seems plain that the Beguins of Languedoc were beginning to be known for their unusual, and possibly dangerous views.[98]

[97] The verb in Latin is *inbeguiniri*. Olivi's letter to the sons of Charles II, *ALKG* 3:539. Raymond-Béranger died young. A slightly earlier use of the word is found in a text edited by Ignaz von Döllinger. In early 1289, a woman of Narbonne named Rixende was accused of being a Waldensian heretic. As Emery was quick to point out, her deposition bears very few marks of anything connected to the Waldensians. Rixende was a visionary, and with her multiple visions of paradise and purgatory, she recalled having seen only Christ, the Virgin, and Saint Francis. She was certainly in contact with a Franciscan milieu, since she claimed to have possessed a letter written by Saint John, which she had received from the Poor Clares of Narbonne, and to have submitted it to a friar at the Franciscan convent, Jacme Moreno. Two of her followers were identified as "biguina," Sicardis and Alissenda. What did it mean in 1289 to be a "biguina"? There appears to have been a Franciscan connection—did it necessarily mean that these two women were members of the Franciscan Third Order? We do not know for sure, since our source is so limited. We do know that in 1305 two other women were listed as "beguina" in a survey of the poor of Narbonne, both of them with what would become the characteristic Beguine prefix of "na": "na Dossa, *beguina*," and "na Guillelma, *beguina*." Richard W. Emery, *Heresy and Inquisition in Narbonne* (New York, 1941), 131n90. The citation comes from A. Blanc, "Le Livre de comptes de Jacme Olivier," *Bulletin de la commission archéologique de Narbonne*, 3–8 (1895–1902): 543. This survey listed a total of 400 women. The record of Rixende's trial appears in Ignaz von Döllinger, *Beiträge zur Sektengeschichte des Mittelalters* (Munich, 1890), 2:706–711, usefully supplemented by a seventeenth-century inventory by Antoine Rocque in manuscript in the library of Narbonne, which provides a few additional details. See Emery, *Heresy and Inquisition*, 105, 130.

[98] "*Concilium Provinciale Anno M. CC. XCIX. Biterris celebratum sub Ægidio Narbonensi archiepiscopo*," in *Thesaurus novus anecdotorum*, ed. E. Martène and U. Durand (Paris,

It would seem that by this time Beguins were becoming a common sight in Languedoc's towns and cities. We do not have any contemporary estimates as to their numbers, but we do know that people could recognize a Beguin when they saw one. One set of witnesses made it clear that Beguins' appearance made them clearly distinguishable. They agreed that a Beguin went barefoot, wearing humble and long clothes, and walked around all day with a mortified face. Some mentioned a cloak with a hood, though there was some minor disagreement as to the exact color or fabric: black, brown, coarse linen, wool, or hemp.[99] The inquisitor Bernard Gui described these clothes, which he specifically called a habit, as brown, made out of *burellum*, a coarse cloth probably similar to burlap. As Gui observed in his manual for inquisitors, Beguins could also be spotted in church by the way they prayed: "praying in church, they often sit hunched over, their faces turned toward one wall or another, or they are prostrate on the ground, hooded. Rarely are they seen kneeling with their hands together, like other men." He also pointed out that you could recognize Beguins by their salutations when they greeted one another: they would say "Blessed be Jesus Christ," or "Blessed be the name of Our Lord Jesus Christ." They also said a particular grace before and after meals. On their knees, one of them would say the *Gloria in excelsis Deo* while the others listened before the meal, and afterwards they would recite the *Salve Regina*, also kneeling.[100] They could not necessarily be distinguished by where they lived, however: those who chose lives of celibacy frequently lived in small communities known as "houses of poverty," while married members might continue to live in their family homes.

Just as is the case with Olivi himself, there has been much controversy regarding the orthodoxy of his followers the Beguins. We know very little about exactly what happened to them in the years immediately following 1299. One prominent Olivi scholar, Raoul Manselli, has interpreted this silence of the sources as an indication that, on further examination, the Beguins of Languedoc were found to be orthodox in their beliefs and left

---

1717), vol. 4, cols. 225–228. I thank Robert Lerner for providing me with a copy of this document. The acts of the council also note that many of these Beguins had taken vows of virginity or chastity, but that these vows "were known to have been violated." This kind of accusation is common in the rhetoric against heretical groups; Olivi himself used it against the Cathars (Burr, *Olivi's Peaceable Kingdom*, 89).

[99] Célestin Douais, *La procédure inquisitoriale en Languedoc au quatorzième siècle d'après un procès inédit de l'année 1337* (Paris-Toulouse, 1900) and Noël Coulet, "Un moine languedocien accusé de béguinisme," *CF* 19 (1984): 365–389.

[100] *Manuel* 1:118–119.

alone.[101] Arguments from silence are always problematic, however, since so many documents have not survived to the present day, and evidence to the contrary may simply have been lost. There are several hints to continued suspicion of the Beguins. In a letter of 1304 to Pope Benedict XI, Arnau de Vilanova referred to inquisitors in the (Franciscan) province of Provence having been sent against the "sons of truth," for instance.[102] Arnau, both a famed medical doctor and an author of suspicious prophetic texts himself (as well as a friend of the Beguins), may well have intervened on their behalf with some rather highly placed patients, that is to say, Popes Boniface VIII and, later, Clement V.[103] In the year 1300, a Provençal friar named Mathieu of Bouzigues "fled" to Rome along with five "Beguins" and thirteen "women" (these are the terms used in the Venetian chronicle that reports the story), carrying books written by Peter Olivi. When Mathieu de Bouzigues made a profession of faith, he did so using terms that are decidedly Olivian in tone: "poor use" is featured especially prominently.[104] The most persuasive argument for the unorthodox nature of the Beguins' beliefs, however, can be found in the source that they accepted as their guide above all, Olivi's commentary on the Apocalypse. Even Olivi's most dedicated modern apologists

---

[101] Raoul Manselli, *Spirituali e beghini in Provenza* (Rome, 1959), 40–41.

[102] Josep Perarnau, "L'*Ars catholicae philosophiae* (primera redacció de la *philosophia catholica et divina*) d'Arnau de Vilanova," *Arxiu de textos catalans antics* 10 (1991): 7–223, at 210.

[103] See Robert Lerner, "The Pope and the Doctor," *Yale Review* 78 (1988–1989): 62–79, and idem, "Ecstatic Dissent," esp. 43–44.

[104] G. Golubovich, *Biblioteca bio-bibliografica della Terra Santa e dell'Oriente francescano*, ser. 1, vol. 2 (1913): 80–81, 96–97. The chronicler seems to place the action in 1299, but the date ("*Bonifacius vero v° anno*") is not actually attached to this particular anecdote, but to the one before (where he recounts Pope Boniface VIII's letter to the Patriarch of Constantinople against Angelo Clareno and Liberato). The anecdote itself simply reads, "*tunc temporis.*" "at that time." Another similar story is told by Angelo Clareno, though the apparent Beguins in flight were from Catalonia: a certain brother Jerome turned up in Venice in 1301 in the company of several women, carrying the books of Olivi. Jerome presented himself as having been sent by the brothers in Catalonia with Olivi's books, and said that the women he was with were his mother and her daughter. According to Angelo, it eventually transpired that the women were not his relatives, and the books were stolen. Burr, *Persecution*, 74. *ALKG* 1:528–529. Two editions of Mathieu de Bouzigues's confession exist: Diego Zorzi, "Testi inediti francescani in lingua provenzale," *Miscellanea del Centro di Studi medievali* 58 (Milan, 1956) 272–278, and F. Delorme, "Frère Mathieu de Bouzigues, Confessio Fidei," *Études Franciscaines* 49 (1937): 224–239. The confession cannot be dated any more securely than between 1298 (Olivi's death) and 1304 (when a pope was last alive in Rome). The confession is orthodox, except in one point, his support of Olivi's position that the lance wounded Christ in the side *before* his death and not afterwards. Though this notion was not declared authoritatively erroneous until the Council of Vienne, it was at least dubious before then, and even Olivi was careful to present it only as a possibility. Burr, *Persecution*, 76.

cannot hide the fact that he deemed the vast majority of the institutional Church in his own day to be nothing more than the minions of Antichrist.[105] Though Manselli considered that it was the persecution itself that propelled the Beguins into real heresy, well before any real inquisitorial campaign was launched against them Olivi's followers viewed themselves as the faithful few who would defend the *true* Church against the carnal forces who were out to destroy her. It is over this point that Manselli's and my interpretations of the events part company most clearly.[106]

Heretics are sometimes thought of as religious eccentrics, readily distinguishable from those who follow the religious mainstream. In the first quarter of the fourteenth century, telling the sheep from the goats was not so simple. Certainly, those who had taken the vows and wore the habit of the Beguins were easy to distinguish at first glance. But it does not appear that they were in any way thought of as outcasts. Many outside the Third Order of Saint Francis sought their counsel, their company, and their friendship, as Bernard Gui noticed. Gui was careful to place among the number of the heretics "other faithful not of the third order, be they clerics, members of religious orders, or laity, as long as they believe and maintain as the beguins do on the aforesaid issues."

Bernard Gui considered belief, not membership in the Third Order, to be the deciding factor regarding who was a Beguin and who was not. What were those beliefs? The "issues" that he elaborates in his manual run the gamut from intransigent views on poverty and belief in Olivi as a saint and in the holy quality of his writings, all the way to believing that the friars and Beguins who died for their beliefs were holy martyrs, that their bones were sacred relics, and that the pope who had condemned them, John XXII, was therefore a heretic himself, not to mention Olivi's "mystical Antichrist." Obviously, these latter beliefs are not those that Beguins could have held before the persecution began. As we make our attempt to understand the Beguin community before persecution, we will try to separate one set of beliefs out from the other.

Besides the widespread belief that Olivi was an uncanonized saint, already discussed, the simplest place to begin is with those beliefs that are related

---

[105] Burr, *Olivi's Peaceable Kingdom*, 76.

[106] Manselli, *Spirituali*, 40–48. For Manselli, the Beguins were thoroughly orthodox in this period, adhering to Olivi as a great master of spiritual instruction, not as a master of apocalyptic or as a prophet of the imminent last days. As I hope my analysis of their beliefs will make clear, they followed Olivi in virtually all of his most radical assumptions. While persecution certainly sharpened their heresy, it did not create it. See also Lambert, *Medieval Heresy*, 206n41.

to poverty. Unfortunately, most of our sources date from after 1322, when John XXII began his assault on the understanding of Franciscan poverty contained in *Exiit qui seminat*, and 1323, when those beliefs were declared definitively culpable with the publication of *Cum inter nonnullos* in November. Thus what was not heretical in 1316, simply the Franciscan Order's widespread understanding of itself, became so by the time the Beguins were being questioned about their beliefs. Nevertheless, it is clear that the Beguins of Languedoc universally agreed that, as Bernard Gui reported:

> Lord Jesus Christ (insofar as he was man) and his disciples as well owned nothing either individually or in common, because they were perfectly poor in this world. Again, they say that having nothing individually or in common constitutes perfect evangelical poverty. Again, they say that having something in common diminishes the perfection of evangelical poverty.[107]

This evangelical poverty was handed down by Saint Francis himself as a model to his brothers: "so that those who profess the aforesaid rule can have nothing either individually or in common beyond the limited use necessary to life, which always smacks of the indigence of poverty and has nothing superfluous."[108] The Beguins also equated the Rule of Saint Francis to the Gospel of Christ: "They say that the Rule of Saint Francis is the Gospel of Christ, or one and the same as the Gospel of Christ,"[109] and evoked the tenets of Olivi regarding the necessary poverty of Franciscan bishops. They also certainly believed in the obligation of Franciscans to wear poor and short habits; though the statement "they say that the pope cannot make dispensation concerning the size and quality of Franciscan habit" clearly dates from after the publication of Pope John XXII's 1317 bull legislating on the matter, *Quorumdam exigit*, the sentiment behind it is certainly older.[110] There are also assertions regarding the sanctity of the vow: anyone who has vowed chastity or virginity can never be released from such a vow. This comes directly from Olivi's *Questions on Evangelical Perfection*.[111]

In a similar manner, by stripping off some—but not all—of the layers of the apocalyptic onion offered up by Bernard Gui and the inquisitorial

---

[107] *Manuel* 1:118–121.

[108] Ibid., 120–121.

[109] Ibid. "Regulam sancti Francisci dicunt esse evangelium Christi aut unum et idem esse cum evangelio Christi."

[110] Ibid., 126–127.

[111] Ibid., 122–123 (vow of poverty), 134–135 (vow of virginity or chastity). See Burr, *Persecution*, 12–13.

processes, we should be able to understand how the Beguins before 1317 understood the unfolding of sacred history. We have seen that already in 1299, the Beguins were saying that Antichrist was imminent. Did that therefore mean that they already considered the entire Church to be rotten from head to toe, and that they were already certain about who was Antichrist? As David Burr has noted, "Olivi's apocalyptic scenario was, in short, a plot line in which the motivation and much of the action were furnished but the names and dates were left unspecified. In the context of 1317 and beyond, a series of people seemed to be auditioning for the major roles."[112] We may certainly push this further back, and point out that the Spiritual friars had begun to feel pressure within the Franciscan Order considerably before 1317. Some of the members of the apocalyptic cast may have been chosen well before the persecution began: the Spirituals certainly saw themselves as the "vanguard of the new age" well ahead of that date. For instance, Bernard Gui reported that the Beguins "claim that at the end of the sixth period of church history—that is, the present period which began with Saint Francis—the carnal church, Babylon, the great whore is to be rejected by Christ just as the synagogue of the Jews was rejected because it crucified Christ."[113] If the Beguins, following Olivi's timetable, were expecting great changes in the early years of the fourteenth century, this was doubtless a topic of discussion among them: when would it happen? how? Therefore, a declaration concerning the role of the Holy Spirit which might sound immoderate to our ears must have seemed distinctly within the realm of the possible, even the imminent:

> Some of them claim that on those elect spiritual and evangelical individuals through whom a spiritual and benign church will be founded in the seventh and last period, the Holy Spirit will be poured out in greater or at least in equal abundance as on the apostles, the disciples of Jesus Christ, on the day of Pentecost during the time of the primitive church. And they say the Holy Spirit will descend on them like a fiery flame in a furnace, and they take this to mean that, not only will their souls be filled with the Holy Spirit, but the Holy Spirit will live in their bodies as well.[114]

By putting together Olivi's insistence that the Franciscan Rule and the Gospel were one and the same with his Apocalyptic vision and its timetable, the

---

[112] David Burr, "Did the Beguins Understand Olivi?" in *PdJO*, 316–317.
[113] *Manuel* 1:144–145.
[114] Ibid., 146–149.

Beguins were able to work themselves into a fervor of impatient anticipation, with themselves and the Spiritual friars at center stage.

THE PATH TO PERSECUTION

This sense of pregnant and fearful anticipation was the mood of the Beguins in March 1313, and they saw the events of the years that followed as proof positive that they had been right. For the Spiritual Franciscans of Languedoc, the deaths of Pope Clement V in April 1314 and of the Franciscan Minister General Alexander of Alessandria in October were an unmitigated disaster. Both of their highly placed protectors (such as they were) were gone. In 1313, it had seemed that the rigorists were firmly and comfortably ensconced in the three convents of Narbonne, Béziers, and Carcassonne. Clement V had at least tentatively approved their practice and reprimanded their enemies, and Alexander of Alessandria had provided them with superiors they were satisfied with. Thus they had been free to run these three convents as they wished, implementing Peter Olivi's poor use in full measure. The truce was of short duration, however. Clement V had never quite managed to publish the decrees agreed upon at the Council of Vienne, and the will to compromise within the order to the end of preserving the peace died with Alexander.

During the two years of papal and ministerial interregnum between 1314 and 1316, forces hostile to the Spirituals (largely within the Franciscan Order itself) seized their opportunity and began to seek an end to any degree of Spiritual autonomy in southern France. In 1315, they forcibly expelled the heads of the convents of Carcassonne, Narbonne, and Béziers and installed new superiors who were entirely unsympathetic to the Spiritual understanding of poor use. These actions brought to a head what had been brewing for some time: an outright, hostile, and occasionally violent break between Spirituals and Conventuals. One expulsion led to another, and the new Conventual superiors of Narbonne and Béziers soon found themselves cast out of their own new convents—an event that was shortly followed by decrees of excommunication. In the towns of Narbonne and Béziers, the conflict soon spread beyond the convent walls and was adopted by the citizens who supported "their" friars, the Spirituals. Many of them took up arms in order to help support the Spiritual rebellion, and some later vigorously protested the decrees of excommunication to papal authorities in Montpellier.[115]

---

[115] The chronology of these events is covered in greater detail in chapter 2 of my dissertation, and also summarily by David Burr, *The Spiritual Franciscans: From Protest to Persecution in the Century after Saint Francis* (University Park, PA, 2001), 168–177.

Two events took place in 1316, however, that would prove to be of great consequence for the Spiritual friars of Languedoc and their supporters. Michael of Cesena was elected minister general of the Franciscan Order at the General Chapter of Naples in May, and after one of the most contested and extended conclaves in papal history, Jacques Duèse of Cahors was elected to the papal see, where he took the name John XXII in August. Neither man was in the least bit favorable to the Spirituals, and both were determined to solve the Spiritual problem.

Throughout the busy fall, winter, and early spring of 1316–1317, the new pope and the new minister general heard a great deal from both sides of the conflict. Not all the epistolary missiles that the Spirituals and Conventuals fired at each other have survived, but some have left a trace in the archives. There were at least three rounds of accusations and rebuttals.[116] The points that were in contention can be summarized fairly briefly: Were the friars schismatic for having thrown out their superiors, or had the superiors unlawfully been imposed upon them? Had the friars used unmerited force in expelling their superiors, or were they simply doing what was necessary? Were the friars spreading heresy by making use of the works of Peter Olivi, or had those works previously been approved? Was it lawful (according to the Franciscan Rule) to collect grain and wine, or were the friars correct in refusing to? Were their habits immodest and squalid, or did they simply imitate the example of Saint Francis? Michael of Cesena made several supplications to the new pope that were read in consistory. Chief among these was a request that the "order of *fraticelli*" be annulled, and also that "Beguins not be reputed to be of the Third Order, lest they disseminate error in that guise."[117]

The tone of all these various petitions and responses can best be described as vituperative: words like "most false," "impertinence," "maliciously," and expressions such as "that is patently a lie" abound. An indication of the level to which their discourse had descended can perhaps best be seen in a response to an accusation that the Spirituals were slandering Bonagratia of Bergamo, one of Michael of Cesena's closest allies:

> They answered with this counsel of a wise man: *Answer a fool according to his folly, lest he imagine himself to be wise*; perhaps it would be better to follow this other counsel of the same wise man: *Answer not a fool according to his*

---

[116] A manuscript in Rome from the first half of the fourteenth century, Vat. Borghesiana 85 (fols. 97r–109v, 124–125), contains a number of these texts, partially edited by Ehrle, *ALKG* 4:52–63 (one passage is edited in *ALKG* 3:449–450). Raimond de Fronsac also provides a catalogue of the various petitions: *ALKG* 3:27.

[117] *ALKG* 3:27, chap. 7.

folly, lest thou be made like him. And so if they are made similar to the fool, they can excuse themselves with Paul, who said, *I am become foolish: you have compelled me.*[118]

It appears that neither side was trying too hard to mince its words. Another phrase summed it all up: "Such are the foundations [of their position]: false, perverse, impious, and unjust."[119]

By the spring of 1317, Pope John XXII was ready to act. Toward the end of April, a coalition of three cardinals wrote a letter to the convents of Narbonne and Béziers, requesting them to doff their distinctive habits and to return to obedience.[120] Only five days later, John followed that missive up with two letters of his own. These were far more serious, since they no longer spoke in general terms but named names and demanded a response: the friars of the short habits were summoned to Avignon.

When the summons came, it was surely no surprise to the friars in Narbonne and Béziers. First they had been warned, and now sixty-one of them were directed to present themselves in Avignon within ten days.[121] Despite the urgency of the summons ("under the pain of excommunication"), they took some extra time, and it was not until the night of May 22 that they appeared before the door of the episcopal palace gates where the curia resided. Though contemporary sources remark on the fact that they did not go to the Franciscan convent of Avignon but instead spent all night outside, this should not surprise us, given the known hostility of many other Franciscans for the Spirituals. They probably decided that a night or two "à la belle étoile" was preferable to finding themselves confined by force. It was the night of Pentecost, and on the Monday they were allowed an audience with John XXII.

It would be difficult to improve on the story of this audience told by Angelo Clareno, who was in Avignon during this period, and possibly an

---

[118] "Quod postea dicitur, dictos fratres diffamasse fratrem Bonagratiam et eius sequasses, gravia crimina imponendo, dicendum quod ea, que responderunt, dixerunt iuxta illud consilium sapientis: *Responde stulto iuxta stulticiam suam, ne sibi sapiens videatur* [Proverbs 26:5]; licet forcitan melius fuisset sequi in hoc aliud consilium eiusdem sapientis: *Ne respondeas stulto iuxta stultitiam suam, ne sibi similis efficiaris* [Proverbs 26:4]. Et sic si similes facti sunt stulto, possunt se excusare cum Paulo, qui ait: "*Stultus factus sum, vos me coegistis*" [2 Corinthians 12:11]. *ALKG* 4:60.

[119] "Qualia sunt fundamenta, falsa, perversa, impia et iniqua." *ALKG* 4:60.

[120] The letter can be found in F. Delorme, "Constitutiones provinciae Provinciae," *AFH* 14 (1921): 432–433.

[121] The summons are printed in *BF* 5:118–120. The names actually add up to 62, but one (*Raymundus de Borditi*) appears twice in the letter to Narbonne.

eyewitness.[122] Certainly, he had a flair for a dramatic story. Through his eyes, it is not difficult to imagine the scene: the wiry and elderly pope in an impressive chair surrounded by advisers, a crowd of angry Conventual Franciscans to one side, dressed neatly, regularly, and perhaps even sumptuously, and sixty-four friars in torn, patched, and short habits to the other.[123] The tension between the two parties would have been palpable, and probably audible as well.

As their first speaker, the Spirituals chose Bernard Délicieux. It is easy to look back at the events that followed and to second-guess that decision, but at the time, he probably seemed a natural choice: Bernard was a comfortable and eloquent speaker accustomed to addressing the high and mighty, and his rhetoric had persuaded many other audiences in the past. And Bernard, whom Angelo described as "a man of great humility, of distinguished wisdom and eloquence," supposedly spoke "prudently, deliberately and effectively,"[124] so much so, again according to Angelo, that the Conventuals were forced to retreat to dirty tactics: instead of denouncing the message, they attacked the messenger. Bernard's past, which included the harassment of inquisitors, the importuning of royalty, and very probably incitement to treason, was loudly evoked against him. The Conventuals maligned him vigorously to his face: "this one who speaks now so boldly against his own Order is a pestilential and malignant man. He has committed evil deeds beyond number. He should not be heard nor permitted to stand in a judgment hall nor to speak against his Order in which there are so many holy men." For they sought to exclude him "with injustice," (said Angelo) "since they foresaw as clear as day that if he were given an audience, for justice and with justice he would prevail." But

[122] Scholarly opinions differ as to whether Angelo's own trial (which resulted in his imprisonment—he was liberated on June 23, 1317) took place before or after the audience of the Spirituals of Narbonne and Béziers. His detailed account of the audience weighs in favor of a later trial, but the sequence of events laid out in his *Historia septem tribulationum* (*ALKG* 2:144–145) places his trial first. Von Auw, *Angelo Clareno*, 135, and Douie, *Nature and Effect*, 63, opt for the later trial, but Manselli, *Spirituali*, 132–134, argues for an earlier one. Gian Luca Potestà has noted the inadequacy of using the *Historia* as a chronology, but does not seem to have been interested enough in this question to formulate an opinion: *Angelo Clareno dai poveri eremiti ai fraticelli*, 9. See the translation of David Burr and E. Randolph Daniel, *A Chronicle or History of the Seven Tribulations of the Order of Brothers Minor* (St. Bonaventure, NY, 2005), 206–210.

[123] According to Angelo Clareno's account, sixty-four were present at the audience. Certainly, some other friars (notably Bernard Délicieux) joined them in their journey to Narbonne, and the total number may even have been larger.

[124] The translation here and in the following passages is from Friedlander, *Hammer of the Inquisitors*, 254.

Bernard's past was too much to ignore, and John ordered him to be taken away and detained.[125]

The next speaker was the lector of the convent of Narbonne, Frances Sans. He was one of the Spirituals' most prominent leaders, writing petitions and acting as a spokesperson for the community to the people of Narbonne. But he, too, was stopped by the crowd: "Lord, nor should this one be heard, since against obedience to his minister and the Order, he has presumed for so long to teach publicly as a lector, and to preach, and to impugn the order to all men." Frances, too, was hauled off to prison. Guilhem de Saint Amans, the leader of the Spirituals of Narbonne, next took a turn, but he was denounced by the others as not having taken care of the order's goods: a denunciation which sent him to prison as well.

By this point, it is clear at least to us that the audience was not going to be decided in favor of the friars of Narbonne and Béziers. But the last straw was the intervention of Geoffroi de Cournon, a respected friar, elderly and sick, a friend and companion of Ubertino da Casale who had spent the winter at the court defending the Spirituals. When he began to speak, the pope, who knew him, mockingly observed that it was quite a surprise to see him there defending the right to observe the rule strictly, when everyone knew that he himself wore five tunics. Geoffroi responded (politely, or so said Angelo) that he was not wearing five tunics. "Are you calling me a liar?" replied the pope. And when the friar responded that no, perhaps the Holy Father was just mistaken, the pontiff sent him off to prison as well, "to see how many tunics he was wearing."

With that, any semblance of an ordinary audience broke down. The friars, realizing that they were going to get no further, cried, "Holy Father, justice! justice!" but all of them were taken into custody; Bernard, Guilhem, and Geoffroi by the pope's men, and the rest of the friars to the Franciscan convent, where Frances Sans was placed "in a cell by the latrines." Though two others were imprisoned within a few days, the struggle was over. Their attempt to win over the new pope had utterly and completely failed.[126]

[125] The story almost seems too good to be believed, but a hostile source, Raimond de Fronsac, paints virtually the same picture, though in somewhat less dramatic terms. *ALKG* 3:28–29.

[126] Raimond de Fronsac's story implies that at least some of the Spirituals did get a chance to speak their piece and to read what he called the "supplication of the rebels." Though Raimond did not mention Frances Sans by name, the list of those imprisoned immediately is otherwise the same as in Angelo's account. *ALKG* 3:28–29.

We can only imagine what life was like for the sixty or more friars who were held in custody in Avignon for most of the following year.[127] From what they said afterwards, it is clear that this was not an ordinary case of being detained for violations of the Rule or other infractions.[128] We may certainly assume that they were not treated with very much indulgence, and they were surely subject to much questioning, threats, and coercion. It is unlikely that they were ever subject to outright torture, since none of them later accused their enemies of that, but the conditions of their imprisonment were nonetheless a significant burden. Angelo Clareno's description of the conditions under which a Catalan friar named Pons Bautugat died in a Franciscan prison around 1302 for his refusal to hand over certain works of Peter Olivi may not apply fully in this case, but it does testify vividly as to the rancor with which members of the community treated the Spirituals:

Fettered with iron shackles and an iron chain, Pons was placed in a fetid, narrow, and dark prison. Affixing the chain to the trunk of a tree, the persecutors confined and bound him so much that, weighed down by the iron, he could fulfill the demands of nature only in the place where he sat. He lay stretched out on bare earth that was covered with his urine and feces to the level of his feet, stinking and filthy, encased in sordid slime. While tossing scant bread and little water to him, the jailors averted their faces. More cruel than beasts and more evil than serpents, they showed no kindness in word or act to a man who, they knew, was truly holy, right to the moment when he died. Finally, Pons fell. While he lay, or rather sat in a reclining position in the stench of his feces and urine, rejoicing in his soul

[127] Though only sixty-one friars were summoned, and Angelo Clareno mentions only sixty-four at the audience with John XXII, it is clear that quite a number of other Spiritual friars came to Avignon, either at Pentecost or later. Of the twenty-six friars turned over to Michel le Moine in November, seven were not among those summoned in April (Arnaut de Felginio, Arnaut Maury, Bernard Aspa, Frances de Badon, Guilhem Guiraut, Philip Ferrier, and brother Serviatius).

[128] In the deliberations over the fate of apostate Spiritual friar Peire Julian in 1329, the guardian of the convent of Béziers argued for clemency, declaring that "he believed that brother Peire Julian had just cause for fear; that is to say since in the order, there were prisons in which the friars of that order punished and were accustomed to punish delinquents who were treated humanely enough, but the brothers who were punished by the Inquisitor of Marseille, of the same order, were more seriously punished, since they had more seriously sinned, and they were placed in harder prisons, and treated less humanely." Doat 27, fol. 168.

and warmed by the fire of love, giving infinite thanks to God, he returned his soul to God.[129]

Once he had the friars in custody, the pope was willing to let the matter rest for some months. Probably he used at least some of the time in study of the issues as became his habit: we are fortunate to have John's personal copy of the Franciscan Rule, with extensive annotations. He was particularly interested in the differences between things *ordered* by the Rule and things that were merely *suggested*.[130] It was not until October, however, that the matter was raised again. On October 7, John XXII issued what was to be the first salvo in his war of decretals against the Franciscan Order, *Quorumdam exigit*.[131]

Quorumdam exigit was two things in one. First, it was a clarification of the interpretations of the Franciscan Rule published by Nicholas III and Clement V, *Exiit qui seminat* and *Exivi de paradiso*. But it was also a kind of loyalty oath, a litmus test for separating out the obedient Franciscans from the rebellious. The tenets described by the bull were simple. First, the "meanness" or "cheapness" of Franciscan habits mentioned in the Rule was to be defined by the minister general of the order and by those to whom he delegated the question. Second, the friars were to preserve grain and wine in granaries and cellars. These two seemingly prosaic issues were to occupy a surprising number of people for years to come. The Spirituals saw Francis's distinctive charism of poverty as the defining element of their order, the most important part of the Rule, and the guiding principle in their place in the history of the Church. In *Quorumdam exigit*, John sought to put poverty in its place; as he wrote: "poverty is great, but chastity is greater, and the greatest of all is obedience if it is preserved intact."[132]

---

[129] *ALKG* 2:300. Translation from Burr and Daniel, *A Chronicle or History of the Seven Tribulations*, 146.

[130] Anneliese Maier, "Annotazioni autografe di Giovanni XXII in codici Vaticani," *Rivista di storia della chiesa in Italia* 6 (1952): 317–332, at 322.

[131] *Extrauagantes Iohannis XXII, Monumenta Iuris Canonici*, ser. B: *Corpus Collectionum*, vol. 6, ed. Jacqueline Tarrant (Città del Vaticano, 1983), 163–181.

[132] "Magna quidem paupertas: sed major integritas, bonum est obedientia maximum, si custodiatur illesa." The interpretation of this oft-quoted phrase has varied, primarily concerning the word "*integritas*." Lambert interprets it as "unity," which would at first glance seem to make sense if we interpret it as the unity of the order, or of the Church (*Franciscan Poverty*, 214; *Medieval Heresy*, 209). Lydia von Auw and Gordon Leff have chosen ambiguity: they translate it respectively as "integrité" (*Angelo Clareno*, 144) and "integrity" (*Heresy in the Later Middle Ages*, 208). Moorman, however, translates it as chastity, as do I (Moorman, *History*, 311). The line following this one in the bull provides the key: "For the first of these is dominated by things, the second by the flesh, and the third in truth by the mind

Would the friars obey? Michael of Cesena himself questioned the Spirituals: in front of witnesses and a notary, he asked each one whether he would
obey the precepts in *Quorumdam exigit*, and additionally, if he believed that
the pope had the power to legislate on the matter.[133] Some of them accepted
John's authority, while others remained intransigent.[134] Those who gave in
were assigned to various (and generally remote) convents in the province
and given sealed letters to deliver to their new superiors upon their arrival.
These letters, which some opened, instructed the superiors to imprison the
friars.[135] But what was to be done with the obdurate brothers? First, John
handed over the two questions asked of the Spirituals to a panel of thirteen
theologians, who all concurred that refusing to agree constituted a heresy.
Each one gave his opinion in his own words, and two of them pointed out
that not only was such a response heretical, but those who gave it pertinaciously were "to be condemned as heretics"[136]

After John received the appropriate verdict from the theologians, he
handed over all the recalcitrant brothers—twenty-six in all—to Michel le
Moine, the Franciscan inquisitor of Provence.[137] By May, Michel le Moine

---

and the soul." If poverty is about things, and obedience is about the mind, then chastity is
more obviously about the flesh than unity, or even integrity. John seems to be playing also
with the idea of the vows of the Franciscan order: poverty, chastity, and obedience.

[133] *ALKG* 3:30.

[134] The interrogation, which is found in BnF MS. 4350, has been edited by Manselli,
Spirituali, 291–296. In this document, twenty-one friars were questioned over two days.
Either this represents only part of the interrogation, and the rest of the friars were interro-
gated on subsequent days, or only the most obdurate friars were questioned at this stage.

[135] The testimony of Alaraxis Biasse, who sheltered some of them, makes this clear:
"They looked at the sealed letters that they bore and saw that their ministers were order-
ing that they be imprisoned in the Convents to which they were sent." Doat 28, fol. 217r.
The fact was also mentioned by Andreas Berenguier of Montagnac, Doat 27, fol. 11r.

[136] *Chartularium universitatis parisiensis*, ed. Henri Denifle, vol. 2, part 1 (Paris, 1891),
no. 760, 215–218. The two most blunt were Raimond Mostuéjouls, bishop of Saint Flour,
and Raimond Robaud, bishop of Marseille. The other theologians included Gui Terré, Michael of Cesena, Arnald Roiard, and Vidal du Four. In the cartulary, Denifle merely dates
the document as "*1318, ante Junii 11*," because on that date, Gui Terré was elected prior
general of the Carmelite Order, and he is not so described. Presumably Denifle posited
1318 because it appears among other charters from that year. However, since the document itself has no date at all, and it was certainly not drawn up in Paris (all of the theologians were present at the papal court in Avignon), it seems more likely to belong in the
window of opportunity between the interrogations of Michael of Cesena in the middle of
October 1317 and the handing over of the twenty-five friars (see below) to the inquisitor of
Provence on November 22. Probably it arrived in Paris sometime in the spring of 1318.

[137] The letter is in *BF* 5:132–133, *Bullaire de l'inquisition française au XIVe siècle et jusqu'à
la fin du Grand Schisme*, ed. J.-M. Vidal (Paris, 1913), 35–37, and Baluze-Mansi 2:247–
248. It is somewhat puzzling that John chose to hand the friars over to the inquisitor of

had succeeded in persuading all but five to recant. On May 7, two weeks after Easter, he issued his sentence. It seems that the five were given every chance to back down and were subjected to numerous entreaties by bishops, cardinals, and masters of theology. One of the five, Bernard Aspa, recanted at the eleventh hour and was sentenced to perpetual imprisonment. The other four, Guilhem Santon, Johan Barrau, Deodat Miquel, and Pons Roca, refused to abjure and were relaxed to the secular arm, which appears to have burned them on the same day in the cemetery of Notre Dame des Accoules, immediately adjacent to the central marketplace of Marseille.[138] It was not a sight anyone could soon forget: four Franciscan friars burned alive because they refused to abandon their short habits and their mendicancy. For some of those who watched, they were dangerous enemies of papal power and authority, and for others, the four friars were martyrs for Franciscan poverty. Public veneration of Peter Olivi and the possibility of his cult achieving any kind of ecclesiastical approval went up in flames with them.

The friars who had abjured at Marseille, like those who had abjured before them, were sent to convents throughout the region. Many of these failed to reach their destinations as they chose instead to flee the region entirely. Fragments from a letter written by some of them soon after the events of May 7 have survived. The letter's tone is defiant: "They were not leaving the order, but only its walls, not the habit, but only cloth, not the faith, but only

---

Provence. Why not Carcassonne, or even Toulouse, since either city was closer to the friars' homes? On other occasions, heretics captured in a region not their own were generally sent home for trial, but not in this case. One reasonable suggestion is that the particular character of Michel le Moine caused him to be selected as the Spirituals' prosecutor. He had been one of the superiors deposed and reprimanded by Clement V in 1312 for his opposition to them, and thus John may have felt that he would be particularly effective in his prosecution (Von Auw, *Angelo Clareno*, 144). Another suggestion by Samantha Kelly is also plausible. King Robert of Naples, who was also count of Provence, was a long-term close friend of Pope John XXII, and John may have sent the rebellious friars to Michel le Moine in Provence knowing that he could count on Robert's support. It was, after all, not the Church that executed unrepentant heretics, but the secular authorities. Samantha Kelly, "A Second Solomon: The Theory and Practice of Kingship at the Court of Robert of Naples (1309–1343)," Ph.D. diss., Northwestern University, 1998, 82–83.

[138] Baluze-Mansi 2:248–251. Sylvain Piron has determined that the relevant portion of BnF MS. 4350 was originally part of a "livre de travail" of the inquisitor Jean de Beaune of Carcassonne, and has published a new edition of the text. See Michael Monachus, "Inquisitoris sententia contra combustos in Massilia," *Oliviana* 2 (2006) *http://www.oliviana.org/document36.html*, and Sylvain Piron, "Un cahier de travail de l'inquisiteur Jean de Beaune," *Oliviana* 2 (2006) http://www.oliviana.org/document26.html, and "Michael Monachus. Inquisitoris sententia contra combustos in Massilia," *Oliviana* 2 (2006), http://www.oliviana.org/document33.html.

its husk, not the Church, but a blind Synagogue, not a pastor, but a preda-
tor." They vowed to return in victory after the death of Pope John XXII,
"just as after the death of Antichrist, the persecutor of the faithful, those
who were on his side will be exterminated by the faithful and ministers of
the true Christ, so after the death of this pope, that is to say, John XXII, we
and our companions, the faithful of Christ, now suffering persecution by the
adversaries of Christ, will appear and we will bring home the victory over all
our adversaries."[139]

From the Friars to the Beguins

John XXII had not waited for the final sentence of the Spirituals to begin
his crackdown on their lay followers in Languedoc, however. On December 30, 1317, he issued a bull authorizing their prosecution. *Sancta romana*
authorized procedures against those called "*fraticelli*, or brothers of poor
life, or *bizzochi* or Beguins" who could be found in parts of Italy, in Sicily, in
Provence, in Narbonne, and in Toulouse. It was no excuse that they called
themselves members of the Third Order, wrote John, since "no such way of
living is allowed in the Rule of the Third Order."[140]

In the cities and towns of Languedoc, upheaval quickly followed this announcement and the auto-da-fé of May 1318. Many men and women were
arrested and questioned by their local bishops or by the inquisitors of Toulouse and Carcassonne. They were asked about their affiliations with the friars summoned to Avignon and about their belief in the sanctity and writings
of Peter Olivi. The inquisitors asked probing questions about the identity of
Antichrist and tested them on Franciscan poverty. How did they feel about
the friars of the short habits? Were they more holy than other friars? Did
the pope have the right to require the friars to keep grain in their granaries
and wine in their cellars?

The responses the bishops and inquisitors heard varied widely. Some admitted that they had believed in the message and writings of Peter Olivi, but

---

[139] Baluze-Mansi 2:272. "Relinquentes in scriptis ea quae sequuntur, videlicet quod ipsi
non dimittebant ordinem, set parietes, non habitum, sed pannum, non fidem, sed corti-
cem, non Ecclesiam, sed synagogam caecam, non pastorem, sed devoratorem. Item quod
sicut post mortem Antichristi persecutoris fidelium exterminabuntur qui fuerint ex parte
ejus a vere Christi fidelibus et ministris, sic mortuo illo papa, videlicet, Iohanne vicesimo
secundo, nos et socii nostri fideles Christi, nunc persecutionem ab adversariis Christi
sustinentes, apparebimus, et de omnibus adversariis reportabimus victoriam."

[140] *Extrauagantes*, 198–204, BF 5:134–135. A second bull, *Gloriosam ecclesiam* (January
23, 1318), was aimed directly at the *fraticelli* of Sicily.

were now prepared to accept the Church's interpretation. These were forced to abjure their heresy publicly and to swear not to help any other heretics avoid capture or question. Others denied any affiliation at all, and they were believed, or held in prison. Still others boldly declared that they, like the four friars burned in Marseille, were prepared to go to the stake to defend their unorthodox beliefs. As more and more men and women became targets of the inquisitors—and especially as some who had abjured their beliefs began to be found aiding and abetting their fellows—the Beguins formed networks of resistance that crossed the length and breadth of Languedoc and even extended across the Rhône into Provence. Pious men and women became fugitives and conspirators on behalf of a cause they held not only dear, but of worldwide historical importance. If these were the last times, as Peter Olivi had predicted and as so many of them believed, it was crucial that they take the right side and fight against the advent and the reign of Antichrist.

In the chapters that follow, we will uncover the heresy and resistance of the Beguins of Languedoc through the stories of the Beguins themselves. There were Beguins in small towns and in the largest of cities, and they used tactics of evasion, persuasion, and defiance in their struggle. It is to those stories that we now turn.

CHAPTER TWO
THE WEAPONS OF THE TRULY WEAK

Do you believe that if the pope ties the tail of an ass on earth, that the tail of the ass is tied in heaven?

—BERNARD DE NA JACMA, *Liber sententiarum*

As the Beguins themselves became the targets of the inquisitors, the initial shock and dismay was transformed swiftly into action. A network of safe houses grew up around the region, and sympathizers assisted fugitives with considerable ingenuity. Though opposition to the inquisitors was rarely overt and never violent, it is nevertheless possible for us to observe the tactics of the Beguins' resistance movement in the years following 1318. In this chapter, we examine the stories of four men and women who exemplify three of the tactics of resistance tried by the Beguins, tactics that we might call the "weapons of the truly weak"—first, the myriad acts of resistance (including jokes like the one in the epigraph) that kept fugitive Beguins alive and believing in the cause; second, the pursuit of martyrdom that kept hope alive; and third, flight to other lands in an attempt to keep the movement itself alive.

Several questions immediately come to mind. First of all, how widespread was this resistance, and how effective? James Given's book on the inquisition of Languedoc (a book that talks about Cathars and Waldensians in addition to Beguins) suggests, correctly, that "open, collective opposition" to the inquisitors was rare, occurring only in unusual circumstances.[1] But Given also observes that the bulk of what he calls collective resistance organized within sectarian boundaries (rather than simply within a village or a kin group) happens to have been among the Beguins. He concludes that Beguins were different from other heretics in two ways. First, they had only recently been declared heterodox, and second, the fact that they already had an organized structure as members of the Franciscan Third Order enabled them to coordinate resistance more effectively. There were "officers" of the Third Order who were well placed to serve as leaders of a resistance, and their regular meetings were also an asset.[2]

It is also useful for us to ask ourselves what we mean when we speak about resistance, especially resistance to inquisitorial prosecution and perceived persecution. An unfortunate preconception is that resistance must always be violent. In the case of the Beguins of southern France, that was most emphatically not the case. Possibly this was due to the injunction against the use of weapons found in both the primitive Rule for the Third Order and Nicholas IV's 1289 revision of that Rule.[3] Though there were many protests, and no doubt many heated arguments, we have no records of the

[1] Given, *Inquisition*, 139–140. When Professor Given presented his conclusions regarding resistance to inquisitors in Languedoc at a seminar at the École des Hautes Études en Sciences Sociales in Paris in March 1998, it was this very distinction between Beguins and other heretics that was first seized upon during the discussion following. Was their resistance qualitatively or quantitatively different from that of the Cathars and Waldensians who constituted the bulk of the heretics prosecuted in Carcassonne, Toulouse, and Pamiers? And to what do we owe that difference? Given, "Les inquisiteurs de Languedoc et leurs ennemis," paper given at the École des Hautes Études en Sciences Sociales, Paris (March 1998).

[2] Given (*Inquisition*, 121) notes that "the Franciscan Third Order to which many belonged was also relatively highly organized; it possessed a rule, elected officers, and held regular meetings." Only one overt reference to this organization is found in the sources— the only Beguin ever referred to as a "minister of the Beguins," Peire de Na Bruna of Belpech, confessed to having gathered the Beguins held together in prison, in order to agree on their common testimony: Bernard Gui, *Le Livre des sentences de l'inquisiteur Bernard Gui (1308–1323)*, ed. and trans. Annette Palès-Gobilliard, 2 vols. (Paris, 2002 [hereafter *Liber sententiarum*]), 2:1314. Nevertheless, it is likely that the frequent meetings, occasionally across communities, such as at the grave of Olivi, facilitated the establishment of a network of resisters.

[3] "Arma mortalia contra quempiam non recipiant vel secum ferant," in the original Rule of 1221, found in Gerald Joseph Reinmann, *The Third Order Secular of St. Francis* (Washington, DC, 1928), 177–185, at 180. "Impugnationis arma fratres secum non deferant, nisi pro defensione Romane ecclesiae, cristianae fidei vel etiam terrae ipsorum aut de suorum licentia ministrorum," in Nicholas IV's *Supra montem*, in *Bullarii Francescani Epitome*, ed. Conrad Eubel (Quaracchi, 1908), 302–306, at 303.

Spiritual Franciscans or the Beguins taking up arms.[4] This was not necessarily the usual course of events for heretics in the Midi. The years of the Albigensian Crusade in the early thirteenth century were filled with acts of violence committed on behalf of the Cathars.[5] Out of 44 separate acts of violence directed against inquisitors or their agents during the century after 1233, none of them were perpetrated by Beguins. One, in fact, was an act of violence (kidnapping and murder) *against* a Beguin, by Cathars.[6] While the Cathars rioted, attacked inquisitorial informants, stoned the Dominican convent of Albi, burned inquisitorial registers, and murdered their enemies, the Beguins did none of these things. Though many aspects of the experience of Cathar heretics and Beguin heretics were similar, the ways in which they resisted varied considerably.

It is tempting to use James C. Scott's term, the "weapons of the weak," to describe Beguin tactics.[7] Given has suggested, however, that the kinds of actions chronicled by Scott, what Given refers to as a "subterranean war...with its anonymous acts of small resistance, foot-dragging, tool breaking and other forms of petty sabotage," did not, and could not, exist in Languedoc. Without a "shared normative universe" encompassing both inquisitors and heretics, such a war would have been fruitless. I do not take issue with his conclusion. Indeed, the acts of resistance we will look at in this chapter tend to constitute what Given calls the "weapons of the truly weak."[8] Nonetheless, I feel that the weapons used by the Beguins of Languedoc, no matter how weak, merit our attention. Their attempts, both individual and collective, to avoid, confound, and escape the inquisitors of Languedoc are attested to in the records of that same inquisition. Taken together, they constitute a window onto the "hidden transcript" of resistance. Though their contempt,

---

[4] The only possible exception to this took place in 1315 when the Spiritual friars took possession of the convents of Narbonne and Béziers in a kind of coup d'état. Each side accused the other of using violence and weapons. *ALKG* 3:26; *ALKG* 4:51–54.

[5] Of course, one might well argue that such violence was brought upon them, not instigated by them. However, the Crusade was triggered by an act of violence, the murder of the papal legate Peter of Castelnau in 1208. Given, *Inquisition*, 12.

[6] Ibid., 113–115. Fearing that a Beguin named Guilhem de Johan was planning to betray them to the inquisitors, two Cathar sympathizers seized him on the bridge of Alliat and took him up into the mountains above the village of Larnat. There they interrogated him, and when he admitted his intent, they threw him off a cliff and into a deep ditch or cave so that he would not be found. *L'Inquisiteur Geoffroy d'Ablis et les cathares du comté de Foix (1308–1309)*, ed. and trans. Annette Palès-Gobilliard (Paris, 1984), 152–154.

[7] James C. Scott, *Weapons of the Weak: Everyday Forms of Peasant Resistance* (New Haven, 1985).

[8] Given, *Inquisition*, 108–109.

their abhorrence, and frequently their hatred were often too dangerous to speak aloud, the Beguins nonetheless succeeded in leaving a record of them through their actions. As Given has noted, this "wide variety of low-profile forms of resistance that dare not speak in their own name" (to use Scott's phrase) depend, by their very nature, on "disguise, secrecy and anonymity."[9] It is sometimes only through the smallest traces that we see them at all.

In this chapter, we investigate several ways that Beguins and Beguin communities managed this abrupt change in the nature of their lives. First we examine the story of a Beguin couple and the community they were part of: their solidarity with each other and with fugitives from across Languedoc, and the actions they took in order to resist the inquisitors. We then look at the case of a Beguine woman martyred in 1321 and the way her death and the death of others like her inspired those who knew her and heard about her and became propaganda for the Beguin resistance. Finally, we look at the case of a priest who chose to flee Languedoc when he could no longer find a way to conceal himself close to home. Together, these stories present a picture of the Beguin world in the early years of their persecution, when the difficult choices were still painful and raw and their sense of apocalyptic doom was at its height.

Most of the stories that I relate here come from the depositions which those accused of heresy made before the inquisitors or their scribes, and which are preserved in the inquisitors' official records or registers. Given the fraught nature of inquisitorial evidence, it is worth our examining the texts themselves, the circumstances under which they were created, and the challenges historians face in interpreting them.

Let us first take a closer look at how and when these registers were compiled. The culmination of the inquisitorial process was the event known as the "General Sermon," a grand and solemn public affair with proceedings in both Latin and the vernacular.[10] It was held infrequently and characterized by an assembly of prelates, often including inquisitors from other regions. The event was advertised in advance, and indulgences were given to the laypeople who attended. Ecclesiastical guests were able to participate in the debate regarding difficult cases, held the day prior to the public event. The accused were assembled in a public space (often the cemetery) to await their sentences. Before these were pronounced, a summary of the heretical sins (the

---

[9] Ibid., 92. The phrase "hidden transcript" comes from James C. Scott, *Domination and the Arts of Resistance: Hidden Transcripts* (New Haven, 1990), 19.

[10] Gui lays out its usual structure in his *Manuel* 2:122–131, and Given analyzes the phenomenon in *Inquisition*, 66–92.

culpa, or fault, an abridged version of their full deposition) was read aloud in the vernacular. In his inquisitorial manual, Bernard Gui wrote that it was customary to include in the *culpa* only as much information as might be useful in a later trial, leaving out details that do not "touch on the substance or the nature of the facts."[11] After the sentences had been read and carried out, the documents relating to the cases were assembled into registers.[12]

These "confessions" or "depositions," as I will call them, were written as third-person narratives, with statements by the accused related in indirect speech ("he said that he believed"). Though it would perhaps be easier for the reader if I converted these indirect statements into direct speech ("I believe") as has so often been done in books on medieval heresy, I have chosen to leave them as they appear in the documents, since use of the first person implies a level of access to the deponent that the historian cannot claim.[13]

There are other issues. The first is a simple linguistic one that also distances us from the original confession. Those who were confessing to the inquisitors spoke in the *langue d'oc*, Occitan, and those who wrote down their confessions translated them on the fly into Latin. When they were read back to the accused, they were translated back into Occitan—and any changes were perforce translated yet again into Latin. We can never be certain that inquisitor and deponent understood one another correctly, or that the documents preserve a fully accurate description of events or beliefs. Another problem is more insidious. As they stood before Bernard Gui, Henri de Chamayou, or any one of a host of inquisitorial scribes and notaries, the subjects were hardly speaking freely. They were under extraordinary pressures: pressures to conform, to confess, and to inform on their friends and neighbors from one side, and pressures to hide their own actions, thoughts, and beliefs, as well as the actions and beliefs of those whom they believed they could protect, on the other.

---

[11] *Manuel* 1:32–33. For a discussion of this point, see Given, *Inquisition*, 348.

[12] Gui does not specify when this was done, but the story of Guilhem Serallier makes it clear that the relevant documents were put together only after the *Sermo Generalis*. Some of these *culpe* have been published in various locations (in Manselli, *Spirituali*, in the *Liber sententiarum* of Bernard Gui, or in other places). Throughout this book, it has been my practice to cite the *culpe* from the most accessible source, using citations directly from the Doat collection only when that was the only complete text available.

[13] Beginning with *Montaillou*, recent books, including Mark Pegg's *Corruption of Angels*, report heretics' statements in the first person. Along with John Arnold, I find this approach essentially dishonest, and misleading to the reader. The inquisitorial record is not a tape recorder. See Arnold, *Inquisition and Power: Catharism and the Confessing Subject in Medieval Languedoc* (Philadelphia, 2001), 5.

They were strongly encouraged—not only with words, but by means of the threat of drastic punishment, and occasionally even torture—to conform to a mold of the model repentant sinner.[14] Probably the most extreme example of this is one taken from another inquisitorial register, that of Bishop Jacques Fournier. In 1321, a leper named Guilhem Agasse confessed to a bizarre and unlikely story of poisoning wells on behalf of the Muslim king of Grenada and the Sultan of Babylon, thereby confirming for the inquisitors the wild stories that were sweeping across France. Guilhem Agasse was certainly tortured, and he told the inquisitor just what he wanted to hear.[15] In his novel *The Name of the Rose*, Umberto Eco describes a similar situation, where his fictional inquisitor "Bernard Gui" exacts a confession in precisely this manner: under the mere threat of torture, the cellarer Remigio confesses to everything that the inquisitor wants and more. Murders, mayhem, and traffic with the devil were all summoned up for "Bernard Gui" just as he and his audience expected. Brother William of Baskerville, Eco's Ockham-like voice of wisdom, tells the credulous Adso: "You see? Under torture or the threat of torture, a man says not only what he has done but what he would have liked to do even if he didn't know it. Remigio now wants death with all his soul."[16] At the remove of nearly seven centuries, however, we are not obliged to believe Guilhem Agasse, whose true story we do not know, any more than we believe Remigio, whom the reader, at least, knows to be confessing to crimes he did not commit.

We must also be wary of using too modern a lens with which to view the phenomenon that provides us with our documentation, medieval inquisition. Recent work by Christine Caldwell Ames has made it abundantly clear that Bernard Gui was not nearly the monster that Umberto Eco describes, and neither were the other inquisitors of Languedoc in this period. He was

[14] Though the use of torture by the medieval inquisitor is usually assumed by non-historians, in Languedoc at least the practice appears not to have been widespread. Intimidation and coercive imprisonment were usually effective enough to extract confessions. Given, *Inquisition*, 53–54.

[15] His deposition is in *Le Registre d'inquisition de Jacques Fournier (1318–1325)*, ed. Jean Duvernoy (Toulouse, 1965), 2:135–147 (hereafter *Registre*). On p. 141, in response to a question from the inquisitor, he said that his initial confession was taken just after he had been tortured, "respondit quod confessionem quam fecit coram magistro Marcho fecit inmediate postquam depositus fuit de tormento." The editor of the text, Duvernoy, questions why Jacques Fournier would have believed such an improbable tale, and observes that Guilhem Agasse's life was probably saved by his confession: in this way, he was condemned to the *mur*, and thus avoided potential lynching by an angry crowd (135).

[16] Umberto Eco, *The Name of the Rose*, trans. William Weaver (New York, 1983), 466–469.

an inquisitor, to be sure, and his mission as an inquisitor was to uncover evidence of heresy, but also and most especially to bring repentant heretics back into the Catholic fold. We cannot use our modern ideas of tolerance and intolerance to judge the inquisitors of the past. As Ames observes, "For this world, in which heresy inquisitions were a site where divine justice, discipline, and violence crystallized here below, one temporized and spatialized point on a putatively eternal spectrum of God's jurisdiction, a binary of tolerance/intolerance is insufficient." Ames has argued persuasively for the *religious* nature of medieval inquisition, and for an understanding of medieval society that can embrace the violent acts of inquisition as legitimate expressions of religious belief. As she observes, "Inquisitors themselves proudly used language of 'persecution' to describe what they saw as the salutary work of re-placing souls in God's right order."[17] We are not obliged to *like* Bernard Gui, but must understand him as something more than a sadistic monster.

All of this means that we must be very careful in how we read and use inquisitorial sources. Many scholars have adopted what we might call a "source-critical" approach. Thus, Carol Lansing, a historian who has written on Cathars in Orvieto, writes: "inquisitorial texts have obvious drawbacks. People's statements about their beliefs were responses to questions shaped by the preoccupations of the inquisitors, shaped in turn by the manuals they used to understand the heresy."[18] John Martin, a historian of early-modern Venetian heresy, questions: "how can historians use an archive of repression to reconstruct the history of dissent? Is not such an archive by its very nature so distortive that we cannot trust it at all? Or, to ask the same question in its most extreme form, does heresy exist outside the act that suppresses it?"[19] In the end, Martin answers his own most extreme question by observing that "not only is there something outside the text; all texts (whether humanist dialogues, papal edicts, or dusty archival documents such as trial transcripts, wills, and tax records) are at least in part products of social and cultural life."[20]

Recently, however, even this moderate, source-critical approach has come under attack by some scholars. Mark Pegg's recent work on Toulouse Bibliothèque municipal MS. 609 is one example. In *The Corruption of Angels*, Pegg suggests reading inquisitorial material in a different way, "listening"

[17] Christine Caldwell Ames, "Does Inquisition Belong to Religious History?" *American Historical Review* 110 (2005): 11–37, at 24.

[18] Carol Lansing, *Power and Purity: Cathar Heresy in Medieval Italy* (New York, 1998), 19.

[19] John Martin, *Venice's Hidden Enemies: Italian Heretics in a Renaissance City* (Berkeley, 1993), 10.

[20] Ibid., 15.

carefully to the nuances of the text, and refusing automatically to categorize the "heresy" of the subjects. He asserts that it is impossible for us to escape the overwhelming bias of the sources: in seeking out heresy in the Laur-agais, the inquisitors actually created it virtually out of thin air. John Arnold's work with the Jacques Fournier register is another example. In an article in the journal *Rethinking History* (notably titled "The Historian as Inquisitor") Arnold questions the "ethics of interrogating subaltern voices." He suggests that by trying to eliminate the inquisitor's biases by criticizing the sources, "making the real inquisitor disappear in order that the 'truth' of the records can be authorized," we encounter an ethical problem: "the positions of historian and inquisitor can become worryingly blurred," and we run the risk of "colonizing the subaltern voice," that is, reading our own concerns into their words.[21] His solution to the problem—how can we avoid "dissolving the Subject" without "colonizing" him or her—is to look at inquisitorial depositions with a different eye, being sensitive to the different voices the deponent uses (not a single voice), understanding that the deponent is in a sense "creating" his or her self for the inquisitor at the very moment he or she is deposing. For Arnold, the confession is "a moment of self-making," and presents an opportunity for us, as "scribes" rather than "inquisitors," to observe the different voices ("subjectivities") so created, and to let the silences and the "heteroglossic" voices speak for themselves.

It is my belief that while we must always be conscious of the problems of interpretation our sources pose, an equally pressing ethical obligation must lead us to try to understand the world and the events that our sources describe. We should not forget that more than a hundred men and women died at the stake professing the beliefs that are recorded in their *culpe*. Caterina Bruschi, who has worked with other inquisitorial sources in the Doat volumes, puts it well when she observes that we cannot see the whole process of our research and writing as simply literary texts. These texts record "the lives, deaths, plots, suffering and feelings of people who really were brought to trial, gave their testimony and for this were condemned."[22] John Arnold further observes: "In feeding off these texts of power, as the historian can only do, there is an ethical demand to return a space for resistance, to forge thus a critical and effective history, even if the recipient of that gift is only a

---

[21] John Arnold, "The Historian as Inquisitor: The Ethics of Interrogating Subaltern Voices," *Rethinking History* 2 (1998): 379–386, at 381.

[22] Caterina Bruschi, "'Magna diligentia est habenda per inquisitorem': Precautions before Reading Doat 21–26," in *Texts and the Repression of Medieval Heresy*, ed. Caterina Bruschi and Peter Biller (York, 2003), 81–110, at 83.

projected fantasy of this historical subject." We cannot claim to know every-thing—there will always be silences that we cannot, and perhaps should not, fill. Historians are not heroes, "defending those otherwise lost by the famous condescension of posterity," as Arnold chides us for sometimes pretending to be, but ignoring the gifts, however tainted, that the historical record has provided us is no less an affront to those "subaltern subjects of the past."[23]

Working with inquisitorial sources in an attempt to understand the events and beliefs that led an individual to be prosecuted for heresy is thus both in-finitely rewarding and famously full of pitfalls. As I have already mentioned, one famous article critiquing Emmanuel Le Roy Ladurie's *Montaillou* states that the inquisitor is not an anthropologist.[24] John Arnold has declared that the historian must not simply be an inquisitor. With that in mind, I find myself drawn closest to the way in which Edward Muir and Guido Ruggiero understand the ethics of the historian's job in the introduction to a collection titled *History from Crime:* "Thus, even as he snitches on the dead, the histo-rian's fundamental obligation is to respect them in their own terms rather than in those of the judicial record that brings their experiences to view."[25]

With caution and respect, therefore, let us now turn to the stories of the Beguins and their resistance.

AT HOME: RAIMON AND BERNARDA D'ANTUSAN

An important stop on the Beguins' "underground railroad" was the home of Raimon and Bernarda d'Antusan of Cintegabelle (Haute-Garonne).[26] Though Cintegabelle is small and isolated today (and merely accidentally famous as the hometown of former French prime minister Lionel Jospin), it was a substantial village in the fourteenth century, home to a surprising number of Beguins. I say surprising because Cintegabelle had no Franciscan convent of its own, and thus the Beguins of Cintegabelle must have been inspired elsewhere and brought their religious practice home with them. Because they had no Franciscan friars to minister to them, the Beguins of Cintegabelle worshipped in their parish church, which was prosperous

---

[23] Arnold, *Inquisition and Power,* 226–229.

[24] See Rosaldo, "From the Door of His Tent: The Fieldworker and the Inquisitor," in *Writing Culture,* ed. Clifford and Marcus.

[25] Edward Muir and Guido Ruggiero, eds., *History from Crime,* trans. Corrada Biazzo Curry, Margaret A. Gallucci, and Mary M. Gallucci (Baltimore, 1994), viii.

[26] This account is based on the testimonies of the Beguins of Cintegabelle, Belpech, Mazères, and Saverdun, who were all sentenced at Bernard Gui's General Sermon of July

enough in the fourteenth century to rebuild its spire in a style still impressive today.[27] One might have expected that the religiously enthusiastic of Cintegabelle would have turned in a different direction: the wealthy and powerful Cistercian abbey of Boulbonne, where the future pope Benedict XII (the inquisitor Jacques Fournier) began his religious career, was less than three kilometers away up the Ariège river. And yet, when Bernard Gui went looking for Beguins in the Lauragais, he found five in Cintegabelle, all professed members of the Third Order of Saint Francis, two of whom were ultimately burned at the stake for their beliefs. The extended community of Beguins may have been larger than it seems at first glance, since Bernard Gui also found seven Beguins in the village of Belpech (30 kilometers away), two in Mazères (23 kilometers), and even one in nearby Saverdun (10 kilometers), the birthplace of Jacques Fournier. Ties among these Beguins appear strong.[28]

We know very little about the secular lives of any of these Beguins, simply because the inquisitors never asked. Raimon spent time working in a vineyard outside of town, which he probably owned, but since many urban residents had their own vineyards even in much larger towns than Cintegabelle, this tells us nothing about his occupation. Despite his vows of poverty, he appears to have been quite well off, and the couple seems to have been childless. If we can judge from other communities of Third Order Franciscans, Raimon and his wife were comfortably part of the social life of Cintegabelle.[29] No doubt they paid their taxes, spoke with their neighbors, bought their provisions at the local market, and took their water from the same well as everyone else. Though Raimon was not called "minister of the Beguins" as was one of his confrères in Belpech, he was one of the leaders of the little group. Alone among the Beguins of Cintegabelle, he was literate (at least in the vernacular), and was accustomed to reading aloud to his wife and fellows from the copy of the Occitan translation of Olivi's commentary

---

4–5, 1322: *Liber sententiarum* 2:1298–1427. Additional testimony was heard from Guilhem Ros at the General Sermon of September 12, 1322: ibid., 1593–1601.

[27] Karl Baedeker, *Southern France including Corsica*, 6th ed. (Leipzig, 1914), 179. Guide Bleu, *Midi-Pyrénées* (Paris, 1989), 609.

[28] Cintegabelle: Guilhem Ros, Peire Calvet, Raimon and Bernarda d'Antusan, and Maria de Sers; Belpech: Raimon de Buxo, Peire de Na Bruna, Peire Morier, Bernard de Na Jacma, Arnaut Pons, Peire Gastaut, and Raimon Esteve de la Cros; Mazères: Bernard Baron and Raimon Julian; and Saverdun: Mathieu Terrin.

[29] Mariano d'Alatri's exploration of the lives of the *pizocari* of Bologna, also members of the Franciscan Third Order, shows us a secure and respected charitable organization, solidly imbricated in the social fabric of the city. "Penitenti francescani di Romagna," *Aetas poenitentialis: L'antico Ordine francescano della penitenza* (Rome, 1993).

on the Apocalypse that he himself owned, probably as part of the weekly gatherings recommended by the Rule of the Third Order.[30] Since there was no Franciscan convent, these meetings would have been held in the Beguins' homes—and Raimon and Bernarda's home was surely used at least from time to time.

An inquisitorial fly on the wall at those meetings would have found plenty to be interested in. Bernard Gui reported that the Beguins would assemble together in their homes on Sundays and on feast days in order to read aloud (or listen to) such works "as the commandments, the articles of faith, legends of the saints, and the *Summa of Vices and Virtues.*"[31] They also read aloud from texts by Peter Olivi, notably his commentary on the Apocalypse, of course, but also very probably short works like those found in an Occitan manuscript now in Assisi. Scholars suggest that this manuscript was written in exactly this part of the Lauragais, and it contains many short instructive and encouraging spiritual treatises that Olivi wrote to inspire his followers.[32] They may have been derived from sermons he gave in Narbonne. After the readings, the Beguins talked about them together: when the provincial council of Béziers accused Beguins in 1299 of gathering together secretly

[30] See *Supra montem* in *Bullarii Franciscani*, 302–306.

[31] *Manuel* 1:110–115. The *Summa of Vices and Virtues* is a well-known work written by Laurent d'Orléans, a Dominican friar, confessor of Philip III. Several translations into various vernaculars existed, but one is particularly relevant. A Catalan translation of the work has been located by Josep Perarnau in a manuscript in Barcelona, also of Beguin origin (Barcelona, Biblioteca de Catalunya, MS. 740). Perarnau, "Aportació al tema de les traduccions bíbliques catalanes medievals," *Revista Catalana de Teologia* 3 (1978): 17–98, at 34. M. Roy Harris, *The Occitan Translations of John XII and XIII–XVII from a Fourteenth-Century Franciscan Codex (Assisi, Chiesa Nuova MS. 9)* (Philadelphia, 1985), 16–18.

[32] The distinguished scholar of historical linguistics M. Roy Harris draws a likely zone of the manuscript authors' origins that begins on the Ariège river near Saverdun, and extends south and east to Fanjeaux and Lagrasse, covering the extreme eastern part of the Ariège and the western zone of the Aude: *Occitan Translations*, 71. This manuscript was formerly part of the collection of the hermitage of the Carcere, outside of Assisi. Among other works of exhortation and spiritual instruction, and in addition to the four *opuscula* of Olivi discussed below and other unidentified *opuscula*, the manuscript contains translations of the *Rules* of both the first and third Franciscan Orders, the *Testament of Saint Francis*, Bonaventure's *Legenda Maior,* and his *Miracles of Saint Francis*, the confession of Mathieu de Bouzigues, and a part of Francesco de Bartoli's treatise on the Indulgence of the Portiuncula. A general study of the manuscript is found in F. Durieux, "Un manuscrit occitan des spirituels de Narbonne au début du XIVe siècle: Essai d'interprétation franciscaine," *CF* 10 (1975): 231–242. For full documentation of all editions and commentary, see my dissertation, "So Great a Light, So Great a Smoke: The Heresy and Resistance of the Beguins of Languedoc," Ph.D. diss., Northwestern University, 2000, 48n77.

and at night to preach, they replied simply and correctly that all they were doing was "talking about God."[33]

What did they talk about when they "talked about God"? The character of four of Olivi's short texts may help us to understand the Beguins' spiritual lives. One, a "thanksgiving," is nearly hypnotic in its repetition of God's blessings, and in its invocation of the miserable station of the "I": a veritable litany of praise and self-contempt. Another is a fourteen-step program for spiritual self-improvement. A third, titled "A Remedy for Spiritual Temptations," warns the spiritual seeker to beware of tempting visions and revelations,[34] and a fourth, "The Soldier in Arms," or *"Lo cavalier armat,"* is a sermon clearly addressed to those in the world with knowledge of worldly things. Its imagery is entirely militant, and it exhorts the faithful to fight like a good knight amid the "traps and perils of these last times."[35] As we have seen, for Olivi and for his followers, the last times were not merely the trope that had been evoked since evangelical times (as in Matthew 24), but were earnestly and urgently felt to be upon them. All of the texts helped the Beguins to live more spiritually in the world—and also prepared them to interpret the cosmic significance of the persecuting events soon to interrupt their lives.

Though Raimon and Bernarda did not mention to the inquisitor that they had traveled to Narbonne in pilgrimage to Peter Olivi's grave, other Beguins of Cintegabelle certainly had. Maria de Sers, a widow, went at least once to the celebration held annually on March 14, and heard a sermon there which inspired her very much. She heard not only that Peter Olivi "was their father and an uncanonized saint," but also that it did not make any difference whether or not the Church ever did canonize him: for "God had canonized him in his life and in his death."[36] She surely spoke about this sermon to her

---

[33] *"Concilium Provinciale Anno M. CC. XCIX. Biterris celebratum sub ægidio Narbonensi archiepiscopo,"* in *Thesaurus novus anecdotorum,* ed. E. Martène and M. Durand (Paris, 1717), vol. IV, cols. 225–228.

[34] Olivi's counsels here would seem to parallel the preference for apophatic rather than visionary experience of God seen so clearly in Marguerite Porete and Meister Eckhart. See Amy Hollywood, *The Soul as Virgin Wife: Mechtild of Magdeburg, Marguerite Porete, and Meister Eckhart* (Notre Dame, IN, 1995), 16–25.

[35] These four *opuscula* are most easily accessible in their Latin forms, edited from Guarnacciano MS. 5230 of Volterra, in Manselli, *Spirituali,* 267–290. Jean Duvernoy has translated them into French in Manselli, *Spirituels et béguins du Midi* (Toulouse, 1989), 239–256. For translations into Italian, and commentary (along with indications of editions and manuscripts), see Peter Olivi, *Pietro di Giovanni Olivi: Scritti scelti,* ed. Paolo Vian (Rome, 1989), 145–192. See also Raoul Manselli, "Opuscules spirituels de Pierre Jean Olivi et la piété des béguins de langue d'oc," *CF* 11 (1976): 187–201.

[36] "Non opportebat quod per hominem canonizaretur, quia Deus canonizaverat eum in vita et in morte, ut dicebant." Maria de Sers, *Liber sententiarum* 2:1374.

fellow Beguins, for all of them testified that they believed exactly this about Peter Olivi. While she was in Narbonne, Maria formed acquaintances with many other Beguins from all over Languedoc, friendships that were soon to be tested.

Raimon, Bernarda, and their companions faced their first real trial in the spring of 1318. One of their friends, another Beguin named Peire Calvet, told the inquisitors in 1322 that he remembered vividly when the news of the burnings of Marseille first reached Cintegabelle.

> It was four years ago in Eastertide when Peire Trencavel came to Cintega-belle and told the Beguins that four friars minor had been condemned as heretics in Marseille by an inquisitor who was of the Franciscan Order; and after this, he, Peire Calvet and the other Beguins began to speak among themselves in many times and places about the condemnation of the friars, saying that they were condemned badly and unjustly and by the envy of the other friars and of the inquisitor of Marseille; that they underwent death for the truth and for the Rule which was the same as the life of the Gospels; and then he and the others said that they were holy martyrs, and so he believed it to be.[37]

Four years later, Peire presented it as a nearly foregone conclusion (the four friars "were holy martyrs, and so he believed it to be"), but in fact, reaching such a conclusion took considerable heated discussion and argument. Their Sunday meetings no doubt became far more lively, contentious, and indeed anguished over how to react or respond to the news. Their strongly held beliefs told them that the execution of the friars was wrong, but they also knew that taking a stand against the papacy was dangerous. While they told themselves that Olivi had predicted exactly this kind of persecution for the last times, they surely feared the consequences of being in such opposition to the established church. But once the Beguins reached the conclusion that the four friars had been condemned unjustly, they took the next logical step.

---

[37] "IIIIor anni erunt in tempore Paschali quod Petrus Trencavelli veniens apud Cinc-tam Gavellam narravit Beguinis ipso audiente quod IIIIor fratres Minores fuerant con-dempnati tanquam heretici apud Massiliam per inquisitorem heretice pravitatis qui erat de ordine fratrum Minorum, et extunc ipse P. Calveti et alii Beguini inter se de condemp-nacione predictorum fratrum multociens et in multis locis loquebantur, et dicebant quod fuerant condempnati male et injuste et per invidiam aliorum fratrum Minorum et prefati inquisitoris Massiliensis, et quod sustinuerant mortem pro veritate sue regule que erat vita evangelica, et tam ipse quam alii dicebant illos esse sanctos martires, et ipse credebat ita esse." Ibid., 1366.

As Olivi had predicted in that vernacular translation of his Apocalypse commentary that they knew so well, they declared that apocalyptic times were upon them, and it was vital to react appropriately.

But what did that mean? From this crucial moment forward, the Beguins began to look at the Book of Revelation (as interpreted by Olivi) as a script for the drama that was playing itself out around them. They already knew that Saint Francis was the Angel of the Sixth Seal (Revelation 7:2), and many of them had been saying for a long time that Peter Olivi was the Angel Whose Face Shone Like the Sun (Revelation 7:2 and 10:1–2). The inquisitors, and the papal power and hierarchy that stood behind them, were a "carnal church" that persecuted the "spiritual church"—that is to say, themselves. Who would they cast in the role of Antichrist? Olivi had predicted two Antichrists, one "major" Antichrist and one "mystical," and both roles were up for grabs. How were they to interpret Babylon the great whore sitting on her throne? Raimon, Bernarda, and the other Beguins were preoccupied by these questions beginning in 1318, and their concern intensified as the inquisitors of Carcassonne and Toulouse turned their attention to the Beguins themselves.

In mid to late October of 1319, more horrifying news reached the communities of Cintegabelle and Belpech. Five Beguins whom all of them had known had been burned, two on October 14 in Narbonne, and three on October 18 in Capestang. The four friars burned in Marseille were more distant figures, but some of these, especially "brother Mai" burned in Narbonne, were beloved friends. The shock and grief soon gave way to debate: were these five, too, to be regarded as martyrs who had died for their faith and were now saints in Paradise? Both Raimon and Bernarda were among those who definitively answered "yes" to this question, and they took their veneration to the next logical level and collected relics from these martyred saints. In the fall of 1321, Raimon traveled to Narbonne, where he saw the burned torso of a virgin martyred at Lunel, but by then he already had a small collection of other bones from other autos-da-fé. He even had a piece of the wood to which brother Mai or his companion had been tied as he was burned. Raimon and Bernarda took their small collection and, having kissed the relics with devotion, placed it with great reverence in a small box inside the coffer where Bernarda kept her precious household things.[38]

---

[38] The story of Bernarda and Raimon can be found in their testimony before Bernard Gui (*Liber sententiarum* 2:1340–1358), as supplemented by the testimony of the other Beguins from the same region in the same volume.

The local Beguins all treated the relics that they had received with similar devotion and reverence, and some even evoked their thaumaturgic power. Peire Morier of Belpech had bones from the Beguins burned in Lunel that he placed next to the lamp which he kept in front of his image of the crucifix. Maria de Sers of Cintegabelle also had several small relics that she kept with her, wrapped carefully in a piece of silk. She once showed them to a friend, who prayed as she kissed them, "if these relics can help me with God, then let them help."[39]

Comments like these briefly evoke the inner world of the beleaguered Beguins. Maria's friend *wanted* to believe that the relics she had in her hands were of real saints—or rather that the "saints" in question were truly saintly—but she still had her moments of doubt. Similar doubts were common among the Beguins. Peire Calvet, for instance, who reported so clearly that he believed the four friars, and later the burned Beguins, to be holy martyrs in Paradise, had many doubts on other points. Did he believe, for instance, that the inquisitor of Carcassonne was a heretic? Not, apparently, until he heard read the confession of a Beguin he had known well (Arnaut Pons of Belpech) who declared that such was the case—and then, Peire declared, "having heard this read, he and the other Beguins hearing it were consoled on that point."[40] But what about the pope? Was he a heretic too? Peire declared that he had wondered greatly about that, but that he was inclined to think he was not. They believed, and yet they doubted, too. They did not blindly follow everything they heard, but exercised their own judgment on many points.

We might wonder why so few of the Beguins took flight to avoid the inquisitors, once they realized the effectiveness of the inquisitors' efforts to suppress their movement. Maria de Sers did, but she left it until the last moment. Her attempt was not very effective, as she was captured in L'Isle Jourdain on the other side of Toulouse. Only one local Beguin, Bernard Baron of Mazères, was more successful, and Bernard Gui excommunicated him *in absentia*, as he had fled and could not be found. There is a hint of longing in the way Bernarda d'Antusan spoke to Peire Tort and Peire Arrufat: "She said that if she and her husband were not so afraid of the oath

[39] "Item predictas reliquias cuidam persone quam in confessione sua nominat ostendit et, ut sibi videtur, eas osculata fuit, dicens quod rogabat dictas reliquias quod si eam peterant juvare cum Deo juvarent." Ibid., 1372–1375. Beguins elsewhere in Languedoc behaved similarly with their heretical relics (see below for the story of Esclarmonda Durban).
[40] Ibid., 1368.

they had sworn, and of the damages their guarantors would suffer because of them, they would willingly go to Jerusalem." Her husband added that he and his wife and many other Beguins believed that if they fled to Jerusalem, they might be able to avoid "the fighting and the wars that would soon destroy the kingdom of France and the carnal Church." But instead, most of them stayed and faced the inquisitors when their time came. The possibility of martyrdom was no doubt part of the tangled thoughts and emotions that kept them in Cintegabelle. Martyrdom was terrifying and enticing at the same time, an opportunity to prove their faith and their confidence of the place in history that God had given them. There would be a glory in going up in flames for such a cause, and the prospect of an immediate heavenly reward surely gave a savor to the taste of martyrdom for these pious men and women. It could be an *imitatio sanctorum*, with the burned Beguins as their model saints. Bernard de Na Jacma of Belpech put it this way: "Likewise, he said that he induced a certain person (whom he named), who was in a sort of passion of fear, that he should commend himself to the Beguins burned as heretics, whom he thought to be martyrs and saints, and that he should be willing to die in that faith in which these Beguins died."[41] In any event, they stayed.

Though it may have been inconvenient for the Beguins of Cintegabelle, Belpech, Mazères, and Saverdun to live so far from the Franciscan centers of Narbonne and Béziers, once the persecution began, that distance became an asset. Though all of them lived openly in their communities wearing the distinctive Beguin habit and associating frequently with each other, they became the targets for local inquisitors only in the spring of 1322, two and a half years after the first burning of Beguins.[42] This gave them the opportunity to help their fellows in a variety of crucial ways. Raimon de Buxo of Belpech, for instance, itemized a considerable list:

> This Raimon did receive and has received many apostate [friars] and took them from place to place.... he knew many others who were believers and

[41] "Item dixit quod ipse induxit quandam personam quam nominat que erat in quadam passione timoris quod conmendaret se Beguinis conbustis ut hereticis quod ipse reputabat esse martires et sanctos, et quod vellet mori in illa fide in qua predicti Beguini mortui fuerant." Ibid., 1338. I thank Richard Kieckhefer for his help with this passage. Bernard was merely imprisoned on the occasion of his deposition before Bernard Gui, but the Wolfenbüttel Martyrology (henceforth WM) makes it clear that he was executed on an unknown future date (see Burnham, "So Great a Light," appendix A, lines 57–58).

[42] The earliest local Beguin taken by inquisitors, Arnaut Pons, was burned in Narbonne in late February 1322, and, given the distance to Narbonne from Belpech, it is likely that he was captured while visiting other Beguins in Narbonne.

who knew the situation of those condemned and he went with them from place to place hiding his habit. He visited the Beguins who were held in prison in Narbonne and were later condemned, and he heard and he knew the words, the counsels, and the discussions of their beliefs. Hiding his habit, he also went with several others to the sermons that the prelates and the inquisitors gave in the province of Narbonne in order to find out what they were doing and saying about the Beguins.[43]

Others did many of the same things. Guilhem Ros of Cintegabelle was one of those who went with Raimon into the "province of Narbonne" looking for information, but as he articulated his goal, it also included, as he put it (and the inquisitorial scribe reported it), "to rejoice in the constancy of those who did not wish to renounce their erroneous opinions."[44]

Most commonly, however, the Beguins of Cintegabelle and the other nearby towns of the Lauragais acted as stops on an underground railroad of sorts. They received, hid, and passed on many apostate Franciscans and fugitive Beguins. Our Raimon d'Antusan and his wife Bernarda did exactly that, as did Peire de Na Bruna and Bernard de Na Jacma of Belpech, Mathieu Terrin of Saverdun, and Guilhem Ros, Maria de Sers, and Peire Calvet of Cintegabelle. Maria de Sers perhaps expressed it best:

> She also saw and associated with many other Beguins and Beguines, both those suspected of the aforesaid errors, and those who were fugitives because of heresy. She ate with them, and gave to them bread and wine and eggs and money. She did not reveal any of them, male or female, nor did she capture them or help them be captured.[45]

Such aid was precious to those who were on the run, and towns like Cintegabelle or Belpech were used as places to continue to articulate and to expound the evolving Beguin message. Bernard de Na Jacma, Guilhem Ros, and Peire Calvet all testified to the inquisitors that they had participated in meetings or conventicles where those fugitives such as Peire Hospital of Montpellier and Peire Domergue of Narbonne, both ultimately burned in Toulouse in September 1322, had read aloud from Olivi's writings on

[43] *Liber sententiarum* 2:1308.
[44] Ibid., 1364.
[45] "Item multos alios beguinos et beguinas de erroribus predictis et aliis loquentes et suspectos et suspectas existentes et fugitivos pro heresi vidit, associavit et cum eis comedit, et panem et vinum et ova et pecuniam dedit eis, nec eos vel eas revelavit, nec cepit nec capi fecit." Ibid., 1374.

the book of the Apocalypse and on poverty. As Guilhem Ros said, it was in such meetings that "he and the other Beguins mutually informed themselves about their erroneous opinions."[46]

Such meetings were not entirely gloomy, however, and another way of resisting can be found in the jokes they told each other. Bernard de Na Jacma of Belpech related that when someone asked him if the pope was able to dispense anything from the rule of Saint Francis, he used to respond by mocking the Petrine formula of Matthew 16:19 in which lay the cornerstone of papal authority: "Do you believe that if the pope ties the tail of an ass on earth, that the tail of the ass is tied in heaven?"[47] Even more than vituperative language, a mocking tone diminished the authority of the Church both for those who spoke and for those who listened. When the Beguins laughed at the idea of the pope tying an ass's tail, they made him seem ridiculous in addition to cruel. Another Beguin foresaw a humiliating end for the papal tiara in an anecdote sure to draw a laugh from a sympathetic listener:

> The Church was founded in humility, purity, and poverty, but these days, it has been changed into the contrary, since the clerics are adulterers, fornicators, and usurers, and they are laying waste to the goods of the Church with their splendid appearances, and great pomp, and with great horses. But the time will come when God will humiliate them, and it will behove them to cover their crowns with muck, or cow dung.[48]

Yet another Beguin made fun of a particular one of their persecutors: "Those Preachers are certainly persecuting the Beguin brothers of penitence, but our Lord Jesus Christ will repay them, and has repaid them already, with a good reward and a fine pay-off. This is clear from the case of brother Johan de Sant Gili, who was persecuting the brothers of penitence—now he's so

---

[46] "Et fuit in conventiculis et congregacionibus in quibus ipse et alii Beguini se mutuo informabant de predictis opinionibus erroneis." Ibid., 1366.

[47] "Credetis vos quod si papa ligaret unam caudam asini in terra quod illa cauda asini esset ligata in celo?" Ibid., 1336. "And whatsoever thou shalt bind upon earth, it shall be bound also in heaven: and whatsoever thou shalt loose on earth, it shall be loosed also in heaven."

[48] "Item quod Ecclesia fundata fuerat in humilitate, puritate, et paupertate, sed in isto tempore mutata erat in contrarium, quia clerici facti sunt adulteri, fornicatores, usurarii, et devastant bona Ecclesie cum superbia, et magna pompa, et magnis equis, sed veniret tempus quod deus humiliaret eos et quod oporteret eos cooperire Coronas suas de bosa, vel stercore bovino." Doat 28, fol. 228v.

sick with gout that he can't even get out of bed!"[49] Gout, the affliction *par excellence* of those living well and (especially) drinking well in the popular imagination, must have seemed a particularly appropriate fate for the persecutors of those vowed to poverty and poor use.[50]

Naturally, the Beguins of Cintegabelle and the surrounding towns also contributed to the material well-being of the fugitives, giving them food of various kinds and money. Bernard de Na Jacma sent ten shillings on one occasion to Beguins imprisoned in Narbonne, and nine silver shillings of Tours on another.[51] Our Raimon d'Antusan of Cintegabelle was even more generous, once sending one hundred silver shillings of Tours and, later, fifty. Even later, he acknowledged having given to Peire Trencavel, the ubiquitous Beguin missionary, a total of three hundred golden pennies, both in golden "agnis" and in florins, on two different occasions. This last sum he delivered as a kind of deposit: should he himself manage to make it to Greece or to Jerusalem (where he clearly believed Peire was going himself), there Peire would help him to establish himself.[52]

The most vivid picture of this underground network comes from the moment at which it all fell apart. In the spring of 1322, Raimon and Bernarda (as well as several others from the region) had testified before Bernard Gui. Though at first, when all of them were held together in the castle of the Alamans near Pamiers, they had made a pact to hide the truth about their faith and the actions they had taken against the inquisitors, eventually all of them spoke with the inquisitor Bernard Gui and told the stories I have recounted here.[53] They all abjured their heresy, and were released to return to their homes while they awaited the judgment of the inquisitors. On the Tuesday after Easter (April 13), however, Raimon came home from his vineyard to discover that in his absence, his wife had entertained Peire Tort and Peire Arrufat, both fugitives from justice, and both disguised. According

[49] "Isti Predicatores multum persecuntur fratres Beguinos de Penitentia, et Dominus Jhesus Christus reddet et reddidit eis bonam mercedem et bonam solutionem; et apparet per fratrem Johannem de Sancto Egidio, qui persequebatur dictos fratres de Penitentia, qui sic infirmatur de guta, quod non potest se movere de lecto." Alexandre Germain, "Une consultation inquisitoriale au XIVe siècle," *Publications de la Société Archéologique de Montpellier* 4 (1857): 309–344, at 334.

[50] Seneca, for instance, wrote: "Bacchus is the father, Venus the mother, and Wrath the midwife of gout." Roy Porter and G. S. Rousseau, *Gout: The Patrician Malady* (New Haven, 1998), 18. The translation is my own.

[51] *Liber sententiarum* 2:1330–1333.

[52] Ibid., 1346, 1350.

[53] Peire de Na Bruna confessed to the pact in his testimony. Ibid., 1314.

to him, he berated her for not turning them in. According to his wife, the men, no doubt friends or Beguin acquaintances from more peaceable times, had entered the house, where one of them greeted her in the manner usual for Beguins: "Blessed be the name of our Lord Jesus Christ," to which all responded "Amen."[54] Bernarda asked her guests about the Beguins of Narbonne, and they told her that twenty-one had been burned on February 28 and that they had withstood their martyrdom "valiantly and strongly." She informed her guests that she and her husband had both sworn to obey the inquisitors and that she was not supposed to talk with any fugitives, but to turn them in instead. Again according to her, Peire denied that they were fugitives at all. As proof, he told her that they had stayed with a Beguin in another town who had been deposed before the bishop of Mirepoix.

While they were speaking together, another Beguin (Guilhem Ros) came into the house, and as all four were drinking a cup of wine together, he informed them that the fugitives had been spotted. He advised that the two Peires had better leave town immediately and cross the bridge to the other side of the Ariège river. Before the two left, however, Bernarda gave them a big slice of cake and two pieces of roast meat.[55]

This incident was the end of the line for the Cintegabelle underground railroad. Peire Tort and Peire Arrufat were taken that very evening by the authorities just across the Ariège, after Guilhem Ros had a change of heart and told the consuls of Cintegabelle where to find them. Raimon, Bernarda, and Guilhem were all taken back to Pamiers to testify again before the inquisitors, and in July all the Beguins of Cintegabelle, Belpech, Mazères, and Saverdun were sentenced. Most of them, including Raimon and Bernarda, were imprisoned in Toulouse. The others, including Guilhem Ros, were sent on to the prison of Carcassonne. These were not, unfortunately, the final sentences for many of them. Though we do not know the full circumstances for most, Guilhem Ros and Peire Calvet of Cintegabelle, Raimon de Buxo, Peire Morier, Bernard de Na Jacma, and Raimon Esteve de la Cros of Belpech all eventually finished their lives on the stake.[56] Whether Raimon and Bernarda ever returned to their home in Cintegabelle, we do not know, but if they did, many of their dearest friends and companions in piety were no longer there.

[54] As Bernard Gui observed in his inquisitorial manual: *Manuel* 1:118–119.
[55] Both stories are found in *Liber sententiarum* 2:1350 (Raimon), and 1354–1359 (Bernarda). In fact, it was Guilhem Ros who turned them in to the town consuls, and his version of the story provides several additional details (1592–1595).
[56] See appendix.

The most emblematic image of heresy and inquisition is that of the stake.[57] Whether we imagine the more than 200 burned at Montségur on March 16, 1244, or Joan of Arc dying alone in Rouen on May 30, 1431 (or Renée Falconetti or Ingrid Bergman for that matter), the picture is much the same: a pile of wood, a stake at the center, and individuals whose agonized faces are gradually obscured by the smoke and the flames. It seems a terrible way to die, a punishment not so much unusual, alas, as fiercely cruel.

And yet we know, because countless books and stories tell us so, that many people actively sought the stake, preferring to die in such a way rather than to renounce the beliefs they held so dear. Not everyone went willingly to the stake, of course, and there are chilling accounts of those who pleaded or begged for their lives or cursed their persecutors through the flames, but the true martyr who embraced his or her fate for the cause is an unforgettable figure, compelling and irresistible.

In the drama of their death, they were witnesses to the truth of the causes they espoused, and their deaths frequently proved to be inspirational.[58] As Tertullian so famously wrote in the third century, "the blood of the martyrs is the seed of the Church."[59] His words have been proven true for many "churches" throughout history.

Esclarmonda Durban was one of over one hundred Beguins who were this kind of inspiration to those around them. Her death on the stake in October 1321 was witnessed by many and heard about by many more. She, the sixteen others who were burned with her in Lunel, and the nearly ninety more who also died for the Beguin cause in Languedoc became martyrs for the truth as they and their fellow Beguins saw it. Understanding the dynamics of how light became smoke, and smoke again light, is vital if we are to understand anything about the Beguins and their struggle.

---

[57] Since Esclarmonda's deposition before the inquisitors has not survived, this account is based instead on the depositions of many others, especially those of the "Beguins of Lodève," Doat 28, fols. 11v–27v, published in Manselli, *Spirituali*, 309–319. Evidence of burnings not mentioned in these depositions comes from the Beguin martyrology (WM). See also Burnham, "Reliques et résistance chez les Béguins de Languedoc," *Annales du Midi* 108 (2006): 352–368.

[58] A thoughtful and probing examination of the phenomenon of martyrdom is Lacey Baldwin Smith, *Fools, Martyrs, Traitors: The Story of Martyrdom in the Western World* (New York, 1997).

[59] Perhaps even more as famously qualified by E. R. Dodds: "provided always that the seed falls on suitable ground and is not sown too thickly." *Pagan and Christian in an Age of Anxiety* (Cambridge, 1965), 133.

Esclarmonda's native town, Clermont l'Hérault, is a fortified market town northwest of Montpellier on the border between the highlands of the Larzac and the vineyards of the plain. Esclarmonda came from a pious family and, like one or, more probably, two of her brothers, was a Franciscan tertiary. It is unclear when she and her brothers Bernard and Johan moved to Lodève, though it was likely when they were adults, since another brother, Raimon (who was not a Beguin), remained behind in Clermont. One good reason to move may have been the presence of a Franciscan convent in Lodève, an episcopal city rather larger than Clermont.[60]

Like Raimon and Bernarda d'Antusan, the Durban siblings had a large circle of like-minded friends and acquaintances between the two nearby cities of Lodève and Clermont. We know a little bit more about the occupations of the Beguins of Lodève than we do about the Beguins of Cintegabelle, and many of them were artisans. Raimon Durban was a smith, but there was also a locksmith, a parchment maker, and a butcher. There were also priests, Franciscan friars, and quite a number of women. In all, the Lodève chapter of the Franciscan Third Order numbered well over twenty-five.[61]

Many of them were married (some to each other), but Esclarmonda appears to have instead taken a vow of chastity, as did at least two other Beguines from Lodève. One was a widow (Ermessendis Grossa, who later moved to Gignac), but Esclarmonda and her friend Astruga both seem to have been virgins. Certainly, their holiness was much admired—one acquaintance from

---

[60] Lodève's convent was founded before 1238. Richard W. Emery, *The Friars in Medieval France: A Catalogue of French Mendicant Convents, 1200–1550* (New York, 1962), 73.

[61] Eighteen Beguins have left depositions or other traces in the Collection Doat: Esclarmonda Durban, Manselli, *Spirituali*, 309–319, WM, l. 26; Bernard Durban, Manselli, *Spirituali*, 309–310, Doat 28, fols. 31r–33r, 115r–116r; Amada Orlach Doat 28, fols. 189v, 193r–194v; Amorosus Lauret, Doat 28, fol. 233v, and Doat 27, fol. 80v; Astruga, WM, l. 27, Manselli, *Spirituali*, 307–319; Berengaria Estorgua, Doat 28, fols. 189v, 194v–196r; Berenguier Jaoul, Manselli, *Spirituali*, 313–315, Doat 28, fols. 31r–33r, 115r–116r, Doat 27, fol. 80v; Bernard Malaura, Manselli, *Spirituali*, 312–313, Doat 28, fols. 33r–36r; Bernard Peyrotas, Manselli, *Spirituali*, 315–318, WM, l. 29, Doat 27, fol. 13r, Doat 28, fols. 194r–195v; Deodat Marcel, Doat 27, fols. 3r–7r; Ermessendis Grossa, Doat 27, fols. 14r–16r, 89v–91v; Guilhem Serallier, Manselli, *Spirituali*, 324–326, Doat 27, fols. 24v, 26r, 39r, 80, Doat 28, fols. 193r, 194v, 233v; Jacma Lauret Amorosa, Manselli, *Spirituali*, 310, Doat 28, fols. 233v–235v, Doat 28, fols. 203v, 31r–33r, Doat 27, fol. 80v; Manenta Rosa Arnaut, Manselli, *Spirituali*, 310–311, Doat 28, fols. 31r–33r, Doat 27, fols. 79v–82r, 97r–98r; Peire de Palasco, Doat 28, fol. 7r; Raimon Rigaut, Doat 27, fol. 24v, Doat 28, fols. 195r–195v; Raimunda Rigauda, Doat 27, fol. 80v, Doat 28, fol. 194v; and Rosa Maur, Doat 28, fols. 3r–3v. There are also 15 unidentified individuals burned at Lunel in October 1321, of whom the majority were probably also from Lodève or Clermont l'Hérault (see WM, l. 22–27). There are also two identified Beguins from Clermont (Berenguier Rocha, and Martin Alegre de San Antonin, Manselli, *Spirituali*, 311–312).

Clermont mentioned their "good life" as a compelling reason for his admiration. Another mentioned their "good life and conduct."[62]

Though the closeness of their sizable community must have made for a warm environment in which to live and to worship, their solidarity was tested early on. The Beguins of Lodève were one of the earliest communities to be rounded up and questioned, well before Cintegabelle. They were not difficult to identify, of course, because they wore distinctive clothing and had made no secret of their affiliation. The bishop of Lodève (like the bishop of Pamiers, Jacques Fournier) took charge of the investigation himself and interrogated the Beguins of both Lodève and Clermont. The questions he asked were those that had brought down the four famous friars burned in Marseille: Did the pope have the authority to force Franciscans to change their clothing (i.e., could a Franciscan be forced to abrogate his vow of "poor use")? Did the pope have the authority to require Franciscans to keep grain in granaries and wine in cellars, as per *Quorumdam exigit?* The bishop also probed them further regarding Franciscan poverty. Were the Franciscans different in any way from other orders regarding poverty? Moreover, what did they think of the friars burned in Marseille? Had they been burned justly, or injustly? Did they consider those friars to be martyrs?

The answers that he heard were quite predictable. The intransigent simply denied papal authority on all three crucial points regarding *Quorumdam exigit,* and further asserted that the four friars had been condemned unjustly and were holy martyrs in Heaven. And in a response that would soon shake up the entire Franciscan Order and not merely the Spirituals of Languedoc, many of them replied that just as Christ and the apostles owned nothing either individually or in common, so the Franciscan Order also owned nothing, even in common.[63] A substantial number of the Beguins of Lodève (Esclarmonda and Astruga among them) were adamant on all of these points and were soon incarcerated by the bishop. Some Beguins who felt unable to swear compliance with the bishop's demands had time to flee the region.

[62] Martin Alegre de San Antonin and Berenguier Rocha, Manselli, *Spirituali,* 311, 312.

[63] Arguments over this last statement opened the second part of the poverty debate of the 1320s. The occasion was the appeal to the pope by the Dominican inquisitor Jean de Beaune and a Franciscan theologian from Narbonne, Berengar Talon, on the orthodoxy of the statement of a Beguin interrogated in Languedoc, who had stated that Christ and the Apostles had owned nothing, either individually or in common. The Dominican found it heretical, but the Franciscan insisted that it had been approved in *Exiit qui seminat.* The conflict appears in the nearly contemporary chronicle of Nicolaus Minorita, *Nicolaus Minorita: Chronica,* ed. Gedéon Gál and David Flood (St. Bonaventure, NY, 1996), 62.

Others, however, confessed such errors of belief, but also professed their desire to abjure these heresies and to be absolved of their errors. Esclarmonda's brother Bernard Durban, the priest Bernard Peyrotas, Berenguier Rocha of Clermont, Guilhem Serallier the locksmith, and many others were among their number. They were absolved, apparently in private with the bishop, released, and soon returned to their lives in Lodève and Clermont. Some of them were given letters to prove that they had passed through inquisitorial hands.[64] As subsequent events make clear, however, not all of these abjurations were fully sincere, and a substantive underground movement of Beguins and their sympathizers soon flourished in Lodève.

Similar investigations were of course taking place across Languedoc, and it was not long before news of Beguin condemnations began to trickle in. First came the three burned in Narbonne on October 14, 1319, who had so upset the Beguins of Cintegabelle, and then three more in Capestang only four days later. Though these were surely distressing to all of them, the first real local blow came in May 1320, when Johan Durban, Esclarmonda's brother, who had fled to points further south and west in Languedoc, was captured by inquisitors and soon burned at a second auto-da-fé in Capestang. It was one thing to envision the death of friars whom the Beguins had perhaps heard give a compelling sermon or to whom they had confessed, but it was quite another when a man whom they had known for most of their lives and admired for his saintly life was concerned. Soon they began to speak among themselves and to concur that the burned Beguins were martyrs in Paradise, just like the friars of Marseille.

Berenguier Jaoul of Clermont, a merchant, remembered those conversations well (though he later protested that he was no expert in such things, being a mere layman). Some of the conversations took place not in Lodève itself, but at the church of San Antonin nearby, where five Franciscan friars were then living. Brothers Frances Aribert, Esteve Seret, Jacme de Cesteramnicis, Jannet of Clermont, and Johan Bauscii may not have been among the friars summoned to Avignon in 1317, but they were devoted to the cause of the Spirituals just as firmly—they all lost their lives for the cause.[65] The writings of Peter Olivi had prepared them to expect to be persecuted, just as Christ himself had been persecuted. The pope had no power to condemn

[64] See Doat 28, 5r, where there is a question as to the binding quality of the abjuration of Bernard Durban, since he had not made a solemn oath. Also, the confession of Guilhem Serralier refers to his having been absolved, struck by a rod, and given a letter to that effect. Manselli, *Spirituali*, 325.

[65] See Bernard Malaura, Manselli, *Spirituali*, 313.

the Spiritual friars for defending the vows they had taken, any more than he could grant them a dispensation from the Gospel itself, because, as they said, the Rule of Saint Francis that they had vowed to live by was itself evangelical. Berenguier later remembered hearing that those who ruled over the Roman Church did so in pomp, pleasure, pride, and arrogance, as opposed to the Spirituals and Beguins who lived in goodness and led holy lives. What is more, these friars and others whom he had known (including the priest Bernard Peyrotas, and the Beguin Frances Bastier) asserted most vehemently that "those Beguins who were burned were burned and condemned because they held these same views and they said and believed that these [burned Beguins] were martyrs."[66]

The years 1320 and 1321 were difficult for the Beguins of Lodève. Those who were imprisoned were transferred to join other Beguins in the diocese of Maguelone, thus taking them far from their families and friends who had previously visited them in prison. Others were still at large, but afraid to talk about the crisis except in whispers among themselves. Bad news continued to arrive. After five were burned in Capestang, two more were burned in Béziers, and several more again in Agde in 1320. In 1321, seven died in Béziers and four in Pézenas. Four of the Beguins of Lodève and Clermont (Berenguier Rocha, Berenguier Jaoul, Bernard Malaura, and the priest Bernard Peyrotas) traveled to either Capestang or Béziers to witness these events, and returned with eyewitness accounts of both the cruelty of the inquisitors and the steady faith of the burned Beguins. They praised them collectively and individually. Bernard Malaura said of the Beguins of Capestang, "never had he seen men die so sweetly."[67] A young virgin of 15 burned in Béziers was praised by many.[68] When he heard the things that Fornier de Floruissac said to the bishop of Agde as he was burned in Pézenas, Bernard Peyrotas was sure that he and all the others had been unjustly condemned.[69] Things were not going well across Languedoc, but in the fall of 1321 the situation in Lodève became abruptly worse when the bishops of Lodève and Maguelone scheduled an execution.

An announcement was made ahead of time, and in early October the Beguins of Lodève still free received a letter from sympathizers closer to Maguelone. The letter told them to come to Lunel, a town on the other side of Montpellier, on the feast of Saint Luke, Sunday, October 18, where

[66] Berenguier Jaoul, ibid., 313–315.
[67] Ibid., 312.
[68] Doat 28, fol. 232r–v, WM, l. 17–18.
[69] Manselli, *Spirituali*, 317.

they would see "the soldiers or the martyrs fighting the good fight."[70] The language was familiar. Peter Olivi's short spiritual tract *Lo cavalier armat* had compared the apocalyptic Christian to an armed knight, equipped with three breastplates, a helmet, a lance, a sword, a shield, and a bow and arrows—each of the weapons representing a different virtue that would be demanded of them in the last times that were upon them. The first breastplate was "a most sharp and robust fervor of faith that always desires war," the second, "a most humble abnegation of all base human sentiments," and the third, "super-excessive confidence in Christ." With a helmet of "filial fear of God," a lance of "an exemplary reputation," a bright and shining sword of "an open and just sentence of truth," and a shield of God's omnipresence, the warrior was ready to do battle, armed also with the bow of Holy Scripture and the arrows of the Words of God.[71] Such a martial image gave strength and purpose to those who faced death themselves and was an inspiration for those who merely watched. This language is, of course, reminiscent of the language used to describe the agony of the early martyrs of the Church.

The Beguins of Lodève heeded the call. On October 18, 1321, several of them were present at the condemnation in Lunel. Though we do not have the program for this particular event, we can imagine the scene nonetheless. General Sermons were very public and grand affairs to which the inquisitors (or in this case, the bishops of Maguelone and Lodève) devoted considerable money and resources. They were "spectacles of punishment," as James Given has observed, where "the church's official version of correct spiritual order was acted out in a grandiose and impressive public fashion."[72] Like the Beguins themselves, the bishops, too, sent out letters across the region, inviting other bishops, inquisitors, and local lords to attend the occasion in order to make it as solemn and impressive as possible. They would have built an imposing catafalque in or near the cemetery of Lunel, and servants would have been dispatched to guard it until the day of the Sermon. There would have been a lavish meal for the guests and a lengthy procession of all the notable attendees as well as those to be condemned. Finally, of course, the secular authority, which was actually to perform the executions, would have prepared wood, vines, shrouds, and ropes to tie those who were to die, and executioners to bind the guilty and set fire to the pyre. Such justice was

[70] Ibid., 318.

[71] Ibid., 287–289. Ingrid Arthur, "*Lo Cavalier armat*, version provençal du *Miles Armatus* attribué à Pierre de Jean Olivi," *Studia neophilologica* 31 (1959): 43–64.

[72] James Given analyzes the idea of the General Sermon as propaganda in *Inquisition*, 71–76. Curiously, he makes little use of this evidence about the importance, cost, and ceremony involved in the General Sermon.

not cheap. For the execution of only four men in 1323, the seneschal of Carcassonne spent a total of £31 3s. 9d. (for comparison, the jailer was paid £12 a year to house a heretic in the Wall of Carcassonne). With such an event, inquisitors could be sure that their message had been made abundantly and magnificently clear.[73]

On the day of the execution in Lunel, the crowds were intense as seventeen recalcitrant heretics (seven women and ten men) were brought out to the cemetery. Though Lunel is now a fairly sleepy agricultural village, in the fourteenth century it was a vibrant and lively place, and doubtless a considerable proportion of its populace came to watch the spectacle.[74] Bernard Durban and his brother Raimon, Martin Alegre de San Antonin, Bernard Malaura, Berenguier Rocha, and Berenguier Jaoul, all from either Lodève or Clermont l'Hérault, were there, though they did not all travel together and likely did not stand together for fear of being recognized. A Beguin from Narbonne, Peire Arrufat, had also come to witness. The crowd was so loud as the ceremony drew to a close that when Esclarmonda asked to have her confession read to her again, Bernard could not even hear the answer of the authorities. The seventeen men and women were bound to stakes, the pyre was lit, and the crowd from Lodève watched their sisters, brothers, friends, and neighbors vanish behind the smoke. As the flames licked around their feet, the Beguins were all stalwart: Berenguier Jaoul later told Manenta Rosa Arnaut, whose sister-in-law had also died that day, "they suffered death most patiently. They did not cry out or say a word, and it was very beautiful to see."[75] Esclarmonda and Astruga were the two that everyone remembered most vividly afterwards. Was it their faces? Their demeanor? All we know is that those who witnessed the execution told their friends that these two, above all, were surely martyrs and in heaven. Astruga, said one, "is Saint Astruga the Martyr."[76]

As the flames died down, the crowds went away, and by earliest morning the cemetery was entirely empty. Where exactly the Beguins of Lodève

[73] The accounts of the seneschal of Carcassonne relating to the inquisition (dating from June 1322 to June 1323) were recorded in Doat 34, fols. 189r–234v, and have been published in *Comptes royaux (1314–1328)*, ed. François Maillard (Paris, 1953), vol. 1. The accounts payable specifically referring to the sermon of April 24, 1323, are found in fols. 219v–224r, and the annual fee for a prisoner is at fols. 226v–227v.

[74] In the twelfth and thirteenth centuries, Lunel was primarily known for the intellectual activity of its famous family of Jewish translators, the Tibbonides, but Philip the Fair's expulsion of the Jews in 1306 put an end to Lunel's Jewish community. David Romano, "La transmission des sciences arabes par les Juifs en Languedoc," *CF* 12 (1977): 363–386.

[75] Doat 27, fol. 81.

[76] "Sancta Astruga et martir." Manselli, *Spirituali*, 314.

had spent the night we do not know, but in the silence before dawn they came back to the cemetery outside of the town to say a final farewell to their friends. What greeted them in the unguarded cemetery was macabre beyond belief. Amid the smoldering ashes of the pyre lay the remains of the bodies of the Beguins, many of them recognizable, and some of them virtually intact. With no one to watch them, they began to collect pieces of their beloved friends as relics, and since the flames had failed to consume the bodies entirely, they took pieces of flesh as well as bones. Peire Arrufat took the entire torso of a woman, perhaps Astruga. Bernard and Raimon Durban took their sister Esclarmonda's heart and some bones and flesh "because of the affection and love that they had for her,"[77] and several others also collected parts of both Esclarmonda's and Astruga's bodies.[78] They put them in a bag, and left before they could be seen by anyone.

The evident popularity of Beguin relics makes us wonder why the cemetery was left unguarded. Given suggests that this "lackadaisical attitude" of the inquisitors may be explained by the fact that the burnings themselves were done by the secular authorities, who were less vigilant than the inquisitors or bishops would have been had they been in charge. I would suggest instead that both inquisitors and secular authorities were simply caught off guard. Though recalcitrant heretics had been burned in Languedoc for over one hundred years, Cathars and Waldensians (who had hitherto made up the vast majority of such executions) do not appear to have been collectors of relics. In the case of the Cathars, this may have been due to their dualist theology: a religion that would not venerate the cross (they considered it a vile memorial of torture and execution) would be unlikely to venerate the burned bodies of their fellows.[79]

Those who had traveled to Lunel soon distributed many of the relics of the burned Beguins, and the "thieves" and those to whom they gave the relics treated them with great reverence. When Bernard Malaura was asked why he had taken them, he said "because here, two good women from Lodève

[77] Ibid., 310.

[78] Bernard Malaura, a butcher by trade, identified the parts he took by their technical terms: "levada" or "mezina" (though ibid., 313, reads "alezina," examination of the manuscript, Doat 28, fol. 18r, reveals that it is clearly "mezina"). It appears that these were either viscera or parts of the torso. J. T. Avril, *Dictionnaire Provençal-Français* (Apt, 1839).

[79] Given, *Inquisition*, 77. In the royal accounts of the inquisition in Carcassonne, mention is made of paying three servants to guard the stand built to shelter the inquisitors during the sermon "for a day and a night," but no mention is made of guarding the execution site after the Beguins had been burned. Doat 34, fol. 221v. Brenon, *Le vrai visage du catharisme*, 65–67.

were burned, and because he believed that all those Beguins had been un-justly condemned, and he believed that they were saved, and holy. Time would reveal, he thought, that they were truly saints."[80] Raimon Durban said something similar: "At the time he took those bones and flesh, he hoped that someday, his sister and the others of her sect who were condemned and burned would be understood to be good."[81] They took these pieces of bones and flesh out of love, reverence, and hope, and brought them back to their homes in awe of what they had witnessed, mixed with their fear of being caught.

The Beguins clearly regarded these as relics, imbued with all the quali-ties expected of saintly flesh. The relic hunters brought them home and enshrined them. Bernard Durban placed them in the wall of his house, and Berenguier Rocha placed a piece of flesh inside a pomegranate skin and kept it on a shelf or table in his house. His companions told him that because it was the relic of a saint, it would not rot: when Berenguier in-spected it some months later and found it corrupt, he told the inquisitor that he had thrown it away.[82] Bernard Peyrotas, who did not attend the burn-ing at Lunel, nonetheless was shown the holy relics: he reverently kissed Esclarmonda Durban's heart and begged Martin Alegre de San Antonin to give it to him or at least to give him half, but Martin refused.[83] Peyrotas already had a small collection of bones from Beguins burned in Béziers: he kissed these, too, and carried them on him "reverently, like the relics of holy martyrs."[84] Jacma Amorosa Lauret, who had not been to Lunel, was also given both a bag of bones and a woman's breast. She claimed to have thrown them to her pigs when she found out that she could be burned for keeping them—but the inquisitors in fact found them in her house and she was forced to identify them.[85] Peire Arrufat, eventually burned in Carcas-sonne, reverently showed the head and torso of the woman's body he had taken in Lunel to Raimon d'Antusan of Cintegabelle, who kissed the head

---

[80] Manselli, *Spirituali*, 313.

[81] "Sperabat tunc temporis quando predicta recepit quod aliquo tempore dicta soror sua et alii illius secte condempnati et combusti reputarentur boni et illa ratione predicta retinebat sed tamen modo non sperat, ut dixit, quod de cetero reputarentur boni, quia videt, ut dixit, quod illi boni homines ita persecutionem patiuntur." Ibid., 318–319.

[82] Burr (*Spiritual Franciscans*, 255) calls this a "do-it-yourself home canonization process."

[83] Both the Durban brothers and Martin claimed to have Esclarmonda's heart, though Martin also acknowledged to the inquisitors (though not, apparently, to Bernard) that the organ he had taken might have been a kidney. Manselli, *Spirituali*, 312.

[84] Ibid., 317.

[85] Ibid., 310.

"out of devotion."[86] Like Bernard Peyrotas, Guilhem Serallier carried his relics on him in a little purse for a year and a half.[87]

The bishops of Lodève and Maguelone had had one message in mind when they designed the drama of the condemnation and execution, but the message the Beguins took away was quite different. This "contested performance," as Given calls it, had a particularly vivid effect on the Beguins, many of whom drew conclusions not to the bishops' or the inquisitors' liking. They saw the heretics being burned not as criminals being justly punished, but as victims of the inquisitors' (and with them, the Church's) might and power. That the burned Beguins should have become popular saints was surely not the inquisitors' intent. But for the Beguins, their persecution was not only a fact which strengthened the resolve of many, it also played directly into the apocalyptic scenario which, prompted by Olivi's Apocalypse commentary, they had come to expect. Persecution was not merely unjust, it was necessary. Not only was the blood of these martyrs the seed of their Church, but it was a necessary and expected sign that the better age was coming. The "apocalyptic eye" with which the Beguins viewed the martyrdom of their fellows strongly colored their perception of the events.[88] In the case of the Beguins, the theater of the General Sermons and the horrifying spectacle of their friends and relatives being burned alive at the stake was neither a deterrent nor a warning. As propaganda for the Beguins, it revealed the carnal character of the inquisitors (and by extension, the Church), denounced its perpetrators as the enemies of the spiritual Church, and aroused even dispassionate believers or sympathizers to conviction and action.[89] As propaganda for the inquisitors, it backfired. Once Beguins started to be burned,

[86] *Liber sententiarum* 2:1342. Another source claimed that he had an entire body. Manselli, *Spirituali*, 315.

[87] Manselli, *Spirituali*, 325.

[88] The phrase is the late Claudia Rattazzi Papka's. As she observes, the Beguins "projected their persecution into the realm of sacred history and thus made further resistance not only imperative, but also sanctifying." She calls this "the Catch-22 of apocalyptic discourse in the Christian mode." Papka, "Fictions of Judgment: The Apocalyptic 'I' in the Fourteenth Century," Ph.d. diss., Columbia University, 1996, 133.

[89] Here I follow Robert Lerner's definition of propaganda: "Egregious propaganda *reveals, denounces* and *arouses;* that is, it communicates truths long hidden or hitherto unknown, identifies enemies and instills emotions of partisanship. Although propaganda can serve to recruit non-believers, it need not be designed primarily for that goal; instead it may aim to sustain the morale of those already converted. Similarly, although it aims to influence conduct, it need not intend to incite violent action" (Lerner's emphases). Lerner, "Writing and Resistance among Beguins of Languedoc and Catalonia," in *Heresy and Literacy (1000–1530)*, ed. Peter Biller and Anne Hudson (Cambridge, England, 1994), 187. Given rightly observes that the inquisitors meant their widely publicized and observed

who among them could doubt any longer that the pope (who implicitly condemned them) was the mystical Antichrist predicted by Olivi? Or that the Church herself was the Whore of Babylon? The bonfires were incendiary in a way the inquisitors may never have anticipated.

The Beguins considered these martyrs to be equal in sanctity and power to the official saints of the church, and in addition to collecting their relics, they treated them similarly to traditional saints in other ways. Bernard Peyrotas, one of the most enterprising of the Beguins in the time of the persecutions, traveled the length and breadth of Languedoc, visiting Beguins and bearing witness to their martyrdom. In Béziers, he saw a little book of parchment in which the names of all the burned Beguins were inscribed.[90] The inquisitor Bernard Gui had also seen such a text and called it a "calendar"; for as he said, "just as the Church of God has the custom of doing for its saints and just martyrs, so the Beguins have written and noted the names of the condemned and the days or calends on which they suffered like martyrs, and they note them in their calendars, and they invoke them in their litanies."[91] Gui probably saw the calendar written by a relapsed Beguin, Peire Domergue, who was sentenced in Toulouse in 1322. Domergue's deposition (obviously transcribed by an inquisitorial notary whose bias is clear) declared:

He had heard, and he knew from memory the names [of those who had been condemned], and he dared to write them down in a litany, which he wrote with his own hand among the holy martyrs and virgins and confessors according to the ecclesiastical custom, saying the litany sometimes aloud, and sometimes quietly, asking the prayers and suffrage of damned men in many times and many occasions, imploring them out of the devotion that he conceived and had for them, and he believed that these prayers were of value with God, as he swore. He inscribed the names of about seventy of these damned men in his own hand in the litany.[92]

---

theater of punishment as propaganda for the "correct spiritual order" (*Inquisition*, 73). This may have worked more effectively on those members of the "audience" inclined to orthodoxy, and on those whose sympathies were inclined to Catharism or to a Waldensian wandering preacher. For those already imbued with Beguin ideas, the inquisitors' message was turned on its head, and became propaganda for the resistance instead.

[90] Manselli, *Spirituali*, 318.

[91] "Item, aliqui ex Bequinis scripserunt et notaverunt nomina predictorum condempnatorum et dies seu kalendas in quibus passi fuerunt sicut martires, ut ipsi asserunt, secundum quod ecclesia Dei de sanctis et justis martiribus facere consuevit, et nomina eorum annotaverunt in suis kalendariis et in suis invocabant letaniis." *Manuel* 1:134–135.

[92] "Postmodum vero prefatus Petrus Dominici confingens se alienatum a sensu predictam sectam et heresim ejusdemque secte, devios sectatores laudans illos quos prius

While such a calendar with the names of the *beguini combusti* integrated with those of more conventional saints does not appear to have survived, Peire Guiraut of Gignac had seen and made use of a litany composed exclusively of Beguin names.[93] Several copies of such a martyrology have survived.[94] Unlike Peire Domergue's calendar, this martyrology contains the names of

condempnatos per ecclesie judicium tanquam hereticos audiverat et sciebat eorumque nomina memoriter retinebat, ausus est conscribere in letaniam quam manu propria scripsit inter sacros martires et virgines ac confessores more ecclesiastico, letaniam dicendo nunc alte nunc demisse dampnatorum hominum oraciones et suffragia pluribus vicibus et multo tempore inplorando ex devocione quam ad ipsos conceperat et habebat et credebat eorum oraciones sibi valere apud Deum sicut in judicio constitutus asseruit medio juramento et letaniam ipsam in qua prefatorum dampnatorum hominum nomina manu sua conscripserat numero circiter septuaginta coram inquisitore perlegit perlectamque ab eodem inquisitor habuit et recepit." *Liber sententiarum* 2:1608. This anecdote begins with a statement that Peire Domergue was pretending to be "removed from his senses" in constructing the litany, which Given takes as an ineffective attempt at an insanity defense (*Inquisition*, 96). As we will see, however, his practice was not very far from the truth, and in fact, such a list of martyrs would appear to correspond directly with the Beguin martyrology (WM, lines 1–44, excluding the wife of Peire Arrufat, who was not burned until 1329), which contains 71 names prior to Peire Domergue's own death.

[93] "He believed that the friars minor who were condemned in Marseille, and the Beguins who were condemned as heretics in the province of Narbonne in the past four years by the judgment of the prelates or the inquisitors of heretical depravity could help him with God. He prayed to them and had prayed to them many times, and he had seen the names of some of them written (by those who had devotion for them, just as to the saints) with the days in which they were condemned and burned." *Liber sententiarum* 2:1624.

[94] Two manuscripts of the martyrology are in Wolfenbüttel and Prague: Herzog-August-Bibliothek, Helmstedt MS. 1006, fols. 12v–13v, and University of Prague IV. B. 15, fols. 304r–315r. I am grateful to Robert Lerner for having brought these manuscripts to my attention, and to Alexander Patschovsky for having generously provided me with his transcription of the relevant folios of the Wolfenbüttel manuscript. The text of the martyrology is included in the proceedings of the trial of two Spiritual *fraticelli*, Johannes Godulchi de Castiglione and Franciscus de Arquata (1354), both of whom were captured in Montpellier and burned in Avignon (see Odorico Rinaldi, *Annales ecclesiastici*, 31 vols. [Bar-le-Duc, 1864–1883], 31:1354). For the Wolfenbüttel manuscript see Otto Von Heinemann, *Kataloge der Herzog-August Bibliothek Wolfenbüttel, Die Helmstedter Handschriften* 3 (Frankfurt am Main, 1965), 3–5, and for the Prague manuscript, Joseph Truhlár, *Catalogus Codicum Manuscriptorum Latinorum* (Prague, 1905), 249, no. 617. An edition of the Wolfenbüttel text is in my dissertation, "So Great a Light," 315–320. All line references are to this edition. Not all copies of the trial of the two *fraticelli* contain the text of the martyrology. A third manuscript contains a related but not identical text, Escorial MS. N. I. 18. The text differs principally in so far as it is organized differently (by city, instead of by day or date) and is thus only a list of martyrs, and not precisely a martyrology used to commemorate the feast days of the martyrs. This text is in the hand of Nicolau Eimeric in a marginal note to an early copy of his *Directorium Inquisitorum*. An edition of the list of martyrs can be found in Jaume de Puig i Oliver, "Notes sobre el manuscript del Directorium Inquisitorum de Nicolau Eimeric conservat a la Biblioteca de l'Éscorial (ms. N. I. 18)," *Arxiu de textos catalans antics* 19 (2000): 538–539.

Beguins and Spiritual friars only, and is not integrated with a more conventional Church calendar of saints. It begins with the four friars burned at Marseille in 1318 and ends with burnings in Barcelona, Carcassonne, and Toulouse in 1347, but it is clear that no one was keeping close track of the burnings in Languedoc after 1323. The martyrology enumerates sixteen of the Languedocian autos-da-fé between 1318 and 1327, and eleven elsewhere or in a later period. Not all of the known events are listed, nor are all the lists of martyrs entirely accurate according to other sources.[95] In sum, however, the names, dates, and numbers of those burned generally match those we know from other sources. At the very end, the total is added up: "altogether there are 113,"[96] but for Languedoc, the named martyrs amount to 90, plus some others not identified precisely. The manuscript not only provides us with the names of many burned Beguins not otherwise identified in the sources, but also testifies to the truth of Bernard Peyrotas's deposition and Bernard Gui's observations. The Beguin martyrs were not merely remembered as treasured friends, but they had joined the saints in heaven whose intercession was particularly sought after. Peire Gastaud of Belpech, for instance, confessed to having sought their intercession several times.[97]

The Beguin martyrology clearly lists those burned at Lunel:

On the feast of St Luke in the *castrum* of Lunel, brother Guilhem Fabre, a priest of God, brother Peter, brother Raimon Camba, brother Peire Alfand, brother Berenguier, brother Nicholaus, brother Rotgier, brother Vesian, brother Guiraut, brother Anuericus, sister Johanna, sister Biatris, sister Basseta, sister Esclamonda, sister Ermessendis, sister Astruga, and one other sister.[98]

---

[95] Those missing are in 1328 and 1329 and an undated burning in Agde before 1323. For those names misattributed, see WM.

[96] In fact, the addition is slightly in error. Even without counting the "and other evangelical paupers," who were said to have been burned at Capestang in addition to two named Beguins, or the "brother Simon the foreigner who died in prison," the count adds up to 114. The figure of 113 was adopted by Johann Lorenz Mosheim (*De Beghardis et Beguinabus Commentarius* [Leipzig, 1790], 499, 632), who doubtless consulted Helmstedt MS. 1006 while it was still in Helmstedt. Wadding says that there were 114 martyrs (1317, no. 44), and thus both figures found their way into Henry Charles Lea's *A History of the Inquisition of the Middle Ages* (New York, 1887) 3:77–78 (Lea incorrectly cites Wadding as "1317, no. 45").

[97] *Liber sententiarum* 2:1390.

[98] "In festo beati Luce in Lunello castro frater Guillelmus Fabri sacerdos dei, frater Petrus, frater Raymundus Camba, frater Petrus Alfandi, frater Berengarius, frater Nicholaus, frater Rogerius, frater Vesianus, frater Guiraudus, frater Anuericus, soror Johanna, soror Beatrix, soror Basseta, soror Esclamonda, soror Ermessendis, soror Astruga et quedam alia soror." WM, l. 22–27.

Like the friars of Marseille, these names joined the names of all those burned for their beliefs in this crisis of the Beguins as martyrs for the cause. One of the most intriguing facts about martyrdom is its elective quality. As Lacey Baldwin Smith has observed, no one can be a martyr without actively choosing death—and the line between suicide and martyrdom is extremely fine. Martyrdom is also intrinsically a political act. As this same author has written:

> Yet martyrdom for all of its religious and teleological overtones is at heart a public and political spectacle. It is the most dramatic symbol of defiance and condemnation that a man or woman can achieve, a display of individuality sealed and sanctified by death. It strikes at the spiritual sinews of society, placing in question the collective integrity and legitimacy of the dominant group.[99]

Though the Beguins of Lodève burned at Lunel have left no documents behind that speak to their choice of martyrdom, some other Beguins left eloquent statements. When Prous Boneta preached to her fellows in 1325, long after the persecution had begun, she told them to be ready to die: "You must free your body for martyrdom if it should come, for the Holy Spirit will do great things, and will give many gifts."[100] Later, instead of abjuring, she declared that "in this belief she wished to live and die."[101] Guilhem Domergue Veyrier recanted his own abjuration, saying that "before he had something else in heart than he had now, and that since the time that God had given him this proposition in his heart, he asserted that he wished to stand and to persevere in it, since God had given it to him."[102] Other obdurate heretics chose similarly. In a dramatic scene at the General Sermon of March 1, 1327, Guilhem Serallier, who may have just discovered that he was to be burned as a relapsed heretic, abjured his previous abjuration, crying out to the assembled luminaries, including the inquisitors of both Carcassonne and Toulouse, that "those who persecute the poor condemned Beguins are persecutors of the life of Jesus Christ! They are the enemies of Christ!" The notaries wrote, "He obstinately persevered in each and every

---

[99] Smith, *Fools, Martyrs, Traitors*, 10.
[100] "Proinde liberetur corpus vestrum ad martirium si opus sit, quia ipse Sanctus Spiritus faciet magna et dabit magna dona." May, "Confession of Prous Boneta," 19.
[101] Ibid., 30.
[102] Manselli, *Spirituali*, 323.

one of the opinions and errors contained in his confession," and Guilhem was handed over to the secular arm and burned forthwith.[103]

As Stanislaw Bylina has observed, it was in their use of vocabulary regarding their experience that the Beguins asserted their belief. Everything depends on one's point of view. Whereas the inquisitors spoke of *condemnation* the Beguins spoke of *persecution*. *Punishment* and *burning* became *martyrdom* and *the martyrdom of fire*. What were *heretics* to the inquisitors were variously *glorious martyrs*, *martyrs for Jesus Christ*, *martyrs and saints*, and *saved and holy martyrs in Paradise*. In one memorable passage, Raimon de Buxo, later himself burned at the stake, compared the four friars burned at Marseille to the four parts or branches of Christ's cross: "in these was the life of Christ, and so consequently, Christ himself was spiritually crucified."[104] For historians, martyrdom and the veneration of those martyrs becomes an important means of understanding the so-called hidden transcript of the Beguins of Languedoc.[105] To themselves and each other, they were not heretics, but the true church of Christ, the Spiritual Church. As Esclarmonda and Astruga felt the flames and breathed in the smoke, they could console themselves (if such a thing is possible) with the knowledge that they had "fought the good fight" with all the armor and weapons that God had given them and that they had freely chosen. As they died "so beautifully," so patiently and well, they became a touchstone for their communities, an inspiration and a way to rally the faithful. For their friends, they were heretical saints, pure and simple.

IN EXILE: BERNARD MAURY

The story of Bernard Maury of Narbonne will take us away from Languedoc and across the Rhône to Provence.[106] When he finally testified

---

[103] "In pleno sermone dixit et asseruit se credere quod illi qui persecuntur pauperes begguinos condemnatos, sunt persecutores vite Iesu Christi et eiusdem Christi inimici.... perseveravitque in omnibus et singulis opinionibus et erroribus in sua confessione contentis, obstinatus in eisdem." Ibid., 324–326.

[104] "Illi IIII^or fratres Minores qui fuerunt apud Massiliam condempnati sicut heretici et conbusti, habuerunt similitudinem IIII^or parcium vel capitum crucis Christi et in eis fuit vita Christi et perconsequens ipse Christus spiritualiter iterum crucifixus." Stanislaw Bylina, "*Martires Gloriosi*: Le martyre et la souffrance chez les contesteurs franciscains en Languedoc au XIVe siècle," *Les Cahiers de Varsovie* 14 (1988): 73–84 at 76–77; *Liber sententiarum* 2:1302.

[105] Scott, *Domination and the Arts of Resistance*, 19. See also Given, *Inquisition*, 108–109.

[106] This account is based on Bernard Maury's deposition, found in Doat 35, fols. 21r–45v, and published in Manselli, *Spirituali*, 328–345. There is also a short papal letter

before the inquisitor of the provinces of Arles, Aix, Vienne, and Embrun in May 1326, he had been a fugitive for three years or more. He was a secular priest from Narbonne and had once been the procurator of the Franciscan convent there, no doubt during the time when Guilhem de Sant-Amans was the vicar (after 1316), since he and Guilhem were close friends. Guilhem, in fact, had sent Bernard to the papal curia in Avignon in 1317 in an attempt to further the Spirituals' appeal to the new minister general, Michael of Cesena, though Bernard's intervention was unsuccessful. Bernard himself was not a member of the Franciscan Third Order, but was one of the many Narbonnese who supported the Spiritual friars and their followers the Beguins. Bernard was well known enough as such a supporter to have been among the very first of the non-Franciscans arrested by the inquisitors in Languedoc in 1319 and had spent nearly a half a year in the archiepiscopal prison in Narbonne, where he had shared his incarceration with many Beguins, including the famous and unrepentant brother Mai.

In early October 1319, Bernard was released from prison and received a penitential sentence.[107] He was given yellow crosses to wear on his clothing, front and back (the sign of a heretic), and told to wear them for a year while he carried out a series of penitential pilgrimages. He first needed to visit the cathedrals or parish churches of Carcassonne, Limoux, Narbonne, and Béziers to publicly confess his heretical sins in each place, and then, at the end of the year, he was to bring letters attesting to his having completed the penances to the papal court of Avignon.[108] He was also to attend mass every week at the church of Saint Just in Narbonne. Of course, he also had to abjure his heresy, express his repentance, and promise never to associate with heretics, to help them in any way, or to continue to believe in their errors.

It seems, however, that he was unable to fulfill these last, crucial requirements. Only a few days after his release, when brother Mai and Peire de Fraxino were burned in the cemetery of Saint Félix in Narbonne, Bernard was already on the scene, ready with a fiery sermon remembered long after-

(March 21, 1327) regarding Bernard Maury's trial published in *Bullaire de l'Inquisition française*, 126–127, but it does not add any information of substance about his activities.

[107] Bernard inexplicably hesitated in his deposition over the exact date of his release from prison and sentence, saying that it was either two weeks before or two weeks after the feast of Saint Luke. Since the auto-da-fé where Mai and Peire de Fraxino were burned took place on the feast of Saint Luke, and others remembered him preaching on that occasion (see below), he may well have obscured the point deliberately.

[108] Though Bernard claimed to have accomplished his penance faithfully, he also noted that he had not visited the churches of either Carcassonne or Limoux, since he had been excused those tasks by a "special favor."

wards by an impressionable young tailor named Peire Esperendiu. "Pour ordi et pour brun voulent lassar cremar aqueste gent marida, sont bien malestruc" ("For grain and for undyed cloth they want to let these poor people burn; they're badly advised"). The thrust of Bernard's sermon seems to have been the injustice of such a severe and grotesque punishment for two seemingly petty things: the right of the Spiritual Franciscans not to keep storehouses of grain, and the right to wear the kind of short, rough, and ragged habits they thought were closest to the spirit of Saint Francis. When Bernard later remembered his own thoughts at this time, he said, "when they were but recently burned, he believed that they had died as good martyrs of God, and in the way to salvation." Though the tailor Peire was neither a professed Beguin at that point nor even a committed follower, he was so impressed by Bernard's sermon that he said to himself, "Hé, santa Maria, vere iste bone gentes moriuntur a grant tort" ("By saint Mary, truly these good people are dying most wrongly"), and that they were condemned and burned unjustly. Despite the evident risk to himself, Peire remained a supporter of the Beguins for three years at least and was ultimately burned as a relapsed heretic.[109]

Bernard was not the only secular priest of Languedoc who was an impassioned advocate for the Spirituals and Beguins. Bernard Peyrotas, the priest from Lodève, traveled up and down Languedoc to witness the burnings of Beguins until his capture in the summer of 1322. He, too, considered the burned Beguins to be martyrs, and as a priest he had a special way to honor their memory. Every day he said mass in honor of the burned Beguins using the common of the martyrs, and even wrote a special commemoration for them, which he said frequently at his morning and evening offices and at other times. He said he knew another priest—possibly even Bernard Maury—who had a similar prayer.[110] This kind of activity was one that pushed the veneration of these martyrs from an ephemeral phenomenon into the timeless zone of the liturgy. Though Bernard Maury, Bernard Peyrotas, or any of the other sympathetic priests we encounter in the sources could only have said their mass and their prayers in private, they did so in the hope and conviction that the burned friars and Beguins were true martyrs.[111]

---

[109] Peire Esperendiu deposed in Carcassonne in August 1325. Manselli, *Spirituali*, 326–328. He was handed over to the secular arm on March 1, 1327: Doat 28, 249v–252v.

[110] Manselli, *Spirituali*, 317–318.

[111] The deposition of Johan Rotgier, another priest, mentions two other priestly sympathizers by name, one of whom had relics of the burned Beguins, and another who had a collection of books by Peter Olivi. Doat 27, fols. 172v–175v, published in Manselli, *Spirituali*, 306–309.

Their priestly authority merely lent such actions more credibility among the followers of the Beguins, or even among those who were uncertain, like Peire Esperendiu.

If Bernard Maury continued to preach in the manner he did in Narbonne, it should come as no surprise that he became sought after again by the inquisitors of Languedoc. Though he was no doubt able to hide himself through the offices of sympathetic Beguins, he eventually chose to flee the region and escaped across the Rhône into Provence, where he was able to remain free for several more years. From our point of view, Languedoc and Provence are hardly very distant from each other. Even in the Middle Ages, it took only a few days to get to Avignon from Narbonne, a distance of almost 200 kilometers. The language spoken was virtually the same, even though we tend to call the one "Provençal" and the other "Occitan." But for the Beguins the division between Languedoc and Provence was crucial, as it was not only a political division, but also an inquisitorial one. By crossing the river, refugees entered not only the lands of King Robert of Naples rather than the king of France, but also lands under inquisitors other than those of Carcassonne and Toulouse. Passage across the Rhône, as we shall see, was common among the Beguins, and due to the lack of effective cooperation between inquisitors of different provinces, perhaps, surprisingly effective.

Besides the question of inquisitorial jurisdiction, there were many attractions to an exile in Provence. Many of the Beguins who made the voyage named St. Maximin as one of their destinations. In 1279, Charles of Anjou had uncovered the body of Saint Mary Magdalen in a crypt there and had begun to build an appropriate shrine for this increasingly popular "apostle of the apostles," who was widely believed to have spent the last 33 years of her life in a cave in the nearby Massif de la Sainte-Baume (also a pilgrimage site, visited even by Saint Louis). By 1316, the new church was functional, if not finished, and was attracting many pilgrims, including Beguins.[112] Other Beguins mentioned Marseille or Avignon, two large cities where a fugitive could find a place to hide among a wealth of other foreigners. While to us, it may seem the height of folly for heretical fugitives to approach the papal court, in fact this was a relatively successful tactic, at least for a while. We might think of it as "The Purloined Letter" factor: that which is hidden in plain view is sometimes the most difficult to find. Avignon was also an enormous city at this time, bulging with people from all over the Chris-

---

[112] For more information on the cult of Mary Magdalen in Provence, see Katherine Ludwig Jansen, *The Making of the Magdalen: Preaching and Popular Devotion in the Later Middle Ages* (Princeton, 2000).

tian world; one stranger more or less was of little consequence. Marseille, a shipping center of great expanse and population, was equally anonymous.[113]

Provence was also conveniently on the way to Italy, and some Beguins declared that they were going on pilgrimage to Assisi or to Rome. A community of exiled Spiritual friars from Narbonne was active in Apulia until the time of the Black Death in 1348, and another community of friars and laymen settled at the hermitage of the Carcere, outside of Assisi.[114] Still others may have gone as far as Sicily, though they are more likely to have taken the sea route.[115] Peire Trencavel appears to have escaped ultimately to Padua.[116] Such a path was not unexpected to the inquisitors of the Midi, of course: Michel le Moine, inquisitor of Marseille, had sent a letter to the Franciscan provincial minister of Tuscany in 1319, asking that any fugitives hiding or passing through the province be caught and submitted to the discipline of the order, "and if need be, with the help of the secular arm."[117] But inquisitors on both sides of the Alps appear to have been far less effective in routing out fugitives than in Languedoc, where the inquisitorial machinery was particularly well developed.

They were so much less effective, in fact, that it was possible for fugitives, strangers after all, to make their homes unremarked in small towns and villages in Provence. Manosque, Céreste, Ste-Catherine d'Aygues, St-Martin de la Brasque, Orange, Brignoles, and Apt are all smaller towns or villages where we know of Beguin refugees in this period. They seem to have scattered by design, and while they kept track of each other's whereabouts, they did not gather in large numbers, no doubt so as not to attract unwanted attention. They do not appear to have unduly feared discovery by their neighbors, though there was always a chance that a single capture of a well-connected Beguin (like Peire Trencavel to name only one) might lead

[113] For a brilliant exploration of Marseille's character and topography in the fourteenth century, see Daniel Lord Smail, *Imaginary Cartographies: Possession and Identity in Late Medieval Marseille* (Ithaca, 1999).

[114] A vernacular chronicle of the second half of the fourteenth century gives many details, including recognizable names of Spiritual friars. Felice Tocco, *Studii Francescani* (Naples, 1909), 520. Assisi Chiesa Nuova MS. 9, originally from the Carcere, was probably written by Occitan-speaking friars living in Italy for a Beguin audience in the 1330s (see chap. 1).

[115] Clifford Backman, "Arnau de Vilanova and the Franciscan Spirituals in Sicily," *Franciscan Studies* 50 (1990): 3–29, esp. 22–24. Sicilian Beguins are mentioned in Archivo de la Corona de Aragón, Reg. Canc. 338, fols. 31v–32.

[116] See below. Fabio Troncarelli, "Pietro Trencavelli, visconte di Carcassonne," *Quaderni medievali* 47 (1999): 14–40.

[117] *Bullaire de l'inquisition*, 38–39n2. The original letter is in Rome, in the Bibliotheca Casanatensis, MS. 1730, fols. 234c (273v)–235v (274v).

to the exposure of the network. When this happened, it was a cue to change residence quickly.[118]

By the spring of 1323 at the latest, Bernard was living in Manosque, the compact market town later made famous by the novelist Jean Giono, who described it as "a tortoise shell in the grass." Giono's hero Angelo, also a stranger to the town in a time of crisis, was forced up to the rooftops to escape the townspeople, but Bernard appears to have found Manosque more welcoming.[119] He was probably drawn there by the presence of a small community of refugee Beguines, Elis Castres, Raimunda Squirola, and a certain Guillelma, with whom he often ate and drank and who cared for him on at least one occasion when he was ill. Such a community gave all of them the opportunity of continuing to speak about the beliefs that had led them into exile. Bernard reported that the three women often "welcomed, recommended, and upheld the doctrine and the writings of Peter Olivi."

One day in July 1323, probably not long after his arrival in Manosque, Bernard received a message from a friend summoning him to Apt, another market town in the center of the Lubéron. His friend was another exile from Narbonne, Berenguier Hulard. Like Bernard, Berenguier had been a prominent citizen of Narbonne—he was even a consul of the Bourg in 1322—but he had become suspect for reasons of his associations with the Spirituals and Beguins and was finally prosecuted *in absentia* in 1325.[120] Berenguier appears to have been well integrated into a community in Apt: there was an inn where he had made friends, and he was acquainted with the inhabitants of the local "house of poverty" where several members of the Franciscan Third Order lived together. As he and Bernard sat in the inn one day, speaking with the owner, in came a face that both Bernard and Berenguier must have been delighted to see: Peire Trencavel, the Beguin of Béziers whose indefatigable missionary activity throughout Languedoc and Provence will be the subject of another chapter. The reunion in Apt opened up the clandestine world of the Beguins in exile for Bernard, and over the course of the next three years, he spent much time traveling with Peire or on his behalf.

Despite the various advantages of Provence, no such exile was without risks, and Peire in particular traveled widely and changed residences frequently. On Peire's request, Bernard sometimes traveled with Peire's daughter Andrea and several other young women—including one from Catalonia—whom Peire

---

[118] See below.

[119] Jean Giono, *The Horseman on the Roof*, trans. Jonathan Griffin (San Francisco, 1982), 190.

[120] Emery, *Heresy and Inquisition*, 166n1. Doat 28, fols. 101v–102r.

appears to have been protecting and hiding. Bernard brought the girls to and from a hiding place in Avignon and various villages in the Lubéron. One of them, a Beguine from Narbonne, died in Céreste, near Apt, in 1324 and Bernard saw her buried. In November 1325, he traveled to Marseille in order to deliver a letter and at the entrance to the city ran into Peire, who was living in rented lodgings with his daughter and one of her companions. Unlikely as this seems, Bernard was not the only Beguin to encounter acquaintances in Marseille while a fugitive; Esteve Gramat of Villeneuve-lès-Béziers, who had been traveling with Peire Trencavel, met a relative there who warned him against associating with such a notorious heretic.[121]

In the end, however, it was the arrest of a Beguin from Apt (we do not know who exactly) that brought the whole house of cards tumbling down. Bernard's friends in Manosque rightly feared that this Beguin might betray them, and moved to Brignoles, near St. Maximin. Bernard changed his name to "Blaize Marty"—similar but different. But the inquisitors were right behind them. When the women were captured in Brignoles, he fled toward Italy, by way of Draguignan, Le Luc, Grasse, and Nice, where he was captured and sent to L'Isle sur la Sorgue near Avignon for questioning. The identity of the inquisitor may have come as a particularly unpleasant surprise: brother Guilhem Astre, one of the Spirituals' most bitter enemies, and rival of Bernard's friend Guilhem de Sant Amans. The two were very likely acquainted from the time of the earliest conflicts. Guilhem Astre was particularly loathed by the Spirituals as he was appointed custodian of the Béziers convent in 1315 only to be ejected by the Spiritual uprising shortly thereafter (he was then made custodian of the Montpellier convent). He was also one of the principal architects of the Conventual response to the Spirituals in the months leading up to the showdown in Avignon in May 1317.

Brother Guilhem, now inquisitor for the provinces of Arles, Aix, Vienne, and Embrun, did Bernard Maury no favors.[122] His grueling interrogation went on regularly for months, and Bernard was moved to Avignon, back to L'Isle sur la Sorgue, and again to Avignon. Obviously, he was questioned about the names and whereabouts of other fugitives, and of Peire Trencavel in particu-

---

[121] Esteve Gramat's deposition is in Doat 27, fol. 9r–10v. He was sentenced to major pilgrimages on November 11, 1328: Doat 27, fols. 89v–91v.

[122] Guilhem had been inquisitor of Provence since 1322. Vidal suggests that brother Guilhem's zeal as an inquisitor pleased John XXII so much that he was not limited to a five-year post as was customary, but was instead confirmed in his post in 1326 with an unlimited tenure. Guilhem Astre was promoted to bishop of Apt in 1332 and died in 1336. *Bullaire de l'Inquisition*, 86–87. I thank Holly Grieco for her helpfulness regarding the career of Guilhem Astre.

lar. He was also questioned at length about his activities and beliefs in the years following his original sentencing in Narbonne in October 1319. Since Bernard had already abjured heresy once in Narbonne, all the inquisitor really needed to establish in order to deliver him to the secular arm and thus ensure his death on the stake, was that Bernard had continued to believe, for example, that the friars burned in Marseille were holy martyrs after his abjuration. Despite Bernard's insistence that five years before "God had placed in his heart that any man who rebelled against the Roman Church would die in mortal sin," and thus that at that point, "by divine illumination," he had ceased to believe like a Beguin, brother Guilhem continued to press him on these points. And in the end, on November 15, Bernard Maury gave in. "Yes," he said:

> When he had heard from Peire Trencavel the aforesaid statements against our lord Pope, that is to say, when he called [the pope] the mystical Antichrist, and said that he was destroying everything that was of God on the earth, that he was condemning and persecuting those who held such beliefs, and that he had no power whatsoever to make any changes in the Rule of St. Francis, and that those who were burned were holy martyrs of God, or in the way of salvation, [Bernard] did believe then that it was all true, all the things that Peire had told him. He no longer believed it was true, but then, he had believed it not only because Peire told him so, but also because Peire Trencavel had quoted to him from the writings of Peter Olivi.[123]

The inquisitors needed nothing more. Four days later, on the feast of Saint Elizabeth of Hungary (herself a member of the Franciscan Third Order) on November 19, Bernard Maury died at the stake in Avignon.[124]

In 1318, the Beguins of Languedoc were a well-established religious group in Languedoc. The members of the Franciscan Third Order were a familiar

[123] "Quando audivit a dicto Petro Trencavelli in istis citrarodonis partibus predicta verba contra dominum nostrum papam, videlicet cum vocabat eum misticum Antichristum et quod destruebat quidquid erat de Deo in terra, pro eo quia condempnabat et persequabatur predictos tenentes dictos articulos et quod non habebat potestatem aliquid immutandi in regula beati Francisci et quod dicti combusti essent sancti martires Dei vel in via salvationis et similia verba superius contenta et scripta, credebat ipse loquens ea esse vera, dixit se recordare pro certo quod tunc ea credebat esse vera, sicut dictus Petrus ea proferebat, sed nunc credit ea [non] esse vera et dicit quod non solum credebat tunc dicta verba esse vera ex eo quia dicebantur per dictum Petrum, sed etiam ex verbis que de scripturis dicti fratris Petri Johannis allegabat tunc Petrus Trencavelli predictus." Manselli, *Spirituali*, 343–344.

[124] Though Bernard's deposition ends without the sentence, his death is recorded in the Beguin Martyrology, ll. 52–53.

sight in the towns they lived in, with their distinctive robes and pious mannerisms. They formed tight communities, gathering regularly for services, often in the Franciscan convent nearby, and for prayer and study sessions, probably in each other's homes. Beguins from one town were familiar with Beguins from another, forming a network of sympathy across the region: frequent gatherings at Olivi's grave brought them together, and they were able to renew old friendships and make new ones annually.

So when the inquisitors rounded up Beguins in the cities and towns of Languedoc, they created a new entity: the Beguin resistance. Despite their likely anticipation of trouble, the actual severity of their persecution was doubtless both shocking and devastating. The resistance of the Beguins, however difficult beneath the watchful eyes of the region's inquisitors, took shape, and motivated a broad spectrum of individuals across Languedoc. The stories of Bernarda and Raimon d'Antusan, Esclarmonda Durban, and Bernard Maury must speak for many others who also participated in that resistance in similar ways.

As the prosecution continued, the fugitives sought one refuge after another—from Narbonne and Béziers to small towns like Cintegabelle, to Toulouse, Carcassonne, and across the Rhône. But as the decade of turmoil drew to an end, it appears that many Beguins found their last place of refuge in a city few of them would have expected, Montpellier.

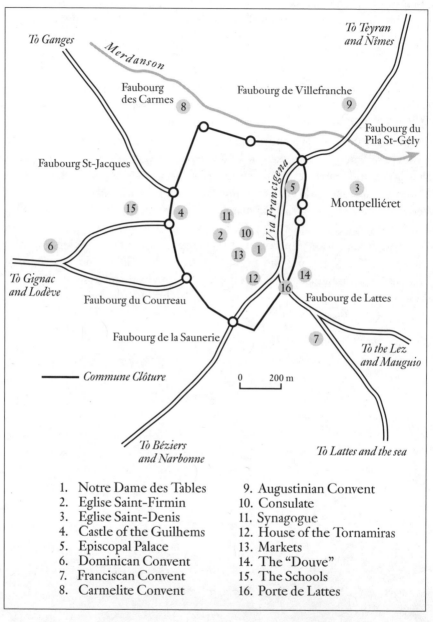

To Ganges

Merdanson

To Teyran
and Nîmes

Faubourg
des Carmes   8

Faubourg de Villefranche   9

Faubourg du
Pila St-Gély

Faubourg St-Jacques

Via Francigena

15   4

11
2   10
13   1

5
3
Montpelliéret

6

To Gignac
and Lodève

Faubourg du Courreau

12   16   14
7

Faubourg de Lattes

To the Lez
and Mauguio

Faubourg de la Saunerie

Commune Clôture

0   200 m

To Béziers
and Narbonne

To Lattes and the sea

1. Notre Dame des Tables
2. Eglise Saint-Firmin
3. Eglise Saint-Denis
4. Castle of the Guilhems
5. Episcopal Palace
6. Dominican Convent
7. Franciscan Convent
8. Carmelite Convent

9. Augustinian Convent
10. Consulate
11. Synagogue
12. House of the Tornamiras
13. Markets
14. The "Douve"
15. The Schools
16. Porte de Lattes

Montpellier at the beginning of the fourteenth century (after Ghislaine Fabre and
Thierry Lochard in *Montpellier: La ville médiévale*, 108).

CHAPTER THREE
AN URBAN UNDERGROUND
Heresy in Montpellier (1318–1328)

He rented a house for the aforementioned Guilhem, paid the rent
(or part of it), and carried him from one hiding place to another
on his shoulders because of his illness.

—Johan Orlach of Montpellier

Once the Beguin networks in places like Cintegabelle, Clermont l'Hérault, Lodève, and Narbonne had been cracked by the inquisitors of Languedoc, the resistance moved to Montpellier. Montpellier must have seemed like the perfect place to hide, because it was one of the last cities any inquisitor would have expected to have heretical sympathies. In so many ways, medieval Montpellier was an anomaly among the cities of the Midi. Unlike Narbonne or Nîmes, Carcassonne or Marseille, Montpellier had no august Roman or Greek past to boast about, no marble antiquities or ancient walls and traditions. Montpellier was the self-made man, the Johnny-come-lately, new money—almost a Horatio Alger hero of the south. As late as the tenth century, the city was no more than a mere farm on a hill, mentioned for the first time in a charter of 985,[1] but by the middle of the

---

[1] Montpellier enters the historical stage in 985 in a charter found in the cartulary of the Guilhems (*Liber instrumentorum memorialium: Cartulaire des Guillems de Montpellier*, ed. Société Archéologique de Montpellier [Montpellier, 1884–1886], 125–126), which documents the donation of a *manse* "at the top of *Monte pestelario*" to the ancestor of the family soon to become the seigneurial overlords of the growing city. A mere hundred years later in 1090, Montpellier was already a town with walls, whose lord participated in a division of property between Montpellier and Montpelliéret, the settlement on the

thirteenth century, it was the undisputed commercial and intellectual capital of Languedoc. By the beginning of the fourteenth century, Montpellier's population had probably risen to 40,000, making it also the largest city in the south.[2]

Such rapid growth seems extraordinary. Montpellier had no particular natural resources and little native industry. It was not a seaport, like Marseille, or on a major river, like Toulouse. To the north, east, and west lay forests and *garrigue* (Mediterranean scrubland) all the way to the Cévennes; to the south, the swampy salt ponds that line the coast. The site was, however, located close to two major roads, the Cami Romieu or "Pilgrims' Road" that led pilgrims to Santiago de Compostella and passed directly through town,[3] and the Roman via Domitia, which crossed the breadth of southern France just north of Montpellier. A third trade route, somewhat less frequented in the Middle Ages, the Cami Salinié or "Salt Road," ran along the Mediterranean littoral south of Montpellier and also probably dated from Antiquity.[4] Montpellier was also only ten kilometers from the Mediterranean, close to the Roman port of Lattes, still used extensively in the Middle Ages. This conjunction of factors certainly helped to make the city a prominent center for commerce, but Montpellier's rise in the commercial world was due also and especially to the far-thinking policies of its early lords, the Guilhems, who actively promoted the city as an international market and as a center of cloth-finishing.[5] The merchants of Montpellier became known as the purveyors of a particularly vivid scarlet cloth, and those who manufactured and traded in textiles, especially silk, were near the top of the social

next hill (ibid., 69–72). For a more detailed introduction to the site of Montpellier and the city's early history see Ghislaine Fabre and Thierry Lochard, *Montpellier: La ville médiévale* (Paris, 1992), 17, and Kathryn Reyerson, "Commerce and Society in Montpellier: 1250–1350," Ph.D. diss., Yale University, 1974, x.

[2] Jacqueline Caille, "L'élan urbain en Languedoc du XIe au XIVe siècle: L'exemple de Narbonne et de Montpellier," *Archéologie du midi médiéval* 13 (1995): 79–90, esp. 84.

[3] According to the twelfth-century text of the *Liber Sancti Jacobi*, the first of the four routes through France that lead to Santiago passes from Saint Gilles du Gard to Montpellier to Toulouse and then to the Somport pass which leads into Spain. Jeanne Viellard, ed., *Le Guide du pèlerin de Saint-Jacques de Compostelle*, 5th ed. (Paris, 1990), 2. The earliest pilgrimage route through Montpellier itself actually took the path of the present-day rue du Pila Saint-Gély, rue de la Vieille Aiguillerie, la rue du Collège, rue de la Monnaie, and rue Jacques Coeur, and exited town by the Grand-rue Jean Moulin, a route as sinuous as the changes in name suggest. By the thirteenth century, however, pilgrims used what is now the rue de l'Aiguillerie, as its name via Francigena would indicate. Fabre and Lochard, *Montpellier: La ville médiévale*, 44–45.

[4] Fabre and Lochard, *Montpellier: La ville médiévale*, 17, map, 22. Reyerson, "Commerce and Society," xii–xiii.

[5] Fabre and Lochard, *Montpellier: La ville médiévale*, 60–67.

ladder.[6] Engaged in trade with Spain, Italy, the Champagne fairs, and as far afield in the eastern Mediterranean as Cyprus and Constantinople, merchants from Montpellier dealt not only in textiles, but also in exotic "spices" coming from afar. Many members of the two most important municipal institutions—the consulate and the Commune Clôture—were cloth or spice merchants.[7] Though the streets in the center of Montpellier may now seem quaintly medieval and provincial, thirteenth- and fourteenth-century Montpellier was the cosmopolitan capital of southern France, a true gateway to the Mediterranean: the market of the Midi.

Such prosperity brought a university, with renowned schools of both law and medicine. Though a charter for the university as such did not exist until 1289,[8] there are many indications that instruction in law and medicine, at least, had been current in the city for 150 years and had an early international reputation (the oldest allusion to medical instruction in Montpellier dates back to 1137, and is found in the life of an archbishop of Mainz). The school of law must be nearly as old as that of medicine, since the famed jurist from Bologna Placentinus probably began teaching law at Montpellier in the 1160s and taught there until he died in 1193. Throughout the twelfth century, Montpellier's fame as a center for medical and legal instruction continued to grow and was mentioned by witnesses as illustrious as the English polymath John of Salisbury, and as exotic as the Jewish traveler Benjamin of Tudela.[9] Illustrious students of the law faculty include Guilhem Nogaret,

[6] The collected works of Kathryn Reyerson are the best introduction to Montpellier's commercial history (see especially Reyerson, *Business, Banking, and Finance,* and *Society, Law, and Trade in Medieval Montpellier* [Aldershot, England, 1995]). Two articles discussing Montpellier as a textile finishing and trading center in particular are Reyerson, "Le rôle de Montpellier dans le commerce des draps de laine avant 1350," *Annales du Midi* 94 (1982): 17–24, and "Medieval Silks in Montpellier: The Silk Market ca. 1250–ca. 1350" *Journal of European Economic History* 11 (1982): 117–140.

[7] The members of the "Commune Clôture" (known as the "*obriers*" or workers) first administered the construction and then the day-to-day functioning and repair of the city's walls and gates.

[8] This is Nicholas IV's bull *Quia sapientia. Cartulaire de l'Université de Montpellier,* ed. Alexandre Germain (Montpellier, 1890), 1:210–213. In 1180, Guilhem VIII declared that those teaching medicine in Montpellier were to be subject to no monopoly of any kind (a kind of academic freedom of the twelfth century). Ibid., 23. Hastings Rashdall takes this document to mean either that neither masters nor the bishop had an exclusive right of granting or refusing the *licentia docendi,* or that no true association of masters existed at the time. Hastings Rashdall, *The Universities of Europe in the Middle Ages,* ed. F. M. Powicke and A. B. Embden, new ed. (London, 1964), 2:122. In 1220, papal legate Cardinal Conrad established official statutes for the faculty of medicine in the city. *Cartulaire de l'Université,* 1:179–183.

[9] *Cartulaire de l'Université,* 1:8–11.

the famous stooge of Philip the Fair who harassed Pope Boniface VIII so effectively at Anagni in 1303,[10] and Petrarch, who studied in Montpellier after 1316.[11] The medical school attracted such renowned doctors as Arnau de Vilanova (physician to kings and popes, and the author of several somewhat unorthodox spiritual tracts for Beguins which were discussed in chapter 1), Guy de Chauliac (Pope Clement VI's physician during the Black Death), and even Rabelais in the sixteenth century.

But Montpellier was far from the heretical hotspots of thirteenth-century Languedoc (Toulouse, Albi, the Lauragais—all in Upper Languedoc), and the inquisitors of Languedoc had not previously been accustomed to traveling much to Montpellier on their business. Both in the Middle Ages and up to the last century, Montpellier had a reputation as a city that was entirely orthodox, a reputation that its inhabitants and leaders promoted successfully enough that one recent historian of heresy has called Montpellier "a Cathar-free zone."[12] Other more traditional historians have offered a rather idealistic explanation of this phenomenon. When the people of Montpellier rejected Catharism, they were not mere papal sycophants attempting to save their city from the ravages of the Albigensian Crusade; they were true believers and genuinely sought to alleviate the suffering of the poor and needy by building hospitals for the destitute. Thus, they did not *need* the Cathars as a corrective to the corrupt Church (as elsewhere in the Midi) since the diocese of Maguelone was already pious and holy enough.[13] Several times over the course of the fourteenth century, the bishop of Maguelone entreated the pope not to allow the inquisitors of Carcassonne to pursue heretics in the city without episcopal accord and cooperation, and with one exception, the popes consistently allowed for such a peculiar privilege. As John XXII wrote in late 1318, "the city of Montpellier in the diocese of Maguelone is clean of the fault of heretical depravity, and our beloved sons the consuls and the people of that city are fixed on the firm rock of the Catholic faith; they lean neither to the left nor to the right, but firmly and faithfully persist in holy devotion to the Roman Church their mother."[14]

---

[10] Joseph R. Strayer, *The Reign of Philip the Fair* (Princeton, 1980), 52–53. Nogaret also taught at the University of Montpellier.

[11] *Cartulaire de l'Université*, 1:13.

[12] Lambert, *The Cathars*, 73.

[13] Augustin Fliche, "La vie religieuse à Montpellier sous le pontificat d'Innocent III (1198–1216)," *Mélanges d'Histoire du Moyen Âge dédiés à la mémoire de Louis Halphen* (Paris, 1951), 217–224. Fliche is echoing the pious enthusiasm of the nineteenth-century ecclesiastical historian Frédéric Fabrège.

[14] Auguste Coulon, *Lettres secrètes et curiales du Pape Jean XXII (1316) relatives à la France* (Paris, 1900), 658–659. Similar letters were written in 1329 and 1379 (*Bullaire de*

Historians have been extremely reluctant to see heresy in Montpellier and, even when confronted with indisputable heretics from the city, have persisted in considering them as isolated and without influence. The most famous heretic from Montpellier, the Beguine Prous Boneta, for instance, whose deposition before the inquisitors is extraordinarily rich and detailed, has generally been treated as a lone eccentric, her message too extreme to attract any support. It is a commonplace among many historians of the Midi, however, that a thread of heterodoxy and rebellion runs virtually unbroken in the region from the Cathars in the thirteenth century to the Protestants of the sixteenth and the Camisards of the seventeenth centuries. Thus, it may not be immaterial to observe that Montpellier was to embrace Protestantism warmly, and became a principal battleground for the wars of religion. Additionally, the city had long had an important tradition of religious toleration, manifested in the cooperation between Jewish and Christian scholars.[15]

The inquisitorial record is not very kind to the pious myth of Montpellier's orthodoxy and its supposedly isolated and eccentric heretics. Like Lodève and Cintegabelle, Montpellier had a local community of Beguins, and they were able to remain active until at least 1325. As the noose tightened around Beguins from elsewhere in the Midi, many of them used this diverse urban environment as a hiding ground. Moreover, it is in Montpellier that we are able to follow a documentary trail that betrays support of the Beguins by individuals and groups who have long seemed untouched by heresy.

We will be aided in our investigation of the Beguins of Montpellier by one of those fortunate accidents that gladdens the heart of the medieval historian. More so than any other city of the Midi, Montpellier has preserved a considerable portion of its fourteenth-century notarial archives in a collection of registers that we might think of as the archives of daily life. Each

---

l'inquisition, 141–142, 443). In April 1330, John XXII gave the inquisitors of Carcassonne jurisdiction over all heretical investigations in the diocese of Maguelone: Doat 35, fol. 85r–86v (the document is cited in ibid., 151, but not printed in full).

[15] Montpellier had an extensive Jewish community from at least the time of Benjamin of Tudela's visit in the late twelfth century to 1306, when Philip the Fair expelled all the Jews from France. The best known example of Jewish-Christian intellectual cooperation is that of Jakob ben Makhir (better known as Prophatius Judaeus), the astronomical writer of the famous Tibbon family of translators, with Armengaud Blaize, the nephew of Arnau de Vilanova, and a prominent Christian physician. See Romano, "La transmission des sciences arabes"; Ernest Renan, "Armengaud, fils de Blaise, médecin," *Histoire Littéraire de la France* 28 (1881): 127–138; Joseph Shatzmiller, "Contacts et échanges entre savants juifs et chrétiens à Montpellier vers 1300," *CF* 12 (1977): 337–344; and Michael McVaugh, *Medicine before the Plague: Practitioners and Their Patients in the Crown of Aragon, 1285–1345* (Cambridge, 1993), 11.

notary (the essential legal counsel for everyday affairs) was required to keep a record of all the documents he created for his clients, and each register thus contains what are essentially the rough drafts of instruments of sale, debt, marriage, and more. Thirteen of these registers (and a substantial deposit of original notarial instruments—the final drafts) survive between the dates of 1293 and 1348.[16] Though these registers are not unknown to scholars (the historian Kathryn Reyerson has plumbed them extensively and expertly in her extremely useful studies of Montpellierain social history), I am the first scholar who has scoured their contents in search of the Beguins—who do, in fact, make their appearances there in some rather surprising ways.

In this chapter, we first examine the story of a young man from a wealthy family who was at the heart of the Beguin community in Montpellier from 1316 until his death in 1325, Peire Tornamira. We are especially well informed about Peire because the complete text of his inquisitorial record has survived, rather than the abbreviated *culpa* we have seen for others of the Beguins. Most important, this means that all of his contacts are named, and this simple fact allows us to trace the web of Beguins in Montpellier much farther than for other cities.

In the second part of this chapter, we take a closer look at one of these notarial documents regarding a Beguine from Gignac named Sibillia Cazelas. By carefully exploring the web of contacts and associations revealed in what seems at first glance to be a simple sale of land and gift of money, we learn a great deal about secret support for the Beguins and expose a plot that has lain hidden in plain view for nearly seven hundred years. The solution to the mystery of this document will help us further to understand the hidden supporters of the Beguins in that supposedly orthodox city of Montpellier.

AT THE CENTER: PEIRE DE TORNAMIRA

If you wander around the trendy shopping district in Montpellier, you are likely to pass through the Plan de Pastourel at the intersection of the rue Jacques d'Aragon and the rue de l'Ancien Courrier.[17] If you look up at

[16] See Reyerson, "Commerce and Society in Montpellier," 1:288–289, for a summary of these registers' contents.

[17] Most of this account is based on the materials submitted for Peire de Tornamira's posthumous "trial" in 1357. The bulk of it is his own deposition before inquisitors, and the rest are the accounts of his activities by unnamed witnesses. The original fourteenth-century parchment, prepared for his family, is in the Archives Municipales de Montpellier (hereafter AMM), Grand Chartrier, armoire D, cassette 1, no. 2, and was published by

the plaque on the wall, you will learn that Plan de Pastourel 22 (a handsome house with a beautifully vaulted rez-de-chaussée) is known as "Le Palais des Tournemires" where Marie de Montpellier gave birth to the soon-to-be famous Aragonese monarch Jaume I "the Conqueror" in 1208.[18] While historians are less certain than most tour guides about the identification of the precise house in question, they all agree that the famed home of the prominent and wealthy family of the Tournemires (or Tornamiras, as the name was written in the fourteenth century) was certainly located on this square.[19] In the fourteenth century, however, a young Tornamira was to cause considerable trouble for the inquisitors of Carcassonne in a unusual and celebrated case that embarrassed his family, led to charges of corruption and cruelty for a member of the inquisitorial team, and eventually preoccupied many of the region's religious leaders with a posthumous trial.

The name "Tornamira" still resounded with civic pride and importance at the beginning of the fourteenth century. Members of the family were especially active as consuls, serving no less than a dozen times in the years before the Black Death. The consulate of Montpellier was born in 1204 as part of the settlement of a crisis of succession. In exchange for their support of Marie de Montpellier and her husband Pere of Aragon, the prominent citizens of Montpellier were granted a "Great Charter" that allowed for the election of

---

Germain, "Une consultation inquisitoriale," 331–344. It is of particular value, since it is one of the few original inquisitorial sources regarding the Beguins.

[18] Any discussion of the medieval city of Montpellier is indebted to two major works. In the nineteenth century, Louise Guiraud published an extensive and erudite monograph titled "Recherches topographiques sur Montpellier au Moyen Age," *Mémoires de la Société Archéologique de Montpellier*, série 2, vol. 1 (1899). Based on this work is a frequently reproduced full map of the medieval city, "Le Montpellier médiéval," by Jacques Fabre de Morlhon, drawn by Lucien Albaret (n.d.). A more recent publication, Fabre and Lochard, *Montpellier: La ville médiévale*, traces the topographical history of the city from its origins to 1500 and a companion volume, Bernard Sournia and Jean-Louis Vayssettes, *Montpellier: La demeure médiévale* (Paris, 1991), is a history of the medieval domestic architecture of the city. This chapter is very deeply indebted to all of these authors, as well as to Marie Gaillard, an enthusiastic, knowledgeable, and patient Guide Conférencière du Patrimoine for the Office de Tourisme and member of the Société Archéologique de Montpellier, all of whom have made the maze of medieval Montpellier, much of it reflected in the modern city, come alive.

[19] Guiraud, "Recherches topographiques," 102. See also Jacques Fabre de Morlhon, *Le Montpellier des Guilhem et des rois d'Aragon* (Montpellier, 1967), 26–30, and Jean Baumel, *Histoire d'une seigneurie du Midi de la France* (Montpellier, 1969–1973), 1:274–279. The identification of the house of the Tornamiras as Jaume's birthplace comes from a contemporary chronicle, published in Claude Devic and Joseph Vaissète, *Histoire générale de Languedoc*, ed. Auguste Molinier (Toulouse, 1872–1904), 6:102. Perhaps because the building itself is more medieval than classical, the Guide Bleu passes over it in silence.

twelve "trustworthy and loyal men" ("*proshomes e lials*") to administer the town. This charter, common enough in an age that saw an upsurge in such municipal autonomy, granted vast authority to the townsmen. The consuls' powers included "the full power of making laws, punishing, and correcting all things which in their view could pertain to the utility of the community of Montpellier."[20] The consuls established themselves in the center of the city—across from the busy markets for fish, grain, meat, and vegetables, a stone's throw from the doors of the pilgrimage church of Notre Dame des Tables, and directly on the main access route to the city from the sea—and ruled over their fellow citizens at the very crossroads of mercantile and religious activity.[21]

The Tornamiras added legal authority to their position as well. One family member, Peire de Tornamira (d. 1301), was both a prominent professor in the faculty of laws and a judge in the king of Majorca's court (the kings of Majorca were the successors to the kings of Aragon as Montpellier's lords), and both his son Marc (d. c.1327) and grandson Johan were also doctors of laws. Their reputation even allowed them to marry into the local minor nobility: Marc's daughter Jacma brought her fabulous dowry of £1,000 with her to her new role as the lady of Boujan (near Béziers) when she married its lord Ermengaut.[22]

Other members of the family were active in other fields. There were clerics, *bourgeois*, priests, and even a tanner.[23] There appear to have been physicians, and Montpellier's medical school had an international reputation second to none. The renowned royal and papal physician Jean de Tournemire of the late fourteenth century may or may not have been part of this family: though he was born at Poujols in the diocese of Albi in about 1330, he lived in Montpellier for many years, and owned at least two houses there.[24]

In the middle of the 1310s, young Peire de Tornamira, a priest, was somewhat at a loss for what to do with himself.[25] He had left his family home (he

[20] Fabre and Lochard, *Montpellier: La ville médiévale*, 101–102. *Thalamus parvus*, article 121, 52–53, and 66. Archibald Lewis, "The Development of Town Government," *Speculum* 22 (1947): 51–67, at 66.

[21] Fabre and Lochard, *Montpellier: La ville médiévale*, 126–127.

[22] *Cartulaire de l'Université*, no. 22, 1:216–217. See also Jan Rogozinski, *Power, Caste, and Law: Social Conflict in Fourteenth-Century Montpellier* (Cambridge, MA, 1982), 162. AMM, BB2, no. 461, fol. 37r (Jacma's marriage contract), ADH 2E 368, fol. 87v (Marc and his son Johan).

[23] AMM, Petit Thalamus, fol. lxxxii; ADH 2E 368, fol. 112r.

[24] Louis Dulieu, *La Médecine à Montpellier* (Avignon, 1975), 1:294.

[25] One account, in an attempt to prove Peire's innocence of all charges of heresy, claims that he was only twelve years old at the time, but this seems rather unlikely, given the statement that he was also a priest. J.-M. Vidal, "Menet de Robécourt, commissaire de l'Inquisition de Carcassonne (1320–1340)," *Le Moyen Âge* 16 (1903): 425–449, at 448.

is of the right age to be a younger son of the lawyer Marc, but we cannot be sure) and had moved to the home of Philip of Majorca, the eccentric brother of Queen Sancia of Naples. Philip, a Paris-educated cleric whose precise ecclesiastical status at this point is unclear, was a strong supporter of Franciscan rigorism. He corresponded regularly with Angelo Clareno (whom he had met in Avignon in 1311) and used his considerable wealth and position to protect many others. He himself was so enamored of poverty and humility that he refused the bishopric of Mirepoix in 1318, despite the personal plea of Pope John XXII that he "take up his burden." Philip's homes in both Montpellier and Perpignan were havens for religious reformers, and in Philip's house in Montpellier Peire de Tornamira soon met with several Beguins who lived together in a "house of poverty" near the Franciscan convent outside the city walls.[26]

Peire was particularly fond of a certain brother Johan Martin, another priest, whom he described as "a good man." The two of them had many talks that had a great impact on Peire, who began to regret his own familial wealth and influence. Johan told Peire that "no one could be saved who was rich, or who had riches." He went on to cite the examples of Christ and Saint Francis, each of whom was "completely poor," and gave as his authority a text from Matthew: "The foxes have holes, and the birds of the air nests; but the Son of man hath not where to lay his head."[27] Johan soon persuaded Peire that he should "begin to do penitence, and to lead a poor life," and thus at Easter of 1316 (April 11), Peire took the Beguin habit, professed himself as a member of the Franciscan Third Order, left the house of Philip of Majorca, and went to live in the Faubourg de Lattes with six other Beguins.

There, no doubt, he participated in the full life of the Beguins. The Faubourg de Lattes was a poor neighborhood with residents who ran the gamut from Franciscans to prostitutes, and back again to Beguins and Beguines.[28] Sometime before the persecution began, Bernard Castillon, a silk merchant of Montpellier who was a substantial benefactor of the Beguins,

---

[26] The basic reference on Philip of Majorca is still the 1910 article by J.-M. Vidal, "Un ascète de sang royal, Philippe de Majorque," *Revue des questions historiques* 88 (1910): 360–403. The letter from John XXII is in Coulon, *Lettres secrètes et curiales*, n456. For Philip's protection of Beguins in Perpignan, see J.-M. Vidal, "Procès d'inquisition contre Adhémar de Mosset, noble roussillonais, inculpé de béguinisme (1332–1334)," *Revue d'histoire de l'église de France* 1 (1910): 555–589, 682–699, 711–724.

[27] Matthew 8:20.

[28] Leah Lydia Otis, *Prostitution in Medieval Society: The History of an Urban Institution in Languedoc* (Chicago, 1985), 25–26; AMM, fonds de la Commune Clôture, inventory, EE 25 and EE26, 4–5; and Kathryn Reyerson, "Prostitution in Medieval Montpellier: The Ladies of Campus Polverel," *Medieval Prosopography* 18 (1997): 217–218.

had bought a house in the *douve*, the area adjoining the ditch outside the walls in the Faubourg de Lattes, for a group of Beguines, who established the "house of poverty" there.[29] The Faubourg de Lattes was a far cry from the neighborhood Peire had grown up in inside the walls, but a suitable place for Franciscans and Beguins with a bent for poverty. Since Peire did not have a trade, he probably begged to help support himself and his companions, an activity that likely scandalized members of his family and their social circle when they came across him at the gates to the city or on the doorstep of Notre Dame des Tables, barefoot, wearing humble clothes made of cheap and coarse fabric, and with a "mortified face." If they saw him at church, things would not have seemed much better: Peire would be sitting with his Beguin companions, hunched over, with his face turned to the wall, or perhaps he would be prostrate on the ground with his hood over his head unlike the rest of the congregation, who were kneeling with their hands together.[30] Peire himself would have rejoiced in the way he was following so closely in the very footsteps of Saint Francis, the son of a rich man.

But Peire had chosen to join the Third Order at a time that could not have been more critical for the Beguins and their mentors, the Spiritual Franciscans. It was at Pentecost 1316 (a mere 50 days after Peire's profession) that Michael of Cesena was elected minister general of the Franciscan Order, and the beginning of August when Pope John XXII was installed. Within weeks, the crisis had begun.

Apocalyptic rhetoric had always been plentiful in the house of poverty of the Faubourg de Lattes, since as we know, the writings of Peter Olivi and especially his commentary on the Apocalypse were the most common spiritual food of the Beguins. As they began to hear of events like the showdown in Avignon in May 1317 and the burnings at Marseille a year later, not to mention the proclamation of *Sancta Romana* that made it clear that the Beguins themselves were targeted, they were swiftly persuaded that they were living in apocalyptic time.

---

[29] Doat 27, fol. 20r.

[30] This description of Beguins comes from the trial of brother Raimon Amiel of the abbey of St-Polycarpe near Limoux, who was accused (unjustly) of being a Beguin in 1337. The trial provides an insight into the popular conception of what a Beguin looked like, as well as the notion that a Beguin was clearly recognizable from his or her appearance. Though extensive parts of the trial of brother Raimon Amiel, preserved at the Vatican, were published by Douais (*La procédure inquisitoriale*), he did not publish the whole. Details from the rest of the trial can be found in an informative article by Coulet, "Un moine languedocien."

When he testified before the inquisitors in 1325, Peire de Tornamira claimed that he had lived with the Beguins of the Faubourg de Lattes only for a few months, until November 1316.[31] Even if that were true, he must have continued to associate with them, for Johan Martin and the others soon indoctrinated him with the full range of heretical opinions. He heard from them, of course, that Peter Olivi was an uncanonized saint whose doctrines were good and holy. He also heard that the papal decretals on Franciscan granaries and cellars were "the destruction of perfection." Since this issue became a matter of heresy only after John XXII issued *Quorumdam exigit* on October 7, 1317, Peire was clearly still in the Beguin orbit after that time. After the four friars died at the stake in May 1318, he agreed with Johan Martin that they were unjustly condemned, and glorious martyrs. When news came to Montpellier that Beguins themselves had been burned in Narbonne and Capestang in October 1319 (news that was surely chilling to a household of men wearing the same habit), Peire was persuaded that they, too, were martyrs in Paradise. All the members of the Franciscan Third Order, Peire included, began to feel like marked men and women. They whispered among themselves that when Pope John had issued *Quorumdam exigit*, he had begun to lose his papal power. Soon they called him the mystical Antichrist, who would prepare the way for the Great Antichrist.

It was at this time that even those outside the Beguin community began to worry for Peire. His friends, and possibly his family, got involved in persuading him to return to a secular life. "After the Friars Minor were burned in Marseille, when the persecution of the Beguins began, and when they began to be condemned, he himself, at the instance and insistence of his other friends, put off the Beguin habit and the society of the Beguins."[32] A mere three weeks later, Johan Martin and another Montpellier Beguin named Bernard Martin were taken by the inquisitorial authorities in Capestang and were burned there in May 1320. Three or four others were later captured in Montpellier and then burned in Lunel in October 1321.

Peire did not become an object of inquisitorial attention at this time, however, despite the damning fact that Johan and Bernard Martin and several of the others told the inquisitors quite plainly that he had been a member of their community and had shared their life and their beliefs. He even visited

---

[31] Germain, "Une consultation inquisitoriale," 338. Peire made two contradictory statements on this subject. He also mentioned that he had lived in a house of poverty in Mauguio for a month, a point later confirmed by Johan and Bernard Martin.

[32] "Ipse loquens, ad insantiam et inductionem aliquorum amicorum suorum, dimisit habitum predictum, et societatem dictorum Beguinorum." Ibid.

them in prison and gave one of the guards a silver shilling of Tours, a quite substantial *pourboire*.[33] His illustrious name may well have protected him. In fact, we know almost nothing about the way he spent the next three years, during which the Beguins of Languedoc were made into fugitives. In these same years, however, Montpellier became the refuge of choice for many of them.

Perhaps the first of the Beguins to use Montpellier as a place to take cover was a priest of Lodève whom we met in the last chapter. Bernard Peyrotas traveled all over Languedoc witnessing his fellow Beguins' martyrdom, and was ultimately himself burned in Lodève in 1323. When he was captured in Montpellier in November 1321, he had been living there for seven months. Over the summer, he had visited the Beguins in the prison at Maguelone who would be burned at Lunel in October (no doubt the same prisoners visited by Peire de Tornamira), ate with them several times, and brought them spiritual comfort. While he was living in Montpellier, he also "knowingly received many fugitive Beguins (who were condemned afterwards) in his room, and ate and drank with them."[34] He testified before the inquisitors in mid-November 1321, long before a second batch of Montpellier Beguins (including Peire de Tornamira) was rounded up beginning in 1325. In their testimonies, many Beguins sought to conceal the names of those who had not yet come to inquisitorial attention. We can assume therefore, that while Bernard was forthcoming with the names of those already dead, he kept silent about the names of his contacts in Montpellier who were still free. It seems likely, therefore, especially given his visits to the same imprisoned Beguins, that he would have at least crossed paths with Peire de Tornamira, and thus the rest of the Beguin community.

That community was certainly extensive: we know of a minimum of 18 individuals prosecuted for Beguin sympathies who were residents of Montpellier, a group nearly as large as that of Lodève. Some of them, like Johan and Bernard Martin, Peire's earliest Beguin contacts, or the Beguines mentioned by Bernard Castillon (and later, as we shall see, the Boneta sisters and their companion), were members of the Franciscan Third Order and lived in houses of poverty with other Beguins, but others never took vows and lived

[33] "Et tunc solvit unum turonensem argenti carcerario, pro vino, qui eos custodiebat." Ibid.

[34] "Item, dum moraretur in Montepessulano, plures begguinos fuggitivos, qui postea fuerunt condempnati, receptavit scienter in camera sua et comedit cum eis." His testimony is published in Manselli, *Spirituali*, 315–319.

on their own.[35] They came from various walks of life. There was a group, for instance, who were all immigrants from the region north of the city and especially from the Cévennes. One of these, Johan Peyre, a tailor, was born in the tiny village of Valfonts, and others (like the Boneta sisters Prous and Alisseta) came from La Cadière or St-Etienne of Bragassargues. Raimon Cambos, another one of Peire de Tornamira's early Beguin contacts, may have come from the remote village of Cambo, now part of the same *commune* as La Cadière.[36] Montpellier, like many prosperous commercial cities, exercised a magnetic pull on its surrounding villages, and many immigrants considered a move to the city as a kind of "gradual upward social mobility," as Kathryn Reyerson has suggested was common.[37]

But immigrants were not the only men and women of Montpellier attracted to the message of the Spiritual friars and the Beguins. Throughout the beginning of the fourteenth century, the popularity and prestige of the Franciscans in Montpellier was growing. Increasing numbers of townspeople began to request to be buried in the Franciscan cemetery, perhaps because the Franciscans engaged in intense activity as confessors and were common at deathbeds. Popularity of the Spiritual message and public support for the Beguin cause may be other factors. Merchants were particularly drawn to associate themselves with the Franciscans—logically, since the Franciscan convent was located on the side of the city most associated with mercantile activity (the Dominicans were on the other side of the city, closer to the schools).[38] Bernard Castillon, for example, was a silk merchant very openhanded with his money and his concern on behalf of the Spiritual

[35] It is probable that the two women called "Na Catherina" and "Na Bodina," mentioned by Peire de Tornamira, were also members of the Third Order, since the term "Na" was used as a term of respect, perhaps equivalent to "sister." Germain, "Une consultation inquisitoriale," 334. See also chap. 4.

[36] Raimon was burned in Lunel. Germain, "Une consultation inquisitoriale," 336; WM, l. 23. There is also a hamlet called Cambous north of Montpellier on the route toward the Cévennes. Guillelma de Mirepoix, also burned in Lunel, and mentioned by Alisseta Boneta, may also have been an immigrant, though Mirepoix is southwest of Carcassonne, at a very considerable distance from Montpellier.

[37] Kathryn Reyerson, "Patterns of Population Attraction and Mobility: The Case of Montpellier, 1293–1348," *Viator* 10 (1979): 257–281, at 271.

[38] See the chart drawn up by Reyerson, "Changes in Testamentary Practice at Montpellier on the Eve of the Black Death," *Church History* 47 (1978): 253–269, at 258. Between 1200 and 1292, only two individuals requested burial with mendicants, and between 1293 and 1345, the percentage more than doubled. In 1347, a year in which there was an especially large number of wills, the Franciscans alone accounted for 34% of all burial requests; in 1348, the year the Black Death struck the city, the mendicants accounted for over half of the burials specified. Reyerson also notes that of the ten references made to

friars and Beguins. He gave many alms, visited many Beguins in prison and brought them food and money, and even rented and bought houses for them. He would have been unable to be so generous had he not been so wealthy: as a silk merchant, he was near the top of the social ladder in the city. His extant business dealings show him engaging in substantial commerce and tell us that he owned a comfortable house in the via Francigena, a central neighborhood.[39]

Johan Orlach was another wealthy and devoted benefactor of the Beguins. Thanks to the survival of his apprenticeship contract, we know that he had apprenticed himself to a draper at the age of 14—and since his mother Maria was a silk merchant, we can assume that he followed her into this most prestigious of the textile trades. Like Bernard Castillon, Maria Orlach owned a house in what seems to have been the silk-trading area of the via Francigena. They may even have been neighbors.[40] Johan Orlach was also part of a prominent family, whose members had been frequently elected consuls since the first days of the consulate, and who had served in many other important municipal positions.[41]

The presence of such a large community of fellow believers in a large and cosmopolitan city led many fugitives to follow Bernard Peyrotas to Montpellier. Two prominent Beguins, one of Narbonne and the other from Lodève,

---

personal confessors in the extant wills, six of these were Franciscans. She also observes that nine requests for burial in the Franciscan cemetery came from merchants. Reyerson does not consider the popularity of the Spirituals to be a factor, though she also observes that the Dominicans do not appear to have been as popular as the Franciscans: ibid., 263–264, 268n68.

[39] See Reyerson, "Le rôle de Montpellier dans le commerce des draps de laine" and "Medieval Silks in Montpellier." Also André Gouron, *La réglementation des métiers en Languedoc au Moyen Age* (Geneva, 1958). Bernard Castillon's deposition is in Doat 27, fol. 203–221v, and his business dealings can be found in AMM, BB1, no. 63, fol. 10v, no. 101, fol. 16v, no. 114, fol. 19r, no. 115, fol. 19r, and no. 116, fol. 19v. Bernard's neighbor in the house on the via Francigena was Astruga, the widow of ben Massip of Narbonne, a Jew (AMM, BB1, no. 393, fol. 87v).

[40] Johan Orlach's deposition is at Doat 27, fols. 24r–26r. His apprenticeship contract is AMM, BB1, no. 108, fol. 183. See Reyerson, "The Adolescent Apprentice/Worker in Medieval Montpellier," *Journal of Family History* 17 (1992): 353–370. Johan's mother's silk dealings are found in AMM, BB1, no. 42, fol. 7r, no. 122, fol. 21r, no. 161, fol. 27r, no. 224, fol. 45r, and no. 254, fol. 50v. Maria Orlach's house was next to a rented house belonging to Guilhem Despuegs, a wealthy knight, and quite obviously in a neighborhood of other silk merchants (the boutique of a silk merchant named Jacme Deodat was almost next door, and Bernard Castillon's house is also mentioned). AMM, BB1, no. 27, fol. 5r.

[41] An Austorc Orlach was on the city's first list of consuls, in 1204. From 1208 through 1292, on nine separate occasions, individuals named Johan, Austorc, or Bernard Orlach were elected to the consulate, and in 1223, a Johan Orlach was bailiff. Baumel, *Histoire*

are known to have taken refuge in Montpellier.[42] Guilhem Domergue Veyrier, a candlemaker of Narbonne, was a prominent leader of the Beguins who was captured in Orange in 1325. But before taking flight across the Rhône, Guilhem Veyrier had apparently spent a considerable amount of time in hiding in Montpellier with his wife, according to the testimony of many witnesses. Several of the Beguins of Montpellier confessed to having eaten and drunk with him, and two Beguins from other cities came to Montpellier expressly to visit him in hiding.[43] Peire de Tornamira certainly visited him at one point when Guilhem was sick at the home of a certain Na Catharina, as several witnesses later recalled. When Guilhem left for Provence in the company of a group of Beguins, his wife Berengaria remained in Montpellier, where she was later captured.[44] Montpellier was a gathering place and a stopping place, where Beguins could expect to find a rest and traveling companions if further flight were necessary.

Not all of them left in time, however. Guilhem Serallier of Lodève may have been too sick to do so when others left for Provence, and he was eventually captured in Montpellier in May 1325. His own testimony is reticent about his movements, but, once again, many deponents recalled meeting with him in the city. Several of them mentioned his lengthy and

---

d'une seigneurie, l:237; AMM, Petit Thalamus: 1208, 1211, and 1216, Johan; 1209, Austorc; 1251, Austorc; 1279, Johan and Austorc; 1292, Austorc. Another member of the family, Guiraut, was elected to the *obriers* of the Commune Clôture in 1261. The name also appears frequently in the Cartulaire of Maguelone: a certain Johan Orlach was the guardian of the castle of Montferrand, north of the city, starting in 1211. *Cartulaire de Maguelone*, ed. J. Rouquette and A. Villemagne (Montpellier, 1912–1924), vol. 2, nos. 313, 314, 348, and 361. Some Orlachs were vassals of count Raimond VII of Toulouse, and canons of Maguelone: *Cartulaire de Maguelone*, vol. 2, nos. 392, 469, and 624, vol. 3, nos. 843 (1292) and 1121 (1301), and vol. 4, no. 1359 (1316).

[42] Two other names of refugees in Montpellier also emerge from the testimony, but there are no further details given: a certain Guilhem Lanternier is mentioned by Peire Massot of Béziers (Doat 27, fol. 13r) in conjunction with Guilhem Domergue Veyrier, and Peire Daissan of Béziers is mentioned by Johan Peyre of Montpellier, also in connection with Veyrier (Doat 27, fol. 22r). Though Peire Daissan testified before the inquisitors in August 1325, and admitted to fleeing with Guilhem Domergue Veyrier, neither he nor Veyrier confessed to the shelter they had received there, no doubt in an attempt to keep their benefactors from further trouble (Doat 28, fols. 213v–215r). Nothing further is known of Guilhem Lanternier. It appears that Biget ("Culte et rayonnement," 304) has chosen to assume that he was the same person as Guilhem Domergue Veyrier, since he identifies this latter figure as a lanternmaker, but this position is untenable, since the text referring to Guilhem Lanternier also mentions Guilhem Domergue Veyrier separately.

[43] Both Esteve Gramat of Villeneuve (near Béziers) and Peire Massot of Béziers visited him (and his wife) specifically. Doat 27, fols. 9v and 13r.

[44] Doat 28, fols. 121r–122v.

incapacitating illness, and two friends from Lodève, Berengaria Estorgua and Raimunda Rigauda, nursed him in Montpellier.[45] Johan Orlach
helped him materially as well, bringing him food and wine, and renting
him a house. He also helped move Guilhem to another lodging when the
first became too dangerous, carrying him on his shoulders because of his
illness.[46]

Though there is less evidence regarding his stay in Montpellier than for
some others, it seems clear that Peire Trencavel, the indefatigable leader of
the Beguins whose story is told in chapter 4, also spent time there in hiding.
Esteve Gramat mentioned his presence there, and Guilhem Serallier mentioned eating and drinking with him.[47] When the bulk of the Montpellier
Beguins were arrested in 1325, Peire Trencavel was still at large after his first
escape from the *mur* at Carcassonne, and it is natural that they would have
sought to conceal any possible information about his comings and goings
(he was only recaptured in 1327).

Another fugitive with a close connection to Montpellier was brother
Raimon de Johan.[48] Raimon was one of the friars originally summoned by
John XXII in 1317, and he accompanied them to Avignon where he was
punished with them by being sent to the convent of Anduze. Like many
other Spiritual friars, he fled the remote convent he been sent to shortly
after the four friars were burned in Marseille. Raimon traveled widely in
the years before he was captured, and through the testimony of many, we
catch glimpses of his activities. He preached in Narbonne, lived secretly in
Béziers, hid for a year in Montréal, traveled abroad to Sicily, and was finally
caught in Gascony, where he lived for up to a year.[49] But he was also very
successful at hiding in Languedoc itself—he spent a total of nine years on

[45] "Dictoque Guillelmo ad habitandum quondam domum locavit et salario vel logerio
partem soluit de uno loco ad alium eundem Guillelmum infermum super humeros suos
portavit, de pecunia, vino, et aliis rebus suis eundem iuvit ad vivendum." Doat 28, fols.
194v–196r.

[46] Doat 27, fol. 25r.

[47] Doat 27, fol. 9v; Manselli, *Spirituali*, 325.

[48] For this section, I rely extensively on David Burr's reconstruction of brother
Raimon's career, "Raymond Déjean, Franciscan Renegade," *Franciscan Studies* 57 (1999):
57–78, esp. 62–68, and also Burr, *Spiritual Franciscans*, 215–221. Raimon's own deposition
is published in Manselli *Spirituali*, 302–306.

[49] Burr, "Raymond Déjean," 10. It is also possible that he traveled to Majorca (his
deposition simply says that he traveled "per diversa loca alia ultramarina et citramarina."
Manselli, *Spirituali*, 302). The trip to Majorca is found in the testimony of Alaraxis Biasse of Sauvian, published in Manselli, *Spirituali*, 319–321. Though Raimon de Johan
is not mentioned by name, it is possible that he was one of the two friars whom she

the run, much of it in his home territory. Though he himself spoke little about his time hiding in Montpellier, many others mentioned having fed him, housed him, or spoken with him.[50]

In 1324, he also appears to have become even more closely acquainted with Peire de Tornamira. That summer, the situation for the Beguins of Montpellier was becoming more dangerous. Guilhem Domergue Veyrier, Peire Trencavel, and others had fled to Provence, and those who remained felt vulnerable. Peire de Tornamira advocated flight for all of them, this time to Sicily by the sea route, and he begged and cajoled many others, including Raimon de Johan, into accompanying him. One day, he invited many Beguins to lunch at the home of a certain Na Bodina, where he talked for hours about the way they would be able to live if only they were to leave Languedoc for Sicily. He himself sold all his possessions to raise cash for the journey, and those who knew him commented on how much he loved the Beguins and their cause. Around the end of June, Peire and Raimon, along with "many other Beguins and Beguines," left Montpellier for Sicily.[51] Leaving for Sicily unremarked, however, was not simple. Some of them left Montpellier by land, and others went by boat through the lagoons that border the Mediterranean. They met in Agde, and thence made their way to Barcelona. A short stop in Sardinia, then Trapani, and finally they went ashore in Syracuse.

At this point, Peire's dream of an easier and better life in Sicily began to fall apart, not because of continued pursuit or an unwelcoming environment, but due to that more mundane travelers' bane, disease. Both Peire and a merchant who had traveled with them became gravely ill. Though it is difficult to be certain, it is tempting to suggest that they were stricken with malaria, which was particularly common in southern Italy. Jaume II of Aragon contracted a fever in Naples that was almost certainly malaria, and there is the well-known case of King Martin the Young of Sicily, who died of malaria in Sardinia in 1409.[52] Peire appears to have been subject to recurring

---

assisted on their way to Majorca, given certain correspondences between their two depositions (see Burr, "Raymond Déjean," 64–66). He was reticent with details throughout his deposition—as Burr observes, "few processes leave us so aware of the fact that what we can learn ultimately depends on what the inquisitors wanted to know and what the defendants were willing to tell them." Ibid., 76.

[50] Alisseta Boneta, for example (Doat 27, fol. 26v), her companion Alaraxis (Doat 27, fol. 30r–30v), Ermessendis Grossa of Gignac (Doat 27, fol. 14v), and Johan Peyre and Johan Orlach of Montpellier (Doat 27, fols. 22r and 24r–26r).

[51] Germain, "Une consultation inquisitoriale," 334–335.

[52] See McVaugh, *Medicine before the Plague*, 9.

fevers, which makes this hypothesis seem even more likely. In any event, he was bedridden for a full month.

By the end of the winter, his enthusiasm for Sicily dampened by his evident frailty, Peire decided to return home. He gave 40 shillings to the ailing merchant, still apparently too ill to travel, and took ship for Montpellier, which he reached by the middle of March 1325. Though some of those who had traveled with him appear to have remained in Sicily, several of his companions, including the merchant and Raimon de Johan, followed Peire back to Languedoc soon thereafter.[53]

The situation for the Beguins had not improved in their absence, but Peire lost no time in making contact again with his friends and fellow believers. Peire was the principal officiant at the secret celebration of the feast of Peter Olivi on March 14 attended by these and many others, which one participant described as "a great feast" (*magnum convivium*—it was paid for by Johan Orlach). Peire blessed the table and said grace before the meal and then read aloud from Olivi's Apocalypse commentary, and also from the short text described in chapter 1, "On the Passing of the Holy Father." They ate and drank, laughed and told stories, grieved for those who had died or were imprisoned, and rejoiced for those who were still at large. Seven years after the destruction of Olivi's shrine and twelve years after Angelo Clareno's visit to Olivi's grandiose feast in Narbonne, the Beguins proved their continued devotion to the man they considered to be a saint. But while none of them could have known that it would be the last such feast they would be free to celebrate together, the shadow of the inquisitors no doubt lay heavy over the meal.

After the return of the others from Sicily, Peire was active in helping to hide and support them. He traveled here and there and eventually found a safe hiding place for his merchant friend at the home of one of Peire's relatives—as safe a place as one could be in these times. From Pentecost to the feast of John the Baptist (a month), they remained safely in hiding. But not even the Tornamiras' influence could help Peire or the others after two fugitives, Guilhem Domergue Veyrier and Guilhem Serralier, were finally caught in May in Provence and in Montpellier. By the end of June, Peire himself was in captivity, and many of his companions soon followed him to prison. Within seven months, at least thirty-nine other Beguins had testified before the inquisitors of Carcassonne, from Narbonne, Lodève,

---

[53] See Backman, "Arnau de Vilanova," esp. 24, and Germain, "Une consultation inquisitoriale," 335.

Montréal, and many other towns and villages across the Midi, including Montpellier.[54]

Because so much of our information regarding heretical activity in Montpellier comes from the depositions of those who were captured in the summer of 1325, it is almost impossible for us to continue to follow the life of the Beguin community in Montpellier after this point. Almost certainly, however, as had frequently been the case throughout the history of the persecution, the Beguins already in custody attempted to protect their own by hiding the identities of many of their numbers and their supporters who were not yet taken or identified. Though certain Beguins did betray their fellows, it was generally preferable to implicate a Beguin who had already died at the stake or one who had fled the region than it was to be the first to mention an unknown conspirator. While it appears that the most prominent members of the Montpellier community (like Peire de Tornamira and Prous Boneta) had been arrested, it is probable that other Beguins, and certainly other less obvious supporters of the Beguins, remained at large, unapprehended by the inquisitors. Na Bodina and Na Catharina, who offered their homes for meals and as refuges, for instance, do not seem to have been captured. Though they hid their assistance even more thoroughly than before the roundup of 1325, many continued to assist the cause, as we shall soon see.

For Peire, however, the long time of hiding and deceit was over. Many of those who were captured around the same time that he was were immediately brought to Carcassonne, where they would ultimately be sentenced.

---

[54] Not all of the depositions contained in the Doat volumes are dated, and it is possible, even probable that at least some of the other individuals sentenced at these General Sermons were also taken in the same period. Thirty-nine dated *culpe* are contained in Doat 27 and 28: in August 1325, the following Beguins testified: Prous Boneta and Bernard Castillon of Montpellier, Peire Daissan of Béziers, Peire Esperendiu of Narbonne, and Raimon Sacouri of Cabezach; in September, Miracla Esteve, Johanna Leona, Arnauda Mainie, Insia Esteve, and Johanna Jouconne of Montréal, Maria and Astruga de Rundaria, Raimunda Arrufat, and Guillerma Civile of Narbonne, and Pons of Sant Gili; in October: Blaize Boyer, Johan d'Almati, and Berengaria Donas of Narbonne, Johan Vascon of Montagnac, Jacma Amorosa Lauret of Lodève, and Amoda Sepian of Limoux; in November: Ermessendis Grossa and Sibillia Cazelas of Gignac, Esteve Gramat of Villeneuve-lès-Béziers, Peire Massot of Béziers, Alisseta Boneta, Alaraxis Bedos, and Johan Orlach of Montpellier, Berengaria Estorgua of Lodève, and Guilhem Quartier of Narbonne; in December, Andrieu Berenguier of Montagnac and his wife Agnes, Amada Orlach of Lodève, Guillerma Berengaria of Montagnac; and in January 1326, Johan Peyre of Montpellier and Peire Monitaur of Narbonne. The *culpe* of Manenta Arnaut of Lodève, Johanna Berengaria of Montagnac, Guilhem Ademar of Narbonne, and Jacma Sobirana of Carcassonne merely specify that they were taken in 1325, but give no month. Peire de Tornamira was captured in June 1325 (and died in prison in October).

But Peire's time in prison seems to have weakened his health and brought on a relapse of the fever that had plagued him in Sicily to such a degree that it was not until October that he began to make the journey.[55] His condition was so grave even then, in fact, that his family and friends were willing to put up the unheard-of sum of £20,000 as a caution, pledging to bring Peire to Carcassonne by a certain day. But Mennet de Robécourt and Raymond Pelat, two of the inquisitorial deputies who were charged with the case, refused to accept the money, and instead took Peire by night to the castle of Loupian (25 kilometers), "half dead" from fever. In the first four leagues, Peire fell three times, "almost dead," off his horse. In Loupian, because he was so ill, and so injured, "almost dead" again, the deputies kept him for three days, but finally proceeded toward Béziers, 40 more kilometers from Loupian. Despite the fact that doctors there told them that Peire was so sick that he would surely die if the journey were to continue and despite the fact that Peire's family renewed their offer of a substantial caution, the deputies placed Peire again on a horse, and they continued to Carcassonne, another 80 kilometers.

He was not yet quite dead when the party reached Carcassonne. Despite the absence of the inquisitor himself, Mennet de Robécourt, also an inquisitorial notary authorized to hear depositions, wasted no time and immediately began to question Peire. He put the ailing Peire on a bed—still clothed and with his shoes still on—and sat himself on the bed to take down Peire's answers to his questions. Present in the room was also the warden of the prison, Jacques de Poloniacho. Peire swore on the Gospels and told Mennet much (but not all) of the story related here, with what difficulty we can only imagine. When Peire had finished telling Mennet about the voyage to Sicily and his activities before his capture, the notary asked him a crucial question: "Had he believed all these things that he had heard from the Beguins, and had now confessed to be true?" Peire responded "No." It is not difficult to imagine the derision in Mennet's voice when he told Peire that that was

---

[55] In 1343, Peire's family alleged that he was already ill when he was captured. Three sources exist for the narrative that follows. The first is Peire's deposition, which tells us in the words of the notary who transcribed it what Peire said (Germain, "Une consultation inquisitoriale," 336–339). The second contains the testimony of two Dominican friars (Johannes Manentis and Jacobus Gormondi) who witnessed the very end of Peire's last deposition—and these confirm the first, while adding additional details (Doat 35, fols. 11r–17r). The final document is a letter from Pope Clement VI to the inquisitor of Carcassonne from 1343, requesting that Peire's trial be reopened. This last letter adds considerable detail regarding Peire's journey to Carcassonne from Montpellier, though it is likely that Peire's family (who had requested the boon from Clement VI) had painted the picture as direly as possible for the pope's ears (Vidal, "Menet de Robécourt," 447–449).

simply not believable. "He had talked with Beguins too much, and had heard too many of their erroneous opinions not to have believed what they said."

Mennet enjoined Peire to tell him the whole truth and not to lie against his conscience. And if simple persuasion were not enough, Mennet also turned to a not very veiled threat. If Peire were to confess fully, then he might be absolved, and then he could receive communion before dying. If he were to die as a good Christian, shriven and having received the sacrament, then all would be well and he would be buried properly; but if not, then Peire would have to be buried in the cemetery "of the dogs and the Jews."

This appears to have hit Peire hard. "And then [Peire] did not wish to respond, but stayed silent a long time." The threat was real and imminent; for Peire by now surely realized his own death was indeed very near. How should he respond? After a long pause, he finally answered: "When he had heard these errors from the Beguins, he had sometimes believed them, and he had held and believed that all of these things were true. But he did not stay continually or constantly in this belief, but sometimes he doubted, and was dubious about them, about whether or not they were true."[56]

David Burr has recently suggested that the Beguins "insisted on making up their own minds concerning things that the church thought it had decided for them." Just as they refused to take the Church's doctrines for granted, so too did they refuse simply to follow any kind of Beguin party line. In such a time of trouble and crisis (or as Burr calls it, in "the heretical briar patch"), they were "doomed to begin making more personal choices." In the years between 1317 and 1325 there were many opportunities for all of them to question what they truly did believe, and many of them did so.[57] I would like to suggest, however, that these decisions were not merely intellectual. For those who had believed strongly in the injustice of the prosecution of the Spiritual friars and the burned Beguins, such decision processes might be more accurately described as anguished doubting. Was everything they had believed in, and died for, wrong? Or was it still right, and would giving in to the Church in Avignon (which they had described for years as the "carnal" Church) be the *true* apostasy? As things fell apart and it looked

---

[56] "Et tunc ipse loquens nichil voluit respondere, sed stetit longo spatio taciturnus. Et post magnam pausum, iterum requisitus quod diceret veritatem plenariam, respondit quod, quando audiebat a supradictis Beguinis errores supra recitatos, ipse aliquotiens credebat eos, et tenebat et credebat in corde suo ita esse verum de omnibus opinionibus supradictis, sed non stabat continue nec constanter in illa credentia, sed quandoque dubitabat et erat dubius in opinionibus supradictis utrum essent vere." Germain, "Une consultation inquisitoriale," 339.

[57] Burr, *Spiritual Franciscans*, 254–256.

increasingly likely that none of them would actually see the splendid Third Age that they had hoped for, it is no surprise that they doubted, and anguished over their decisions in the face of death. Peire's agonized deathbed words of both belief and doubt are a potent testimony to the difficulties faced by all of the Beguins.

Mennet was still not satisfied with Peire's answer to his question. Just as two Dominican friars entered the room (they had been hastily summoned as witnesses), Mennet was asking Peire whether when he had been across the sea with brother Raimon, he had been a believer or not. One of the two friars, who had never seen Peire before and did not know anything about him or his situation, asked Jacques de Poloniacho if he knew who was "brother Raimon," and Jacques informed him that it was Raimon de Johan. Peire again told Mennet that sometimes he had believed and sometimes not, but also added "that when the Beguins were condemned, and were condemned by experts, and religious men, and great clerics, he himself began to doubt his belief and was dubious, and when he returned from overseas with brother Raimon, he was still in that doubt." Peire went on to say that "he himself did not have faith in these opinions unless he could look at them eye to eye and verify them, or unless he knew them to be approved by holy scripture, and that he still was of the belief that did not believe those opinions except so far as they were approved by holy scripture."[58]

Not even this answer was good enough for Mennet, who in frustration demanded why he had not revealed or accused these "apostates and Beguins" if he had not believed in their errors. Peire merely repeated his previous answer, and then asked for something to drink. The warden went to fetch chicken broth, but Peire asked for well-watered wine, and a servant mixed it for him and brought it to him. Peire drank a little and then lay back down on the bed, but did not and could not answer any further. He was dead. They brought in two doctors, who tried to administer theriac and eau-de-vie, but to no avail.[59] The feather they placed in front of his

[58] "Quod aliquo tempore fuerat in illa credentia et aliquando non, sed dubitabat in illa credentia, et non stabat constanter in ea pro eo videlicet, quia vidit postea ut dicebat quod ad condempnationem dictorum condemnatorum vocabantur periti religiosi, et magni clerici et de consilio eorum condempnabantur, et ideo dubitare incepit, et dubius fuit in credentia supradicta dicens, quod adhuc erat in dicta dubitatione quando rediit cum fratre Raimundo de Ultramare, ita quod non habebat fidem in dictis opinionibus nisi videret eas oculo ad oculum verificari, vel nisi sciret eas per sacram scripturam approbari, et quod adhuc erat in tali proposito quod non credebat dictis opinionibus nisi inquantum videret eas per sacram scripturam approbari." Doat 35, fol. 13r–v (the testimony of Johannes Manentis).

[59] Theriac was a compound originally developed by Galen, but "improved" over the centuries, and believed to be a potent curative in the Middle Ages (and up to the nine-

mouth did not move. Peire would not be answering any more of Mennet's questions.

Mennet was true to his promise and buried Peire in unconsecrated ground, an action that enraged the Tornamira family. Over the course of the next three decades, they carried on a campaign to have Peire's reputation restored and his body re-interred. Almost immediately, they had the two Dominican friars questioned as to Peire's last moments, though they were frustrated by the fact that while both attested to Peire's evident illness and his apparent sanity, they also affirmed that Peire had not asked for the sacraments of either confession or the Eucharist. In 1343, three years after Mennet de Robécourt had been convicted on unrelated charges of cruelty and corruption, they managed to enlist the assistance of Pope Clement VI, but while Clement appears to have been utterly persuaded of the cruelty and injustice of Mennet's treatment of Peire, the process seems not to have gone anywhere. In 1357, however, the Tornamiras managed to convene a "court" of 27 ecclesiastical dignitaries in Montpellier. The court consisted of those educated in civil and canon law, and theology, many of whom were members or leaders of the three local mendicant convents: the Franciscans, Dominicans, and Carmelites. They assembled in the Bishop's Hall in Montpellier before Vespers on December 21, where they listened to a reading (and simultaneous translation) of Peire's entire dossier of depositions and witnesses' testimonies.[60] At the end, they were given a chance to debate, and then to express their opinions regarding several questions. Was Peire a heretic, or a heretical believer? Was he a fautor, or abettor of heretics? Was he truly doubtful about his beliefs? Had he perjured himself? Was he truly excommunicated? Did he die impenitent? Ought his body to be buried in unconsecrated ground? Was the trial truly just?[61] Esteve Trucha, a doctor of both laws, led the crowd with his eloquently stated opinion that the answer to all of these questions, except to the fifth (was he truly excommunicated), was no, and that even his excommunication ought to be regarded as having been lifted, given his penitent death. Twenty-four of those present mostly

---

teenth century). At the end of the thirteenth century, the medical faculty at Montpellier became especially interested in its composition and medicinal action, and Arnau de Vilanova (d. 1311) wrote a treatise on its proper use. It included opium and the roasted skin of vipers, among dozens of other ingredients. Nancy Siraisi, *Medieval and Early Renaissance Medicine: An Introduction to Knowledge and Practice* (Chicago, 1990), 118–119. Arnau de Vilanova, "Epistola de dosi tyriacalium medicinarum," in Arnau's *Opera medica omnia*, vol. 3, ed. Michael R. McVaugh (Barcelona, 1985), 55–91.

[60] Germain, "Une consultation inquisitoriale," 331–333.

[61] Ibid., 339–340.

agreed with him, with the exception of the two members of the Order of Preachers, both of whom dissented, saying that Peire was "a heretic, who was excommunicated, and died impenitent; his trial was just, and he was also a fautor or abettor of the heretics."[62]

In the end, Peire's family got what they wanted: a posthumous acquittal from charges of heresy, or at the least an admission that Peire had died in communion with the church. They were able to take home a splendid parchment copy of the entire trial, a parchment that now resides in the Archives Municipales de Montpellier. One wonders how much of the experts' decision to acquit Peire was due to their actual conviction and how much to the importance and influence of Peire Tornamira's family. One does not like to allege outright corruption where there is little or no evidence of such, but Esteve Trucha's eloquent statements on Peire's behalf seem hardly to match the evidence, all of which points to Peire's life as a Beguin fautor and believer, who never really had the chance to repent before he died untimely, his death hastened by a particularly cruel inquisitor.

With Peire's death in October 1325 we reach the end of the most accessible part of the story of the Beguins of Montpellier, but the story was not yet entirely over. Many suspects were arrested in 1325 and 1326, but not all, and others continued to espouse Beguin beliefs even behind the walls of their prison. There were still others who never came before an inquisitor and whose names were never mentioned by those who did. It is in search of these last that we turn to the story of Sibillia Cazelas.

ON THE FRINGE: SIBILLIA CAZELAS

It was looking to be a fine Monday morning when the Montpellier notary Johan Holanie closed up his shop, and accompanied the two women down the carreria Daurada (or Goldsmith's Street) toward the Porte de Lattes. He nodded occasionally at acquaintances, perhaps including some of the city consuls, who would have been winding up their year's business, getting ready for the election later in the week.[63] It was still Lent, and so the meat market was closed, but the fishmongers, and the greenmarket across the street from the consulate were doing a fine business.

---

[62] Ibid., 340–343.

[63] This story is based on Sibillia's testimony before the inquisitors (Doat 27, fol. 16r–18v), the testimony of other Beguins such as her friend Ermessendis Grossa (Doat 27, fols. 14r–16r), and many documents in the notarial registers of Johan Holanie, notary of Montpellier, particularly register ADH 2E 368, July 7, 1327–April 3, 1328.

The first fresh spring greens were coming in (dandelions, wild asparagus, and fennel), he noticed, and even the first of this year's garlic. He idly hoped his wife would pick up some of the grey mullet—the season had just begun, and he was tired of sardines.[64]

Once out of the Porte de Lattes, they made their way through the douve and the Faubourg de Lattes over toward the Franciscan convent.[65] Not far away from the convent itself, they entered a field—Peire de la Gautru's if he remembered correctly—where several others shortly joined them. He was not acquainted with them all, but friar Bernard de Bordelas, whom he did know, made introductions all around.

Master Holanie had come out of the city with his client Sibillia Cazelas, a widow from Gignac whom he had done work for previously, and her friend Ermessendis Grossa, also from Gignac. Friar Bernard was there with two of his fellow Franciscans, and they had brought with them an older woman who was vaguely familiar to Holanie, as well as two younger men, one of whom was introduced as her son. She was Gaucelina, dowager lady of Teyran, and he was her eldest son Guilhem Jacme. The other man was a glassmaker whom Holanie knew slightly, Peire de la Rueyra. Holanie finally realized that he had seen Lady Gaucelina at the church of the Friars Minor once or twice.

Soon they got down to business, and Holanie made notes in his register for two acts. First was a simple gift from Lady Gaucelina to his client Sibillia Cazelas of a rather large sum, £300. Second, Lady Gaucelina and her son sold all their lands in St Etienne de Cazevieille and in the valley of Montferrand to Peire de la Rueyra for another large sum—well over £200. Money changed hands, and Gaucelina handed over a small rock to Peire, symbol of her lands. Holanie wrote down the names of the three friars as witnesses, promised the various parties that he would have clean copies of their documents the following day, gathered up his register and ink bottle, said farewell, and headed back into the city. His client and her friend stayed behind to speak with the friars and Peire de la Rueyra, and Lady Gaucelina and her son mounted two horses held by a servant on the edge of the field and headed north, toward Teyran.

As he rehearsed his steps through the Faubourg and the douve, through the Porte de Lattes and up the carreria Daurada to his office, Holanie reflected on what an odd morning it had been. He wondered why they had not all just come to his office

[64] For information on the earliest of the Mediterranean greens, and the tastiest of Mediterranean fish, see Patience Gray, *Honey from a Weed* (New York, 1986), 118–141 and 188–204.

[65] The douve, or *degua*, was the poor neighborhood closest to the "ditch" outside the city's walls.

instead of dragging him all the way out to Peire de la Gautru's field. Sibillia had said something about Lady Gaucelina not wanting to fight the crowds in the city, but it still seemed rather strange. And what an odd transaction! He had never yet recorded a simple gift like that between individuals, and of such a large sum, too. It was more money than he usually recorded in a month! He hoped he had gotten the formula right—he would have to check. The land sale at least made some sense: Holanie knew that glassmakers were always looking for new woodlands to feed their furnaces—and Cazevieille was good country for that, and close to the glass factories. Still, the whole business was a little bit strange, even fishy. He thought about asking some of the more experienced notaries on the Notaries' Square, but then reflected that his clients had paid him for his professional discretion, after all, and it was really none of his business. At this stage of his career, he would not want to get a reputation for a loose tongue.

As he opened his shop, he saw a party of four approaching from the direction of the horse market. This was a good day! Three clients already, and the noon bell had not even rung. He ushered them in with a smile, and promptly forgot all about his musings.

This imaginative reconstruction of the morning of March 21, 1328, is less fanciful than it may seem. The notary Johan Holanie did write such acts in his register that morning and noted that he had gone out to Peire de la Gautru's field to record them.[66] Though I might have gone a bit far to suggest that the young notary preferred grey mullet to sardines, if Master Holanie had asked questions of himself such as those I have suggested on the way back to his office, they would not have been unwarranted or inappropriate. There was indeed something strange, something fishy going

---

[66] ADH 2E 368, fols. 144v–145r. Holanie recorded seven acts that day in his register, a higher than usual number. The acts involving Sibillia were the second and third of the day. The fourth (fol. 145r) was the sale of a white mule to an innkeeper of Montpellier by a man from Villeneuve-lès-Maguelone (with two witnesses), and was transacted within the walls in the "king's part" of the city, presumably at Holanie's usual place of business. The exact price Peire de la Rueyra paid for Gaucelina's land is unknown, though it is in excess of £200—the top right-hand corner of the page has been eaten away by rodents, and the rest of the sum is missing. Simple donations between living persons are indeed unusual in Montpellier, and somewhat rare in any case. Though he suggests that the register he is studying is atypical, John Pryor observes that such donations are also unknown in the 1248 Cartulary of Giraud Amalric of Marseilles: *Business Contracts of Medieval Provence: Selected Notulae from the Cartulary of Giraud Amalric of Marseilles, 1248* (Toronto, 1981), 172–173. I owe the conjecture that 1328 was relatively early in Holanie's career not only to the fact that register 368 is the first of his four surviving registers, but also to my observation that his clientele became more wealthy and exclusive over time, as recorded in his later registers (the last register ends in February 1344).

on with these two acts—something that we will now explore in further depth.

To do so, we need to begin with Holanie's client, Sibillia Cazelas, and her relationship with the Beguins. Sibillia, the widow of a merchant named Guilhem Cazelas of Gignac, had at least two children, a son by the name of Johan who was an adult by the 1320s, and a daughter. Though she does not seem to have been a member of the Franciscan Third Order and thus "officially" a Beguin, she was very much connected with Spiritual and Beguin circles.

Her involvement in those circles began long before such involvement became criminal. For centuries, the strongest religious influence on the small market and viticultural town of Gignac had been the nearby Benedictine abbey of Aniane (a mere six kilometers away), founded in the eighth century by King Louis the Pious's famed adviser and monastic reformer Benedict of Aniane. But around the turn of the fourteenth century, the Franciscans founded a convent in Gignac, thus enlarging their influence in the region. Gignac was approximately halfway between Lodève (where there had been a Franciscan convent for over sixty years) and Montpellier, whose convent was even older.[67] Sibillia was one of those in the town who were particularly attracted to the new friars and the spiritual messages they brought, and she was not alone. Though not many texts about the Beguins of Gignac have survived to the modern era, Sibillia's friend Ermessendis Grossa had vowed chastity under the influence of the Spiritual friars back in 1305. The two friends seem to have traveled together in Franciscan circles.[68] Another member of the Franciscan Third Order from Gignac, Peire Guiraut, was one of the Beguins who had visited Raimon and Bernarda d'Antusan in Cintegabelle and was captured in Caujac, just across the Ariège river. Peire and both of his companions were handed over to the secular arm in September 1322 as obstinate and pertinacious heretics and burned at the stake.[69]

Though we do not know how large the community was in Gignac, at least some of the friars there must have been partisans of Peter Olivi and the Spiritual friars because when Sibillia's daughter was afflicted with scrofula

---

[67] Emery, *The Friars in Medieval France*, 73–74.

[68] Ermessendis was an immigrant to Gignac from Lodève, and it is unclear from her testimony in which town she was living in 1305. Doat XXVII, fol. 14r.

[69] *Liber sententiarum* 2:1608–1633. They also appear in WM, l. 54. Peire had been traveling with Peire Hospital of Montpellier and Peire Domergue de Hounoux of Narbonne.

(an affliction of the lymph glands of the neck often tubercular in nature), she thought to take her to Narbonne to Olivi's shrine.[70] Many years later, even as Sibillia expressed her adherence to orthodox beliefs regarding Olivi and the Spirituals, she continued to insist that she was still certain that it was Olivi's prayerful intercession that had cured her daughter, and that Olivi was surely in Paradise. A grateful mother (or perhaps a mother who fears that miracles once granted can always be withdrawn) remembers.

Nor was Sibillia's involvement with the Spirituals limited to acting on behalf of her daughter. She was acquainted with one of the four friars later burned in Marseille, and she had also confessed to one of the Spiritual friars who recanted in Marseille, but later fled as an apostate. Since the mid-1310s, she had also been friendly with some of the Beguines of Montpellier, with Na Prous Boneta, her sister Alisseta, and their companion Alaraxis Bedos. She had visited them occasionally in Montpellier, and one of them had visited her in her home in Gignac. Her friend Ermessendis, who also knew the Boneta sisters, had Beguin contacts in Mauguio. Like many Beguins, their spiritual acquaintances were scattered across Languedoc and they did not hesitate to visit them from time to time.

Because, so far as we know, only one other Beguin from Gignac (Peire Guiraut) was ever caught by inquisitors (and he was caught in the company of Beguins from Lodève, Montpellier, and Narbonne, not in Gignac itself), Sibillia and Ermessendis might well have escaped inquisitorial attention entirely had it not been for their acquaintance with Na Prous Boneta. After Prous related her tale of visions and her personal apocalyptic importance, the inquisitors were particularly vigilant regarding her contacts, and it seems that Ermessendis's name came up somehow. When she was first asked about her familiarity with Prous, Ermessendis affected a wide-eyed innocence, but eventually told what she clearly hoped would be a plausible story.

Ermessendis had traveled to Montpellier with her friend Sibillia, and when the two of them arrived, they heard some extraordinary rumors about Prous. A friend told them:

> Na Prous said she had received the Holy Spirit and possessed God's grace as perfectly as the Blessed Mother of Christ; that she could go everywhere throughout the world and people should follow her; that wherever she went the Holy Spirit followed her; that whoever did not believe in her would die a bad death; that this same Na Prous had come to such a state that she had not

---

[70] Scrofula was also known as "the king's evil," and the "royal touch" was believed to cure it.

confessed for a long time because, she said, the sacraments of the church no longer contributed to salvation, and those who wished to have God's grace and be baptized in the Holy Spirit must now be baptized with earth entirely nude, like a child who emerges from the belly of his mother.[71]

Ermessendis was shocked, she said, and since no one, not even Sibillia, would go with her, she went alone to see Prous, to tell her that her beliefs were fatuous, to castigate her, and to beg her to renounce her errors. But Prous was adamant and reiterated her confidence in her visions to Ermessendis. Ermessendis claimed afterwards that she quickly made the sign of the cross, verbally commended herself to Christ and his Passion, and fled.

We may well wonder about the veracity of Ermessendis's story. The inquisitors certainly did. They questioned her about a person's duty regarding heresy, and Ermessendis acknowledged that she had known it was her duty to make an accusation to the authorities if she heard someone speaking such heresies. Yet Ermessendis had not turned Prous in and concealed her knowledge of Prous's heresy. How could she have done such a thing? they asked, to which she finally responded that she had not thought about whether she was doing a good thing or a bad thing, but simply wanted to flee all evil. It would be hard to blame her for not wanting to get involved, if such were truly the case, but the inquisitors were well known for not tolerating such excuses.

In the course of her confession, Ermessendis mentioned Sibillia's name, and Sibillia was soon asked to give her version of the story. At first, she too denied that she had ever even heard of Na Prous and her assertions. But eventually, she gave quite a detailed account of them, stating that she had heard it from someone she was speaking with. And once she was in a confessional mode, she kept right on, detailing her previous involvement with the friars of Narbonne and the things they had told her, her pilgrimage to Olivi's grave, and her belief that those who had died at Marseille, Narbonne, and elsewhere had been condemned unjustly and were "holy and glorious martyrs."

---

[71] "Ipsa naprous dicebat se recepisse spiritum sanctum, et habere gratias Dei ita perfecta sicut beata mater Christi habuerat, et quod ipsa poterat ire per mundum ubique, et quod gentes debebant eam sequi et quod quocumque ipsa iret Spiritus sequeretur eam, et quod qui non crederet ei moreretur mala morte, et quod in tantum devenerat ipsa naprous quod steterat per magnum tempus quod noluerat confiteri, quia dicebat quod sacramenta Ecclesiae non erant salutis, nec aliquid proficiebant ad salutem animae, et quod oportebat et quod quicumque vellet habere gratiam Dei, et baptisari in Spiritu Sancto quod de terra sicut puer qui exit de ventre matris suae baptizatur totus nudus." The translation of Ermessendis's deposition is by David Burr, "Ermessende" (http://www.history.vt.edu/Burr/heresy/beguins/Ermessende.html)

Like so many others, both Sibillia and Ermessendis said they repented of their heretical sins and wished to be absolved. But there is an odd note at the bottom of Sibillia's confession: "she is believed to have confessed badly."[72] Such an observation is nearly unique in the inquisitorial corpus, but seems to mean that the inquisitors believed Sibillia had still more to confess. And yet, when the time came for both women to be sentenced in November 1328, some three years after their initial depositions, both were given the lightest possible inquisitorial punishment, a mere slap on the wrist.[73] Out of nineteen living heretics condemned that day, only Sibillia and Ermessendis received the mildest of inquisitorial punishments: minor pilgrimages without crosses. One Beguine (Prous Boneta) went to the stake, twelve others went to prison (including four who were to be held in chains and in solitary confinement), one was given so-called major pilgrimages, and the rest were all given yellow crosses to wear as well as being required to make the same pilgrimages as Sibillia and Ermessendis. All Sibillia and Ermessendis had to do in order to be absolved of their sins was to travel to certain relatively nearby pilgrimage shrines, such as Puy Vauvert, Notre Dame des Tables in Montpellier, Notre Dame in Sérignan, Saint Gilles in Provence, Saint-Guilhem-le-Désert, Saint-Maximin, and la Baume (or grotto) of Sainte-Marie-Madeleine.[74] Had they been sentenced to "major" pilgrimages, they would have had to visit Rome, Santiago de Compostella in Galicia, Canterbury, Cologne, Rocamadour, Notre Dame of Paris, Saint Denis and Saint Louis in the Île de France, Saint Martial and Saint Leonard of Limoges, Chartres, Pontoise, Sully, Castres, and Bologna in Italy, in addition to the sanctuaries required for minor pilgrimages.[75] Sibillia and Ermessendis had to travel for a few months, but they might have had to travel for a lifetime. Additionally, they were not required to wear that telltale sign of a repentant heretic, yellow crosses sewn onto their garments, front and back. The yellow

---

[72] "…dixit se poenitere male confessa reputatur."

[73] Doat 27, fols. 89v–91v.

[74] The sermon of November 11, 1328, does not specify exactly what the inquisitors meant by "minor pilgrimages" on this occasion. The list I have provided comes from the sentence of Johan Torrozelle of Narbonne from February 1324. Doat 28, fol. 163r. In fact, this list may be longer than that required of Sibillia and Ermessendis. In 1322, Bernard Maury was asked only to visit the cathedrals or parish churches of Carcassonne, Limoux, Narbonne, and Béziers. Manselli, *Spirituali*, 330. The case of Johan Torrozelle was an especially complicated one, since he had been a prominent partisan of the Spirituals (he was one of the consuls who protested in 1316), but had turned informant, and had helped capture three Beguins. See Emery, *Heresy and Inquisition*, 132n.

[75] This list comes from the General Sermon of September, 1329. Doat 27, fol. 195r.

crosses were deeply resented by those who were sentenced to them, not only because it made them subject to public ridicule, but also because many of those so marked found it difficult to find work and to make a living.[76]

The punishment, in this case, does not really seem to fit the crime, especially considering the inquisitors' conviction that Sibillia at least, despite her admission of a continued belief in the sanctity of Peter Olivi, had "confessed badly." Naturally, this preferential and undeserved easy treatment makes us speculate, and speculation takes us rather quickly to a suspicion of corruption. Corruption within the inquisitorial system was hardly unknown in Languedoc. The most famous example of attempting to obtain better treatment in exchange for money occurred in Pamiers, where just a few years earlier, Bernard Clergue claimed he had spent 14,000 solidi (or £700) trying in vain to free his infamous brother Pierre, the small-time, libidinous Napoleon of Montaillou, from the inquisitorial prison.[77] Bernard gave bribes to the lord of Mirepoix, the reeve of Rabat, a relative of the count of Foix, the archdeacon of Pamiers, and an inquisitorial notary and spy, Arnaud Sicre. Jacques Fournier, the future Pope Benedict XII and bishop-inquisitor of Pamiers, may have been implacable, but was the inquisitor of Carcassonne less so?

Corruption also occurred on lower levels. Bartholomeu Adalbert, a notary of the inquisitor of Carcassonne, was condemned of corruption by the inquisitor of Toulouse at the very same General Sermon when Sibillia and Ermessendis were sentenced. When we realize that the notary who took down Sibillia's deposition was Mennet de Robécourt, who not only drove Peire de Tornamira to an early grave but was also convicted of corruption in the case of a certain Jew of Lombers in 1340, we wonder even more.[78] Mennet's only biographer, Jean-Marie Vidal, baldly describes him as "incompetent, malevolent, and greedy,"[79] and Vidal did not even suspect him in Sibillia's case, which he appears not to have noticed. But how would two such widows, both advocates of apostolic poverty, have come up the necessary amounts of liquid cash to grease greedy inquisitorial palms such as those of Mennet de Robécourt?

[76] Given, *Inquisition*, 85–86, 103.

[77] Ibid., 121; *Registre* 2:82–83. Pierre Clergue, a priest, was the lover of at least a dozen women in Montaillou, and also a Cathar heretic who betrayed his enemies to the inquisitors, whether or not they were actually guilty of heresy. He was also notably short of stature. See Le Roy Ladurie, *Montaillou*, esp. 54–58.

[78] Vidal, "Menet de Robécourt." In addition to his mistreatment of Peire de Tornamira, Mennet was also accused of falsifying testimony, and of using violence and torture against innocents.

[79] Ibid., 435.

For that, we need to return to the scene in Peire de la Gautru's field in the spring of 1328, and the extraordinary gift that caused Master Holanie to wonder. Three hundred pounds was a large sum of money indeed (the price of a large house in a good neighborhood inside the walls of Montpellier),[80] and the circumstances unusual, to say the least. On no other occasion in his surviving registers did Holanie record such a "simple gift between living persons." Another way in which it was unusual was the fact that it all took place in a field outside of town. Nowhere else in Holanie's register (or in any other surviving notarial register from Montpellier before the Black Death) does a transaction take place in such circumstances. Generally speaking, notaries met their clients in their homes or offices, and occasionally at the homes of prominent individuals or those on their deathbeds.[81] A desire or a need for a certain degree of discretion is one plausible explanation, though it is somewhat unclear exactly who was being protected. Sibillia? Or perhaps the others who wished to avoid being seen with her.

The gift is also unusual because of the parties who were present and, in particular, those who acted as witnesses, the three Franciscan friars. Franciscans are not commonly found in the notarial registers of Montpellier, and Holanie's four surviving registers contain only sixteen separate occasions when Franciscans appear, nine of which are in this particular register, and eight of which involve Sibillia or Peire de la Rueyra, the glassmaker who bought Gaucelina's land.[82] Sibillia, who also conducted more orthodox business with Master Holanie (calling in debts, which also raised more cash), was always accompanied by at least one friar, and two transactions done on

[80] For example: in 1333, Bernard Roardi, merchant, and several members of his family sold a large house, with its cellars and attached outbuildings to Guilhem de Calvinhac, moneychanger, for £230. The house was located in the center of town, near St Firmin, next to the "Notaries' Square." Its neighbors included a house belonging to the wife of the notary Arnaut Bodon, and another one belonging to Guilhem Marc, *domicellus*. ADH 2E 370, fol. 61v. Many other houses in Montpellier sold in the registers went for much less money. A table in Reyerson, "Land, Houses, and Real Estate Investment in Montpellier: A Study of the Notarial Property Transactions, 1293–1348," *Studies in Medieval and Renaissance History* 6 (1983): 39–112, at 61, demonstrates that many houses in Montpellier sold for under £100 and indicates an overall average of approximately £130, though if we discount a single sale of a house for £800 in 1331 as highly unusual, the average falls to closer to £80. In any event, a gift of £300 was substantial.

[81] Master Holanie very rarely left the town of Montpellier on business. In September 1327, he registered an act at the home of a certain Peire Arnaut in Mirevals, a town some 15 kilometers from Montpellier along the lagoons (ADH 2E 368, fol. 38v).

[82] Franciscans appear as witnesses nine times in this register, but only three in register 369, two in 370, none in 371 and twice in 372 (these are Master Holanie's only surviving registers). Franciscan Jacme d'Aspras does appear in an additional act of register 368 as the recipient of a gift of money (£30). ADH 2E 368, fol. 36r.

her behalf (though without her actually being present) were recorded at the Franciscan convent itself.[83] It appears that Sibillia was able to call on the resources of the Franciscan convent, or at least of individual Franciscans, to an extraordinary degree. That she had been strongly allied with the Franciscan convent of Montpellier before her arrest is hardly surprising given the strength of her Beguin convictions and her frequent contacts with the Beguins of Montpellier. Prous Boneta, for instance, continued to worship at the church of the Friars Minor in Montpellier at least until Easter of 1321, and very probably beyond that.[84] It seems rather more surprising that the Franciscans of Montpellier would welcome the presence of a soon-to-be-convicted Beguin heretic in their midst in the winter and spring of 1327–28, when the persecution of John XXII was at its height. Less than a year before, in March 1327, two of the Beguin ringleaders who had spent considerable time in Montpellier, Guilhem Domergue Veyrier and Guilhem Serallier, had been turned over to the secular authorities, and burned in Carcassonne. Twenty-nine other Beguins were sentenced along with them. Though none of the twenty-nine were from Montpellier itself, at least one native of Montpellier was released from prison during this sermon and probably returned to her native city, not only with the news, which would certainly have circulated quickly in any case, but also as a living and visible reminder of the severity of the inquisitors as she went about her business with those vivid yellow crosses on her clothes.[85] One would think that it was hardly a time to be caught flirting with heretics in Languedoc. Nor was the Montpellier convent particularly known for its tolerance for the Beguins—Raimon Rouvier, adamant opponent of the Spirituals, had been guardian in 1316 and was an important figure in the suppression of the Béziers and Narbonne convents. Guilhem Astre, who was later appointed inquisitor of Provence and who prosecuted the priest Bernard Maury, was another former official of the convent of Montpellier.

And yet, though the leadership of the convent of Montpellier had long been hostile to the Beguins, the circumstances we have been studying suggest

[83] ADH 2E 368, fols. 21v, 24v, and 133v.

[84] May, "Confession of Prous Boneta," 7.

[85] Johanna, the daughter of Pons Medit of Montpellier, who was released from prison "with crosses" (Doat 28, fol. 189v). Though many of those released with her had been sentenced at the General Sermon of February 24, 1325 (Doat 28, fols. 96r–174v), Johanna was not, and must have been sentenced at a General Sermon whose records have not survived. Thus we know nothing about her crimes or associates, though several of the others who were released with her are known Beguins. At least two sermons had been held in Carcassonne in 1323, and probably one in 1322, and she was most likely originally sentenced at one of these.

that other friars there were more tolerant. The fact that the Franciscan Order as a whole was now (1328) embroiled in its own controversy with Pope John XXII, the controversy over evangelical poverty which would lead Michael of Cesena to flee imprisonment in Avignon in May in the company of William of Ockham and Bonagratia of Bergamo, may have led to a softening of their position. All the friars, Conventuals as well as Spirituals, now saw their understanding of their own Rule and order shaken by the papacy; the earlier differences between them may not have seemed so grave after all. The debate over granaries and cellars and appropriately ragged habits was pointless when the papacy put in question the very idea of Franciscan poverty and denied the Franciscan claim that their poverty was in any way different from the poverty of orders who had communal property.[86] The evidence we have in hand here suggests that individual Franciscans may have supported the Spiritual position on poverty and certainly appear to have aided the clandestine actions of the Beguins.

One of the Franciscans had somewhat more to risk than the others. Bernard de Bordelas was singled out by Master Holanie as being not only from the convent of Montpellier, but also from Montpellier itself. Brother Bernard was probably already known to the notary, since several other members of the Bordelas family did business with him.[87] Bernard's family, all apparently merchants, was also very prominent in the affairs of Montpellier, and members of the family had held elected positions in the city several times, as recently as 1313.[88] They were also wealthy: when a certain Raimon de Bordelas, junior (who would be named consul in 1305), drew up a will in 1301, he enumerated an impressive estate, including over £2,000 in specified legacies and an untold amount of real estate. He appointed as his executor

[86] For more information on the "Poverty Controversy" see Douie, *The Nature and Effect of the Heresy of the Fraticelli*, esp. 153ff. Also Lambert, *Franciscan Poverty*.

[87] A Peire de Bordelas, merchant, appears three times in this register (ADH 2E 368, fols. 50v, 111v and 112v), and Jacme, Raimon, Mathieu, and Galhard de Bordelas, all also merchants, appear several times each in this and later registers (ADH 2E 368, fols. 88v and 144r, ADH 2E 369, fols. 22r and 23r, ADH 2E 370, fols. 59r and 104v, and ADH 2E 371, fol. 2r).

[88] In 1258, Johan de Bordelas was elected as a replacement consul, and in the following year elected as an *obrier*. He was re-elected to the consulate in 1266 (AMM, Petit Thalamus, fols. lxxvi r–v, fols. lxxvii r–v; AMM, Thalamus de la Commune Clôture, fol. 12). A Peire de Bordelas was elected consul in 1276 and re-elected in 1279, but died in office (AMM, Petit Thalamus, fols. lxxviii–lxxix). A Bernard de Bordelas makes an appearance at the Commune Clôture in 1288 (AMM, Thalamus de la Commune Clôture). Individuals named Raimon de Bordelas were elected to the consulate four times, and once as bailiff (the consulate's most important position), between 1298 and 1312, and twice elected to the Commune Clôture, in 1305 and 1313.

a prestigious figure: Johan Marc, doctor-in-laws, professor at the university, representative of the city to Philip the Fair, and eventually, royal judge in Nîmes, a family friend or acquaintance who contributes to our appreciation of the family's prestige.[89]

In 1320 and 1321, Raimon de Bordelas had also been in the public eye, though not in a particularly flattering manner. Raimon had been sent on a municipal mission to the city of Aigues Mortes, but was shortly thereafter found abusing the public trust. Though Raimon and his two companions had done the city business they were expected to do in Aigues Mortes, they had taken their own sweet time returning, and had conducted business of their own at the city's expense. When the fraud was uncovered, the affair was appealed first to King Philip V, and from there to the judge of Béziers, who settled it in the consulate's favor. Raimon de Bordelas and his companions were ordered to repay the sum of £14 tournois to the consulate.[90] But cheating on one's expense accounts is not nearly as serious a crime as heresy, and it may have been Bernard de Bordelas's desire for secrecy (for himself, the Franciscan Order, and also his family) that led the sundry group to gather in Peire de la Gautru's field.

Or it may have been Lady Gaucelina's. The dowager lady of the small hilltop village of Teyran north of Montpellier surely did not wish to risk

[89] AMM, EE 840. Maurice de Dainville and Marcel Gouron, eds., *Inventaire. Série EE: Fonds de la Commune Clôture, et Affaires Militaires* (Montpellier, 1974), 167. If brother Bernard had been a priest before joining the Franciscan order it is possible that this Raimon de Bordelas was his brother, since Raimon's will mentions a brother who was a monk in Marseille, another brother who was a secular priest, and a sister in the Cistercian monastery of Saint Félix de Montceau, but apparently no living children. The summary of the will in the inventory is imprecise, and conflates two different women named Cecilia (one a sister and one an aunt) into one. Rogozinski, *Power, Caste, and Law*, 163–164. AMM, Grand Chartrier, armoire E, cassette 1 (Louvet 1998). Another copy of this procuration is found in AMM, BB7, no. 1102. We catch a further glimpse of the family's wealth due to an unfortunate incident in 1339, when a certain Peire de Bordelas took refuge from the law in the Dominican convent of Montpellier due to debts contracted at the fairs of Champagne, and was eventually forced to hand over all his business records and reveal his assets. His wife Eustacia's property (her dowry and its augment) is particularly impressive: the real estate alone amounts to a dozen houses in addition to fields and vineyards. ADH 2E 375, fols. 129v–136r.

[90] The 1320 letter from Philip V to the judge of Béziers is Louvet 3750 (Grand Chartrier, armoire H, cassette 5), and the 1321 settlement by the judge of Béziers is Louvet 3405 (Grand Chartrier armoire G, cassette 6). An additional document, which shows Peire and Mathieu de Bordelas to have been in Genoa in 1309, contracting debts to be repaid at the fairs at Bar, can be found in Renée Doehaerd, *Les relations commerciales entre Gênes, la Belgique et l'Outremont d'après les archives notariales génoises aux XIIIe et XIVe siècles,* vol. 3 (Brussels, 1941), document 1658.

being caught in the act of aiding and abetting a heretic. After all, £300 was a sum large enough to be difficult to explain away as mere alms for the poor, and many individuals had already found themselves in inquisitorial prisons for gifts of much less—Jacma Amorosa Lauret of Lodève, for instance, was sentenced to perpetual imprisonment in 1327 on account of the wheat, figs, grapes, and dried pears that she had sent to a fugitive Beguin, along with a mere three or four pennies and a few sausages given "for the love of God."[91] Gaucelina's family was respectable and comfortable, and she was risking a great deal with her gift. We might wonder why, if the risk was so great, was such a clandestine and culpable gift recorded at all? The reason no doubt lies in the fact that Gaucelina needed to sell her land, possibly her dowry, to a glassmaker in order to have such a large sum to give to Sibillia. The glassmaker needed official title to the land in order to exploit it. We can assume, however, that if such a substantial donation from one noblewoman resulted in a tell-tale document, donations from others more cautious did not.

This single strange transaction can also lead us to additional important conclusions. Support for the cause of the Beguins was wider than we could ever have known from studying inquisitorial records alone. In Montpellier, at the very least, we have found pockets of supporters never even suspected by the inquisitors (Bernard de Bordelas, Gaucelina of Teyran, Peire de la Rueyra). Not only that, but these supporters came from groups who have not previously been identified as having any connections to the Spiritual Franciscans or their followers. Most scholars have reported that support for the Beguins came exclusively from the cities and towns of Languedoc, and that such support was greatest among artisans.[92] But Gaucelina was a member of the minor landed nobility of Languedoc and came from a small village. Brother Bernard de Bordelas came from an extremely wealthy and influential merchant family and was, moreover, a Franciscan friar. The survival of these few records in Master Holanie's register is therefore precious in our understanding of the depth of support for the Beguins in Languedoc, even after such effective campaigns of repression had already taken place.

[91] She had already abjured and been sentenced to wearing crosses three years previously, and was thus technically a relapsed heretic. Doat 28, fol. 234r. Burr, *Spiritual Franciscans*, also notes the seeming injustice of this incident, but does not mention the wheat or the fruit, 256–257.

[92] Especially Jean-Louis Biget, "Autour de Bernard Délicieux: Franciscanisme et société en Languedoc entre 1295 et 1330," *Revue d'histoire de l'église de France* 70 (1984): 75–93, and "Culte et rayonnement."

We can break the history of the Beguin community of Montpellier down into three distinct chronological phases. The first is the one we know least about, from the community's origins to the first arrests and burnings in 1319. In this period, we know that there were at least two Beguin "houses of poverty" located in the poor neighborhood of the douve, close to the Franciscan convent, and that the Beguins benefited from the patronage of such luminaries as Philip of Majorca. It was in this period that Peire de Tornamira, a priest and member of an elite family, put on the habit of the Beguins and lived in houses of poverty both in Montpellier and in nearby Mauguio. We would expect that this community would have resembled those elsewhere in Languedoc during the same period, as described in chapter 1. Closely allied to the Franciscan convent, they were distinguished by their clothing and their practices and drawn together by their devotion to their patron "saint," Peter Olivi, and by their passionate belief that the Church was teetering on the brink of a new age. Their certainty that Antichrist was near, their practice of a strict and uncompromising poverty, and their belief that they had an important role to play in the script of the end times appear to have won them friends and benefactors in the community like Bernard Castillon and Johan Orlach.

As in the rest of Languedoc, the dynamics of the community changed radically after the burnings first in Marseille, then in Narbonne and Capestang, and especially in Lunel, where a number of local Beguins lost their lives. From this point on, the Beguins of Montpellier were necessarily suspect and went into hiding. After the burning in Lunel in the fall of 1321 until the roundup of Beguins in the summer of 1325, Montpellier was an important urban underground. Its relative anonymity protected those prominent Beguins who had fled there, like Guilhem Domergue Veyrier or Guilhem Serallier, with the significant assistance of the natives. Important regional leaders like Bernard Peyrotas or Peire Trencavel also passed through the city. Natives of the city, such as Johan Orlach or Peire de Tornamira, were able to use their wealth and their familial resources to hide these fugitives and to assist them materially.

We do not know what led individuals like Gaucelina of Teyran or Bernard de Bordelas to become involved with the Beguin resistance. These were men and women with a seemingly more peripheral involvement with heresy, yet who nevertheless risked their reputations and possibly their lives to support the Beguins with donations of money and with help in a difficult situation. It is possible that the severity of the repression (well advanced by 1328) evoked sympathy in groups who had hitherto not become involved—and it is also possible that they had been involved all along, and it is by chance that we have caught them only at this late date.

Such significant involvement of members of the Franciscan convent of Montpellier is especially intriguing, because so unexpected. Our evidence enables us to ascertain that in Montpellier at least, by 1328, a certain number of Franciscans were willing not only to forgive the Spirituals and their lay followers the Beguins, but actually to support those still in hiding or already imprisoned. A debate among the inquisitors and the inquisitorial counselors in June 1329 highlights this uncomfortable change on the part of the Franciscans. The case was that of brother Peire Julian, Franciscan of the convent of Béziers, a captured fugitive, who was possibly to be relaxed to the secular arm and burned at the stake as a relapsed Spiritual. In the midst of a heated debate, brother Guilhem de Salvella, guardian of Peire's convent, pleaded for clemency, arguing that when he apostatized, Peire had had good reason to be afraid of the treatment of his own brethren and of the severity of their prisons, and so his running away should not be dealt with too severely. On the one hand, brother Guilhem emphasized his order's severity toward malefactors, and on the other, he sought clemency for Peire.[93] In the late 1320s, members of the Franciscan order were forced to tread a fine line between orthodoxy and heterodoxy, particularly in the matter of the interpretation of poverty, the crux of Spiritual and Beguin belief, but also at the very core of the Franciscan Order's belief system. The friars of Montpellier may not have been able to speak out in public, but at least some of them were willing to act in private in support of the Beguin heretics who sought their aid.

The picture that emerges is one of a highly heterogeneous Beguin community, whose members ranged from recent immigrants to the city to members of the local nobility and members of the mercantile and intellectual elite. Mercers, drapers, glassmakers, and Franciscans all appear to have supported the heretics, even under the threat of persecution. The city of Montpellier, far from being an orthodox stronghold loyal to the papacy to the end, was thus riddled with heretical undercurrents and people who struggled in secret to keep the Beguin movement alive. Though the lack of documentation means that we are unable to trace Beguins in Montpellier after 1329, it is clear that they continued to resist longer and more effectively than historians have been aware. And if this is true of Montpellier, we may also expect that it

[93] Doat 27, fol. 168r–v. Due to the sharp disagreement among the counselors, a decision regarding the matter was referred to another day, and Peire Julian's resulting sentence has not survived.

was true of other Beguin cities, like Narbonne, Béziers, and Carcassonne, as well. Though the inquisitorial prosecution was devastatingly effective, it did not eliminate all of the Beguin believers.

Keeping a beleaguered faith alive against such strenuous opposition took strong personalities, and resourceful individuals. Peire de Tornamira, Sibillia Cazelas, Esclarmonda Durban, Raimon and Bernarda d'Antusan, and Bernard Maury were all important to the Beguin resistance and to the successes of the underground movement, but none of them were considered by their fellows or the inquisitors to be the true leaders of the Beguins. Some of those who had been leaders, of course, were martyred early on—like brother Mai, for instance—but others continued to lead and began to lead as the inquisitorial web tightened. It is to these leaders that we turn in our next chapter.

CHAPTER FOUR
HERETICS, HERESIARCHS, AND LEADERS

I am a leader by default, only because nature does not leave a
vacuum.

—DESMOND TUTU

eresy is in the eye of the beholder. When Esclarmonda
Durban withstood her death at the stake so patiently,
she did so because she did not think of herself as a
heretic, but as a faithful Christian who died to protect
and preserve the true faith of Christ. Many Beguins told inquisitors that they
believed the inquisitors themselves (and the authorities behind them, up to
and including the pope himself) to be the real heretics, in that they unjustly
persecuted and condemned those who were only struggling for good. Peire
Guiraut, for instance, told Bernard Gui that "he believed the bishops, priests
and inquisitors who condemned these Beguins, as well as all those who gave
them advice about this condemnation, to be infidels and heretics, if they persevere pertinaciously in this error. And the current Lord Pope John XXII has
made himself an infidel and a heretic if he knew the confessions of these Beguins, and if it was with his knowledge and consent that they were condemned
as heretics, and if he persevered in this pertinaciously and wishes that others
persevere."[1] Peire turned the vocabulary of the inquisitors ("persevere perti-

---

[1] "Item credit esse infideles et hereticos episcopos seu prelatos et inquisitores qui con-
dempnaverun predictos Beguinos tanquam hereticos et etiam illos qui in predicta con-
dempnacione dederunt consilium si in hoc pertinaciter perseverunt. Item quod dominus

naciously," for example) on its head. As we have already discussed regarding martyrdom, the vocabulary changes according to one's point of view. Esclarmonda felt she was *persecuted*, but the inquisitors felt strongly that in *prosecuting* her, they were upholding God's law and preserving God's Church.

The same problem of language emerges when discussing the personalities of those the Church deemed to be heretics. A strong and charismatic leader, unyielding in faith, capable of rallying support for his or her cause, was of course the very worst possible type of heretic, called "obdurate" and "pertinacious." The inquisitors also had a special name to describe such individuals, a term enshrined in canon law and used by inquisitors as a particular mark of opprobrium and shame: heresiarch. Canon law defines "heresiarch" as follows: "He who defends the error of others is much more damnable than those who err, because not only does he himself err, but he prepares and confirms the stone of offence of error for others. Whence, the teacher of error is said to be not only a heretic, but also a heresiarch."[2]

Who were the heresiarchs of the Beguins? Surely the ultimate heresiarch was Peter Olivi himself, and his body ("relics" to his followers, mere bones to the inquisitors) was spirited away from Narbonne at the very beginning of the conflict to be burned like a live heresiarch, with the ashes thrown into the Rhône.[3] We might have expected to hear the "ministers" of the Beguins, those individuals chosen by their congregations as teachers and

---

papa Johannes XXIIus qui nunc est erravit et factus est infidelis et hereticus si scivit confessiones predictorum Beguinorum, si de sua sciencia et consensu fuerunt tanquam heretici condempnati et si in hoc pertinaciter perseverat et vult quod alii perseverent." *Liber sententiarum* 2:1622.

[2] "Qui aliorum errorem defendit multo est dampnabilior illis, qui errant, quia non solum ille errat, sed etiam aliis offendicula preparat erroris et confirmat. Unde quia magister erroris est, non tantum hereticus, sed etiam heresiarcha dicendus est." *Corpus Iuris Canonici*, ed. Emil Friedberg (Leipzig, 1879–1881), I, 999. C. 24 q. 3 c. 32. That this definition was known in the south of France can be discerned from its inclusion in a list of statements regarding heretics, all taken from Gratien, appended to a treatise on heresy by the thirteenth-century Benedictine bishop of Marseille, Benedict d'Alignano, found in a fourteenth-century manuscript. BnF MS. 4224, fol. 448a. "xxiiii q. vult hereticus vel qui magister erroris est non tantum hereticus sed heresiarcha dicendus est." Benedict d'Alignano was bishop of Marseille from 1229 to 1267, and he wrote the tract before his resignation from the episcopate to become a member of the Franciscan Order. *Gallia Christiana*, 2nd ed., vol. 1 (Paris, Rome, 1870), col. 653. Licia Porcedda kindly examined the manuscript on my behalf. This definition was also used by inquisitors in a Bohemian trial that dates from between 1335 and 1343. "Zwei Rechtsgutachten zum Inquisitionsprozeß gegen den Brünner Goldschmied Heynuß Lugner," in Alexander Patschovsky, *Quellen zur Böhmischen Inquisition im 14. Jahrhundert* (Weimar, 1979), 289, 302.

[3] Biget, "Culte et rayonnement," 296. The original citation is found in Francisco de la Peña's commentary in Eymeric, *Directorium Inquisitorum* (Rome, 1578), 2:77.

leaders, called heresiarchs, but the only man identified as a "minister of the Beguins" in the surviving records, Peire de Na Bruna of Belpech, abjured his beliefs and was sentenced to the Wall as a mere heretic.[4] The inquisitors of Languedoc were more capable than we are of determining who had truly acted as a leader and who had backed down from any position of authority and leadership under pressure.

The Spiritual friars are another logical place to look for Beguin here-siarchs, and one of the most active of the fugitive friars, brother Raimon de Johan, was indeed sentenced to perpetual imprisonment in solitary confine-ment as both a heretic and a heresiarch in 1328. David Burr has compared brother Raimon to Graham Greene's "whiskey priest" hero of *The Power and the Glory;* like the priest, Raimon can hardly explain or understand himself why he spent so long—nine years—in his fugitive underground ministry. Greene's priest described how it all happened this way:

> The fact is, a man isn't presented suddenly with two courses to follow—one good and one bad. He gets caught up....I thought I'd stay till next month, say, and see if things were better. Then—oh, you don't know how time can slip by.[5]

Raimon has slipped in and out of these pages, acquainted with almost every-one, a ubiquitous but unassuming conspirator, teacher, confessor, and friend. But in the end, faced with the stake, Raimon recanted and abjured his heresy. We can only imagine what that abjuration meant to him. Did he feel he had betrayed everything he had stood for? Or did he instead regret the heretical choices he had made before? As Burr suggests, Raimon de Johan was one of those flawed heroes who do so much of the real work of history.[6]

Wherever we look for them, leaders or heresiarchs were few. In the over-whelming atmosphere of fear and uncertainty, it was near impossible to find those who were both fearless and certain. What made some men and women into leaders is a subject perhaps more suited to psychology than history, but in the case of the Beguins it is one we can explore fruitfully for two of the Beguin heresiarchs. The subject is particularly interesting because one of these heresiarchs was a woman, Prous Boneta of Montpellier.

---

[4] *Liber sententiarum* 2:1310, 1420.

[5] Burr, "Raimond Déjean," 77–78. Graham Greene, *The Power and the Glory* (New York, 1940), 263–234.

[6] Burr, "Raimond Déjean," 78. Burr also discusses the "case history" of Raimon de Johan in *Spiritual Franciscans*, 215–221.

As early as 1310, opponents of the Spiritual Franciscans accused the rebellious friars of being "followers of dreams and fictitious visions" and suggested that they "unduly frequent meetings of women, especially Beguines, on the pretext of sanctity."[7] Accusations of libertinism against one's enemies are hardly unique to the Franciscan conflict, of course. As Malcolm Lambert has observed, accusations of sexual license against those perceived as heretics (including the early Christians) are among the most persistent of all tactics with which to tarnish an enemy's reputation.[8] Olivi himself used just such an accusation against the Cathars.[9] And accusations of believing "fictitious visions" (which if not inspired by God, might well be inspired by the Devil) often go hand in hand with libertinism.[10]

Peter Olivi was aware that this accusation was common against his followers, and the seventh of his *Questions on Evangelical Perfection* was devoted to helping his friars combat such unjust suspicions. Olivi provides a list of six suggestions as to how to determine what kinds of association or conversation with women ought to be avoided. Whom are you meeting: someone young, or old? rich, or poor? Where: in a secret or solitary location? in a place with a bad reputation? When: during the day or night, or at what time of night, and for how long? How often: rarely, or frequently? Why: do you have a good and sufficient reason? In what manner are you talking: in an ordinary fashion, honestly or dishonestly? are you colluding together, or do you touch each other too familiarly? For the convenience of his brothers, Olivi even provided a little mnemonic device to help them determine what was and was not suspicious: a catchy Latin tag that prompted the friar to think about "why, where, when, who, how, and how often." The original Latin even scans as a hexameter: *"causa, locus, tempus, persona, modus, numerusque."*

---

[7] "Si sint sompniorum vel fictarum visionum sectatores; si nimis frequentant colloquia mulierum potissime Beghinarum sub specie sanctitatis." This comes from the response by Raimond de Fronsac to Ubertino's defense of the Franciscan *Regula bullata* before the Council of Vienne, *ALKG* 3:102. A similar accusation (though in response to chapter 6 of the Rule) is found in the same volume, 119: "they audaciously preach erroneous opinions and fictitious visions" ("opiniones erroneas et visiones fictas audacter modo predicant").

[8] Lambert, *Medieval Heresy*, 164–166.

[9] Burr, *Olivi's Peaceable Kingdom*, 89.

[10] Lambert, *Medieval Heresy*, 164–166. Gregory the Great, for example, was suspicious about dreams, suggesting that many dreams were caused by "the hidden enemy by way of an illusion," "ab occulto hoste per inlusionem." Gregory the Great, *Dialogues*, ed. Adalbert de Vogüé (Paris, 1980), 3:172. See also Norman Cohn, *Europe's Inner Demons: An Enquiry Inspired by the Great Witch-Hunt* (New York, 1975), esp. 32–42; Wendy Love Anderson, "Free Spirits, Presumptuous Women, and False Prophets: The Discernment of Spirits in the Late Middle Ages," Ph.D. diss., University of Chicago, 2002; and Nancy Caciola, *Discerning Spirits: Divine and Demonic Possession in the Middle Ages* (Ithaca, 2003).

In such matters, as in sobriety and temperance, our actions always lie some-where on a scale leading from perfect and blameless observance all the way to culpable disobedience, and it is not practicable to provide universal rules. Because not all contact with women is illicit—there are times when for a Franciscan, it is simply part of the job—not all conversation or association could, or should, be avoided.[11]

Women played an important role. Though it does not appear that women were over-represented in the Beguin movement, neither were they neces-sarily excluded from intense participation.[12] Arnau de Vilanova's *Lesson for Narbonne*, written in the vernacular, and among the texts frequently read aloud in the weekly meetings common to groups of Beguins, pointed out that true knowledge of Scripture was not always found by those who sought it through philosophy and through the schools: "The apostles and all the disciples (who were without number, and among them many women), who had learned no philosophy, knew more true theology than all the masters that ever were, through grace, and through the inspiration of the Holy Spirit."[13] Furthermore, the progressive nature of Olivi's view of history may also have been appealing to women who were deeply drawn to matters of

[11] There are two versions of the *Questio*, both of which remain unpublished. There are eight manuscripts. I have drawn these examples from version A, in Emmen's transcription, but the arguments in version B are similar. Assisi, Com. 589, Capestrano, 21, Montefano, 19, fol. 33v, Vat. Borgh. 46, fols. 38va–40ra (version A), Vat. Borgh. 357, fols. 34rb–36va (version B), Vat. Borgh. 358, fols. 44v–45r (version A), Vat. Lat. 4986, fols. 21v–22v (version B), and Florence Laurentiana Plut. sin. 3, carta 181 (fol. 150a–d). I am grateful to Sylvain Piron, who called the *questio's* subject matter to my attention, to David Flood, who made available to me a typescript transcription and partial edition of the Vatican and Florentine manuscripts by A. Emmen, and to David Burr, who allowed me to borrow several microfilms.

[12] Women constituted only 29.6% of the total number of Beguins of whose existence we are aware. As John Mundy has observed, however, "the documents speak quaveringly about the participation of the middle classes, in hushed tones about the poor, and in a whisper about women who, as always, are insufficiently represented." John Mundy, *Men and Women at Toulouse in the Age of the Cathars* (Toronto, 1990), 2. Jean-Louis Biget cal-culates the percentage of women as 37%, but he did not have access to the Beguin mar-tyrology and certain other sources. Biget, "Culte et rayonnement," 302. For a full list of the 213 Beguins I used to make my calculations, see Burnham, "A Prosopography of the Beguins and Spiritual Friars of Languedoc," Oliviana 2 (2006), http://www.oliviana. org/document37.html.

[13] "Primerament, en los appòstols e en tots los dexebles (que foren sens compte, e hac-hi multes dones), que hanc no appraneren en philosophia, e saberen més de vera theologia que tots los mestres que ara sòn, per gràcia e per influcció del Sant Esperit." This is the *Lliço de Narbona*, in *Obres Catalanes* 1:164. Arnau's Catalan would presumably have been comprehensible throughout Languedoc, situated at the linguistic crossroads of Provençal, Occitan, and Catalan.

piety and theological speculation. In the Age of the Spirit, it was expressly understood that the humble were to see their spiritual understanding increase.[14] Who, after all, had more to gain in this Age of the Spirit than women? The story of Prous Boneta, a woman whose apocalyptic visions were simultaneously shocking and familiar, will help us to understand the charismatic, mystical, and inspirational elements of leadership among the Beguins.

Not all Beguin leaders, however, were charismatic visionaries, and it would be a mistake to take Prous Boneta as in any way typical of the overall makeup of the Beguin movement and its leadership. Female visionaries are all too easy to dismiss as individualistic, unusual, or simply unimportant.[15] The figure of Peire Trencavel, a member of the Franciscan Third Order who has left no personal statement in the form of a deposition or confession, was nevertheless a leader who appears continually through the eyes and the reports of others. Throughout the years of their persecution, Peire struggled constantly to keep his fellow believers alive and safe and to protect the sources of their beliefs and ideas, Olivi's writings, from destruction. He tirelessly crossed and re-crossed Languedoc and Provence in his efforts to outwit the inquisitors. In Peire's story, we can see the compelling nature of Beguin belief for those who were not driven by the demands of their visionary experience, but who nevertheless risked their lives to keep the belief and their fellow believers alive.

As we examine the two poles of Beguin leadership, we will see revealed the fundamental problematic of the Beguins: radical and apocalyptic on the one hand, though with a spirituality and practice only minimally divergent from the norm on the other. Peire Trencavel and Prous Boneta were Beguin leaders at opposite ends of this spectrum, and also represent another divide: the one was a man of action, and the other was a woman of many words. Both were full of conviction as to the rightness of their cause. We will begin with the woman whose visionary authority made her into one of the last and most radical leaders of the Beguins of Languedoc.

[14] Burr, "Olivi, Apocalyptic Expectation," 280. Lerner, "Ecstatic Dissent," 56–57.

[15] As the philosopher Grace Jantzen has observed, female visionaries are perceived as particularly dangerous to the male status quo, because a "true access to the mysteries of God" is a kind of power. Therefore, "what counts as mysticism will reflect (and also help to constitute) the institutions of power in which it occurs. Put starkly, the church...will exert its power to determine who counts as a mystic, excluding from that category any who are threatening to its authority." Jantzen, *Power, Gender, and Christian Mysticism* (Cambridge, 1995), 14.

What kind of young woman would take a vow of chastity at the age of nine, and then maintain it for the rest of her life?[16] The same kind of young woman who could believe not only that Jesus was her sole lover, but that, in her, God had conceived the Holy Spirit, just as he had conceived Jesus in Mary. Through a series of visions in the early 1320s, Prous Boneta of Montpellier came to believe that it was through her and in her that the beatific Third Age of the Holy Spirit would begin—no one could be saved who did not believe in her and her role in the economy of salvation. God "put on flesh in the body of a virgin, and in her herself, Naprous, he has put on words," she told the inquisitor, and she said God told her, "You are the *donatrix* of the Holy Spirit."[17] Prous went to the stake willingly, even eagerly, in November 1328, and died there impenitent, convicted as a obdurate and pertinacious heretic and heresiarch.

Prous's deposition is as shocking to us as it must have been to the inquisitors and scribes who heard it and transcribed it. Though many of the ideas were the same as those they had heard time and again from the Beguins of Languedoc, Prous spoke them with a decisiveness and a fervor that must have left her auditors breathless. Furthermore, her understanding of the meaning of the present apocalyptic moment went far beyond the interpretations of even the boldest Beguin they had heard so far. It was not simply that the end times were upon them, but she herself held the key to their eschatological future. Knowing that it would lead to her death, Prous did not simply answer the inquisitors and their questions; she preached to them, telling them that there was a new dispensation, and a new order to the world:

> Again, the Lord told her that just as God ruled the Church through two
> bodies of flesh, that is, the bodies of Christ and of his mother the Vir-
> gin Mary, so in the same way he henceforth rules the church through the

---

[16] This story is based on Na Prous's own testimony before the inquisitors in Doat 27, fols. 51v–79v, published in May, "Confession of Prous Boneta." A translation into French can be found in Manselli (trans. Duvernoy), *Spirituels*, 274–289. Though the translation in Elizabeth Petroff, *Medieval Women's Visionary Literature* (New York, 1986), 284–290, is heavily abridged, a full English translation by David Burr is available on his website: (http://www.history.vt.edu/Burr/heresy/beguins/Prous.html). Prous's sentence, Doat 27, fol. 95r–96v, is published in Lea, *History of the Inquisition*, 3:653–654. Some of the material that follows also appears in my article "The Visionary Authority of Na Prous Boneta," in *PdJO*, 319–339.

[17] "De virgine cepit corpus suum, et de ipsamet Naprous cepit verbum," "Item quod Deus dixit sibi: beata virgo Maria fuit donatrix Filii Dei et tu eris donatrix Spiritus Sancti." May, "Confession of Prous Boneta," 29, 11.

two bodies of spirit given to the aforesaid friar Peter of John [Olivi] and to her who is speaking, Na Prous, both of which spirits are one, as she said....Once they have known these things, they cannot be saved otherwise, and whoever does not believe in the words of Na Prous shall die an eternal death.[18]

She welcomed her martyrdom, for in it she was utterly assured of her place in the history of salvation:

Again, she claimed that the Lord told her Christ took his body of flesh from a poor virgin so that poor people and rich would not be afraid to find fault with him and finally crucify him...and in the same way Christ took a body of spirit in a poor virgin so that poor and rich would not be afraid to find fault with him and persecute him and finally to crucify him in the spirit, because, as God told her (as she claims), he took his body from a virgin, and from her, Na Prous, he took the word, for as much as Christ was vituperated in the body which he took from the Virgin, it is necessary that he be vituperated the same amount in that body of words of her speaking, that is, in the spirit.[19]

Extravagant claims such as Prous's may lead us to suspect not merely vainglorious heresy, but even madness or insanity. Some historians who have written about Prous have called her "delirious" or even "psychopathic," while another has simply lumped her together with eccentrics, madmen, and "suggestible women."[20] We have already observed that, as in the case of Esclarmonda Durban, her yen for martyrdom might be seen as a product of

[18] "Item quod dixit sibi Dominus quod quemadmodum ipse Deux rexit ecclesiam per duo corpora carnis, scilicet corpora Christi et eius matris Mariae virginis, eodem modo reget de caetero ecclesiam per duo corpora spiritus dati fratri Petro Joannis praedicto et etiam spiritus dati ipsi Naprous loquenti, qui spiritus ambo sunt unum, sicut dixit....Postquam ea sciverint, aliter homo non posset salvari; in super quod qui non credat eiusdem Naprous verbis, morte morietur aeternali." Ibid., 22–23.

[19] "Item dixit et asseruit quod Dominus dixit sibi quod ipse Christus cepit corpus suum carnis ex una paupere virgine, ut pauperes et divites non timuerunt eum vituperare et finaliter crucifigere...et quod a simili ipse Christus cepit unum corpus spiritus in una paupere virgine ad finem quod pauperes et divites non timeant ipsum Christum vituperare et persequi et finaliter crucifigere in spiritu, quia, ut Deus sibi dixit, ut asserit, de virgine cepit corpus suum, et de ipsamet Naprous cepit verbum, quia tantum quantum Christus vituperatus in corpore quod cepit in virgine, ita oportet quod tantum vituperatus sit in illo corpore verborum ipsius loquentis, scilicet in spiritu." Ibid., 29. The translation is by David Burr (see above).

[20] Lea, *A History of the Inquisition* 3:82; Manselli, *Spirituali*, 247; Lambert, *Medieval Heresy*, 188n42. Other general histories of heresy and prophecy have also given Prous

the "demons of her mind," as one scholar has put it.[21] Prous's visions, which we will examine shortly, merely compound the problem. Still, we must remember that while the modern world is uncomfortable with the idea of religious visions and a desire for martyrdom, the medieval world was willing to accept them both as genuine, provided the visions could be ascertained to come from God, and not from the Devil, and the desire for martyrdom for an authentic cause.[22] Prous knew that others would question her, and would think she was simply out to make herself seem important, but she "would prefer to be cut in pieces with swords or that lightning from heaven should fall upon her and lay her stretched out upon the ground than to say such things about herself," she said, "but because God wishes and commands her, she must do the will of God and say them."[23]

Reading (or hearing) her words, it seems almost unimaginable that anyone could have believed her to be what she claimed to be: the herald of the new Age, a John the Baptist for the Age of the Holy Spirit. And yet, when he sentenced her, Henri de Chamayou called Prous a heresiarch, a leader of heretics, which means we must look for evidence that others saw her visions and her commitment as genuine and sent from God. There are three points that we must consider. First, we will see to what extent Prous's extraordinary testimony has its basis in the Olivian and Joachite traditions. Second, we will establish how the reception of her message among her contemporaries was conditioned both by the development of these ideas in the Beguin communities in the Midi and by the atmosphere of persecution. Finally, we will see how Prous exercised a significant influence over the heretical conduct of both men and women, owing to the authority of her visions.

---

short shrift. Though Gordon Leff considered Prous to have been influential (especially with women) because of the revelatory nature of her views, he provided no details of that influence: *Heresy in the Later Middle Ages: The Relation of Heterodoxy to Dissent, c. 1250– c. 1450* (Manchester, 1967), 213. Marjorie Reeves juxtaposed her discussion of Prous with a more thorough analysis of another heretic whose followers considered her to be the Holy Spirit, Guglielma of Milan, and called Prous's doctrine "strange" and "ill-assorted": *The Influence of Prophecy in the Later Middle Ages*, 248.

[21] "It is only too easy to argue that the martyr was in fact a sick and disjointed personality, as much the hapless product of a divided and floundering society as of the demons of his own mind, scarcely deserving of our admiration, let alone the name of martyr": Smith, *Fools, Martyrs, Traitors*, 14.

[22] See Anderson, "Free Spirits, Presumptuous Women, and False Prophets."

[23] "Quia plus voluisset, ut asserit, frustratim lacerari cum ensibus vel quod fulgur de coelo descendisse super eam et eam stravisset super terram, quam dicere talia de se ipsa, et quod plus voluisset dicere de una alia creatura sed, quia ita vult et mandat sibi Dus, oportet hoc ipsam dicere et facere Dei voluntatem." May, "Confession of Prous Boneta," 27.

Prous Boneta, the daughter of Duran Bonet,[24] was born and baptized in the parish of St. Michel of La Cadière, about 40 km north of Montpellier, no later than 1297.[25] La Cadière, despite its seemingly royal name (Cadière is derived from *cathedra*, or throne) is a tiny place even now, and in 1293 it had only 35 households, or probably close to 175 inhabitants.[26] Prous seems to have had two sisters, Alisseta and Stephana, and an extended family in La Cadière, including cousins close to her own age.[27] Her father was a respected man in the village who was asked to serve as a witness for an important royal inquest. In July and August 1293, when dozens of inhabitants of the villages in the region gathered in the town of Sauve to acknowledge the feudal dues they owed, Duran Bonet witnessed approximately 45 of these acknowledgments. Since he did not swear himself, we may assume that he had no land under royal jurisdiction.[28]

[24] Her deposition calls her "filia Durandi Bonet de sancto Michaele de la Cadyera" (ibid., 7), but her sentence reads "filia quondam Stephani Bonet de Sancto Petro de la Cadiera" (Lea, *History of the Inquisition*, 3:653).

[25] Prous's deposition informs us that she has lived in Montpellier since she was seven years old (May, "Confession of Prous Boneta," 7), and her sister Alisseta declares that she has lived in Montpellier for 22 years. Since it seems reasonable to assume that the two sisters moved together to the city, according to Alisseta's 1325 deposition, that would have been in 1303. Prous, therefore, must have been born in approximately 1297.

[26] The inquest of Guillaume de Nogaret in 1293 regarding dues owed to the king in this region counted 35 *feux* in La Cadière; at an estimate of 5 inhabitants per *feu*, La Cadière would have had 175 inhabitants. L.-J. Thomas, "La population du Bas-Languedoc à la fin du XIIIe siècle et au commencement du XIVe," *Annales du Midi* 20 (1908): 469–487 at 487.

[27] Her sister Alisseta testified before the inquisitor of Carcassonne: Doat 27, fols. 26r–30r. We can only tentatively identify Stephana Boneta as Prous's and Alisseta's sister, since while her laconic sentence has survived, her deposition has not. Also from St. Michel de la Cadière, like Prous and Alisseta, and also an inhabitant of Montpellier, Stephana was sentenced to the Wall in September, 1329: Doat 27, fols. 186r, 225r. A marriage contract from a generation later helps us to determine that while Duran Bonet and his daughters left La Cadière for Montpellier around 1302, other members of the family stayed put. In 1325, a Laurent Bonet of La Cadière gave his daughter Poncia in marriage to a certain Guilhem de Artigolis of the same parish. He also had two other daughters, but no sons. Nor can the family of Laurent Bonet be the only ones who remained behind in La Cadière, since the family name continued in the village until the middle of the twentieth century. On a visit to La Cadière in the summer of 1997, I found the late nineteenth-century grave of a certain "Jean Bonnet" located in the Protestant half of the cemetery. According to a retired schoolteacher in the village, the Bonnet family was "traditionally" Protestant, and lived "down by the route Nationale."

[28] This inquest was required because Philip the Fair had traded the rents from the *baillie* of Sauve to the bishop of Maguelone for the "Bishop's part" of Montpellier, later the "King's Part": *Cartulaire de Maguelone*, vol. 3, 521–575, nos. 856–968 (July 29–August 4, 1293). Not all of those who swore were identified by their village (including an Esteve Bonet), but also from La Cadière was a Peire Bonet. Another of the men to swear was

This does not mean, however, that the family was destitute. At least one other Bonet from La Cadière (Peire) did have to swear, and other members of the family seem to have been comfortably well off, though hardly affluent.[29] But in 1303, Prous's family left La Cadière and moved to Montpellier, where there were many other immigrants from this region of the southern Cévennes. They no doubt quickly found themselves a place in a community within the city of similar immigrants. Though many immigrants were looking for social or financial advancement, the Bonets may also have had a motive that was not in the least economic. The family was certainly religious and of a Spiritual Franciscan and Beguin persuasion. In 1306, when Prous was only nine and Olivi had been dead only eight years, they traveled together to the celebration of the feast of Peter Olivi, held at his tomb in the church of the Franciscans of Narbonne. While it is possible that the Bonets first encountered the Spiritual Franciscans after their move to Montpellier, a Franciscan convent had been established in Ganges around 1297, and thus they may have had their first introductions to the movement while still in La Cadière (nine kilometers from Ganges), and simply relocated to the larger Beguin community in Montpellier.[30]

---

a Bernard Bedos of Bragassargues, almost certainly the father of Alaraxis Bedos, Prous's companion. The original acts were not assembled in any single register of the cartulary, but scattered across several. Duran Bonet appears as witness to nos. 878–926. Bernard Bedos of Bragassargues appears in no. 887, and Peire Bonet swore in no. 897.

[29] The provisions of Poncia Boneta's marriage contract from 1325 are instructive. Her dowry consisted of all her father Laurent's goods, both movable and immovable. His reservation of £40 usufruct for himself and his wife in their lifetimes, and his provision of a £20 dowry for one of his remaining daughters and £15 for another, make it seem likely that the family was of comfortable, though not substantial means, since the family fortune must have amounted to some £75 in addition to the goods, land, and perhaps also money given to Guilhem de Artigolis as the dowry of what appears to have been the eldest daughter. ADH 2E 364, fol. 44r, dated August 26, 1325. This document is found in a notarial register of Ganges, the closest town to La Cadière likely to have had a notary in the fourteenth century. I thank Liberto Valls, Conservateur of the Archives Départementales de l'Hérault, for his generous help transcribing this difficult and heavily damaged page of the register. According to Jean Hilaire, who has studied all of the region's marriage contracts, the date of this marriage contract (1325) is in the middle of a period of dotal "stability and opulence," where dowries under £100 were in a distinct minority in Montpellier. Though Hilaire suggests that the average dowry in the region of Ganges was "much lower on average" (as we would expect in a more rural area), he suggests that the region nonetheless followed the general pattern of Montpellier. Jean Hilaire, *Le régime des biens entre époux dans la région de Montpellier du début du XIIIe siècle à la fin du XVIe siècle* (Montpellier, 1957), 59–61.

[30] Emery (*The Friars in Medieval France*, 73) attests to the presence of a Franciscan convent in Ganges only as of 1302, but a record in the *Cartulaire de Maguelone* allows us to move that date back to 1297 (*Cartulaire de Maguelone*, vol. 3, no. 1044).

It is clear that Prous, at least, was "beguinized" at a very young age. In June 1305, at the age of nine, she took a vow of virginity and when she told this to the inquisitor, she emphasized, "and I have maintained it."[31] Nine months later, when she was taking part in the feast of Peter Olivi, she had a revelation that God had "given birth to her in spirit," and he gave her three gifts: tears, a sweet aroma, and a warm feeling.[32] These three "gifts" are classic signs of sanctity—Prous clearly believed that Olivi was a powerful saint, capable of great miracles. From the age of nine or ten, therefore, Prous had been a committed member of the Beguin community and a supporter of the claims to sanctity of Peter Olivi.

Beyond these two events, we know little of Prous's young life (at her arrest, she would have been approximately 28 years old). Her father was certainly dead by 1328,[33] and it appears that Prous had lived in her own home for at least ten years in 1325.[34] She did not live alone, but with her sister Alisseta and a companion named Alaraxis, also an immigrant to Montpellier from the same region as the Bonets.[35] Though none of the three make their situation explicit in their depositions before the inquisitor, we can surely refer to their joint home as a "house of poverty." Prous herself was a member of the Franciscan Order, and those who knew her always called her "*Na* Prous*," using a term of respect often accorded to other professed members of the order.[36] It is probable that Prous herself, at least, was illiterate,

---

[31] "Et servavit." May, "Confession of Prous Boneta," 10–11. Though nine seems young to commit oneself to the celibate life, Prous was not the only fourteenth-century figure to do so. In their study of medieval saints, Donald Weinstein and Rudolph Bell found that a very large proportion of female saints vowed chastity around the age of seven. Caroline Walker Bynum has written about this disproportionate number of saintly women committed to celibacy at an early age: unlike men, women tended to see religious commitment as a steady progression to sanctity. Donald Weinstein and Rudolph M. Bell, *Saints and Society: The Two Worlds of Western Christendom, 1000–1700* (Chicago, 1982), 19–47, 123. Caroline Walker Bynum, *Holy Feast, Holy Fast: The Religious Significance of Food to Medieval Women* (Berkeley, 1987), 24–25.

[32] "In tali die ipse dominus Deus concepit ipsam Naprous in spiritu; et quod ipsa die, eadem qua ipsa fuit in Narbona supra sepulcrum dicti fratris Petri Joannis, ipse Dominus peperit eam in spiritu, et dedit sibi ipse Deus tria dona, scilicet fletum seu luctum quandiu stetit super dictum sepulcrum, secundo, maiorem fragrantiam vel odorem quam unquam ipsa sensisset, tertio et ultimo, unum calorem temporatum et ita dulcem ac si fuisset sibi proiectus unus mantellus super humeros et involuta fuisset circumquaque." May, "Confession of Prous Boneta," 10–11.

[33] He is termed deceased in Prous's sentence: Lea, *History of the Inquisition* 3:653.

[34] Doat 27, fol. 16v.

[35] Alaraxis was from Bragassargues, also in the diocese of Nîmes. Doat 27, fols. 30r–33r.

[36] "Na" was short for *domina* or *domna* (i.e., "Mistress," or "Lady") and was probably a simple honorific, perhaps used to indicate a professed Beguine (the masculine equivalent

since she described her religious practice as repeating the *Pater Noster* (Our Father) instead of saying the offices of the Church: this was what the Rule of the Franciscan Third Order prescribed for the unlettered.[37] The three women no doubt worked with their hands, making enough money to live "a poor life," as Bernard Gui put it.[38] Though we can only speculate about their precise occupation, other young women from the Cévennes came to Montpellier specifically to work in mercery or to do needlework, and such occupations for immigrant women were common enough in Montpellier that they even became the subject of fiction. In the thirteenth-century romance *Escoufle* by Jean Renart, the heroine in search of her lover establishes a sewing shop for wimples, linens, and trinkets in Montpellier whereby the lovers are reunited.[39] We do know that the home of these three immigrants was also a center for Beguin activity in Montpellier: both Alisseta and Alaraxis refer to a number of Beguins who ate and drank with them,[40] and Sibillia Cazelas, whom we met in the last chapter, had been meeting Beguins at Prous's home for ten years.[41] Needlework, cloth finishing, ribbon

---

"En" does not appear to have been used in this way). In Montpellier, several Beguin women were called by this title (see Germain, "Une consultation inquisitoriale," 334, "Na Catharina," and 338, "Na Bodina"). Emery also notes the existence of two poor women in Narbonne in 1305 called "na Dossa, beguina and na Guillelma, beguina": *Heresy and Inquisition*, 131. It is important to note that in this context "Na" did not imply wealth or nobility, but simply deference. In Montaillou, the title was used in reference to women who were perceived as matriarchs of peasant clans: Le Roy Ladurie, *Montaillou*, 29, 35, 37, and 42. For Beguins, it seems to denote a woman who was a professed member of the Third Order of Saint Francis.

[37] May, "Confession of Prous Boneta," 9. *Supra montem*, in *Bullarii Franciscani Epitome*, ed. Conrad Eubel (Quaracchi, 1908), 302–306.

[38] *Manuel* 1:114–117. Reyerson has suggested that many female immigrants to Montpellier worked in the food trades, in needlework, and with precious metals: "Patterns of Population Attraction," 271–272.

[39] In February 1294, a young woman named Maria, daughter of the deceased Raimon *de Tintor*...(the name is partially illegible) of Valleraugue, a Cévennes mountain town east of the Mont Aigoual in the diocese of Nîmes, apprenticed herself to a certain Duran Orlach and his wife to learn to make silken cords and other items of their business. Indications in the text make it likely that this Duran and his wife were part of the same silk merchant family to which Johan Orlach, Beguin, belonged. AMM, BB1, no. 367, fol. 8ov. The text of *Escoufle* reads "Alons a Monpellier manoir./ Si louons la .j. tel manoir/ Ki bien souffise a nostre afaire./ De touailes, de gimples faire/ Nos paistrai je bien ambedeus./ Fait Aelis: S'en iert mes deus. /Bien sachiés que jou referoie/ Joiaus de fil d'or et de soie." Ysabiax and Aelis establish themselves in Montpellier to make napkins, wimples, and ornaments of gold thread and silk. Jean Renart, *L'Escoufle: Roman d'aventure*, ed. Franklin Sweetser (Geneva, 1974), 175, ll. 5451–5458.

[40] Doat 27, fols. 26v, 30r–v.

[41] Doat 27, fol. 16v.

making, and other types of mercery like weaving (the "classic" occupation of heretics) were sedentary and quiet activities often practiced communally, where extended conversation might lead to religious topics.[42]

Prous and her companions were not picked up in the first round of arrests in Montpellier in 1319–1320. We do not know why. Probably they were more discreet about their participation in the Beguin movement than some others, and those who were arrested did not betray them. The three women appear to have lived through the early stages of the persecution unharmed, though many of their acquaintances and friends were imprisoned, and some of them burned at the stake.

But in the spring of 1321, Prous Boneta conceived of a change in her role as a Beguin. On Good Friday, April 17, she was in the church of the Franciscans in Montpellier. After the usual service, she remained in the church contemplating the passion, and felt herself to be transported into the first Heaven, where she encountered Jesus Christ, both in the form of a man and in his divinity.[43] He showed her his heart, which she saw was pierced with holes like a lantern, and streaming with light like the sun. He gave her his heart in spirit.[44] In vain, she protested that she was unworthy of such an honor; for Christ responded that he would do even more for her if she would be faithful to him.[45] Coming close to him, she placed her head on his body, and saw nothing other than the light streaming from Christ himself. Weeping and sobbing, in the greatest fervor and love for God, she found herself placed gently back in her seat in church. On successive days, she had additional visions which assured her further of Christ's special love for her, and

[42] Grundmann asserted that "weavers did not become heretics, heretics became weavers," but weaving and similar textile pursuits, where several artisans might work together in a room, were an ideal opportunity for speaking together at length and in depth, and thus at least some weavers also became heretics. One example is the Cathar perfect Prades Tavernier, who was a weaver before he became a heretic. Herbert Grundmann, *Religious Movements of the Middle Ages*, trans. Steven Rowan (Notre Dame, IN, 1995), 15; Le Roy Ladurie, *Montaillou*, 6.

[43] "Vidit dictum Jesum Christum in forma hominis et in divinitate sua." May, "Confession of Prous Boneta," 7.

[44] "Dedit cor suum in spiritu." Ibid.

[45] This is a short macaronic passage, whose precise meaning remains obscure, but which we can perhaps construe in this manner: "*ne sunt de mi Seigneur tant gratias causes; et Christus respondit: si bien les ty donneray maiours sol que tu mi fiees fizels*" (ibid.). *Gratias* may be better understood as *grant*, as it appears later in the text (ibid., 10), and makes more sense. "Are there about me, Lord, such good reasons (to choose me)?" and Christ's response, "So many that I will give you much more if you will be faithful to me." I am indebted to John Dagenais for his help and suggestions with this passage.

told her of her special place in the economy of salvation: "just as the blessed virgin Mary was the *donatrix* of the son of God, so you will be the *donatrix* of the Holy Spirit."[46]

These first visionary experiences are familiar, reminiscent especially of other mystical experiences that might seem particularly female.[47] When she was transported to the first heaven, Christ first gave her his heart, much as a lover might. In response, "she drew near to him, and put her head on the body of Christ." Later, in the churchyard, she was caught up in ecstasy again, this time in response to an encounter with "the one man from whom she wanted to turn away"; perhaps Christ, her protector, helped her to avoid an unwelcome suitor.[48] When she was praying, she called out "friend, friend, friend!" ("Amice amice amice"). There is even an erotic dimension to certain passages: he told her many times, "I leave now completely, and I come again, for I have chosen you, and made my chamber in you."[49] She converses so familiarly with God and so intimately, telling him of her fears of being too great a sinner for such an honor[50] and her fears of falling into the sin of pride,[51] that we are drawn into her intensely personal relationship with God. The notary transcribed certain passages in Prous's deposition in the first person and in the vernacular, which preserves for the reader a hint of this intimacy.[52]

This intimacy is played out with God's responses to Prous. Though God may seem abrupt with her when he answered her call to her "friend": "And you, what do you want?" he nonetheless spoke to her gently thereafter, "I know whom I have chosen."[53] On another occasion, the three members of the Trinity came together to her: "one of them began to run, and on his way put himself on the neck of her who is telling this, and another placed himself on her right arm." Arm in arm with the triune God, she heard the

---

[46] "Beata virgo Maria fuit donatrix Filii Dei et tu eris donatrix Spiritus Sancti." Ibid., 11.

[47] Caroline Walker Bynum has, of course, written about the "feminization of religious language" beginning in the twelfth century, where "images taken from uniquely female experiences" are used also by men. See for example, Bynum, *Jesus as Mother: Studies in the Spirituality of the High Middle Ages* (Berkeley, 1982), esp. 135–146.

[48] May, "Confession of Prous Boneta," 8.

[49] "Ego tociens vado et revertor, quia in te sumpsi et feci cameram meam." Ibid., 10.

[50] "Domine, ego sum verum nihil, quia sentio me peccatorem, et peccatum est nihil" ("Lord, truly I am nothing, for I feel that I am a sinner and sin is nothing"). Ibid., 8.

[51] "Domine Deus custodias me ab illo peccato superbie per quod Lucifer angelus corruit de coelo." Ibid., 11.

[52] For example, ibid., 7, 10, 11, 29.

[53] "Et tu, quid vis," "ego scio quid elegi." Ibid., 9.

gift of the Holy Spirit confirmed and strengthened: "now this promise has been made complete, when I had promised to you saying that I would give you more, because now you have the whole Trinity."[54] "Every day and night and every hour she sees God in the spirit and he never leaves her," reported the notary.[55] She was continually affirmed in her prophetic purpose through the intimacy of her relationship with God the Father, Christ, and the Holy Spirit.

And yet we would seriously misrepresent Prous's ideas if we assumed that the substance of her visions was entirely gendered female. She also extensively uses images and vocabulary taken directly from the Apocalypse. Prous declares that it is she herself who destroys the serpent of Revelation 12 who tries to persecute Mary;[56] the Spirit given to her will govern the Church along with the Spirit given to Peter Olivi;[57] it is she who holds the rainbow above her head;[58] and she herself is the horse of Revelation 19:10, ridden by Jesus Christ, who leads the army of God into battle with the Beast.[59] While Francis was the angel who carried the sign of the Living God, and Peter Olivi was the angel whose face shone like the sun, she herself was the angel who held the keys to the abyss: "the abyss will be shut and closed for those who believe in these words, the words of her speaking, and for those who will not believe, the abyss will be opened."[60] Prous was the angel who "laid hold on the dragon the old serpent, which is the Devil and Satan, and bound him for a thousand years."[61] It is with Prous herself that the glorious reign of the Spirit would begin.

The boldness of her declaration that she is the angel with the keys to the abyss reminds us of the declarations of Guiard de Cressonessart, who called himself the Angel of Philadelphia, a title he took from Revelation 3:7–13. Guiard, called *beguinus* by the inquisitors of Paris, was prosecuted for heresy in 1310 with Marguerite Porete, the author of the controversial mystical text

---

[54] "Nunc completum est illud promissum factum quando tibi promiseram dicendo, maiores dabo tibi, quia nunc habes totum Trinitatem." Ibid., 10.

[55] "Item dixit quod omni die et nocte et omni hora vidit Deum in spiritu, et numquam ab ea recedit." Ibid., 29.

[56] Ibid., 20.

[57] Ibid., 22.

[58] Revelation 10:1. This is the same angel whose face is like the sun; May, "Confession of Prous Boneta," 25.

[59] May, "Confession of Prous Boneta," 25.

[60] "Item dixit quod abyssus erit cantata et clausa illis qui credent verbis suis, scilicet ipsius loquentis; et illis qui non credent verbis suis erit abyssus apperta." Revelation 20:1; May, "Confession of Prous Boneta," 29–30.

[61] Revelation 20:2.

The Mirror of Simple Souls.[62] Like Prous, Guiard believed that he was called by God to a special role; in his case, "saving the adherence to the Lord," and defending those, like Marguerite Porete, whom he believed to be part of the "Church of Philadelphia." Guiard, too, believed that his special illumination had come to him in prayer while he was in the lower chapel of the Sainte-Chapelle. His assertion that he had been given the office of the Angel of Philadelphia twenty years prior to that illumination reminds us of Prous's claim that on the day she took her vow of virginity at the age of nine, "God conceived her in spirit," and nine months later, at Olivi's tomb, "he gave birth to her in spirit."[63] Both Guiard and Prous apparently regarded their whole lives as preparation for their God-given missions, and also saw themselves as guarding the threshold of a new dispensation. Revelation 3:7 declares: "These are the words of the holy one, the true one, who holds the key of David; when he opens none may shut, when he shuts, none may open." Guiard interprets this "open door" as the "opening of the meaning of scripture,"[64] a phenomenon which for Olivi, whose influence on Guiard is likely, marked the age of the Spirit.[65]

Though the worst of the persecution in Montpellier was yet to come, in the spring of 1321 nearly 30 Beguins and Spiritual friars had already died at the stake.[66] The Beguins of Languedoc were witnessing what they surely interpreted as the beginning of the end times. Disciples of Olivi surely remembered that the third age was meant to be a time of spiritual illumination that would be granted most especially to the humble. We can see this clearly in a number of passages in Arnau de Vilanova's *Alia Informatio*, which he apparently wrote for the Beguins of Barcelona.[67] Arnau warned Beguins about inquiring intellectually into the nature of God: "when he inquires or seeks the truth in such matters through human reason, a person can bring

---

[62] Robert E. Lerner discusses this case in detail in "An 'Angel of Philadelphia' in the Reign of Philip the Fair: The Case of Guiard of Cressonessart," in *Order and Innovation in the Middle Ages: Essays in Honor of Joseph R. Strayer*, ed. William C. Jordan et al. (Princeton, 1976), 343–364.

[63] Ibid., 348; May, "Confession of Prous Boneta," 10. "In tali die ipse dominus Deus concepit ipsam Naprous in spiritu; et quod ipsa die, eadem qua ipsa fuit in Narbona supra sepulcrum dicti fratris Petri Joannis, ipse Dominus peperit eam in spiritu."

[64] Lerner, "An 'Angel of Philadelphia,'" 348.

[65] See Oriana Cartagegia and Perarnau, "El Text Sencer de *L'Epistola ad Gerentes Zonam Pelliceam* d'Arnau de Vilanova," *Arxiu de Textos Catalans Antics* 12 (1993), 7–42.

[66] See appendix.

[67] Arnau de Vilanova, *L'"Alia Informatio Beguinorum" d'Arnau de Vilanova*, ed. Josep Perarnau (Barcelona, 1978).

on the devil."[68] For Arnau, it was better to be blind, deaf, and mute in all such matters so as better to remember the passion of Christ through faith alone. *Curiositat* was perilous, but *humilitat* was pleasing to God.[69] Arnau emphasized God's preference for the humble and the unlettered by citing the example of Saint Francis, who refused the priesthood and "did not wish to have the preeminence or the dominion of the doctorate, nor the dignity of the prelacy, in order to shun any occasion of conceit or pride."[70] It is probable that these very words were read aloud in the Beguin circles frequented by Prous, further establishing the right of the humble to spiritual insight.[71] That this activity was made culpable by the condemnation of a number of Arnau's works (including the *Alia Informatio*) in 1316 merely emphasizes the importance of the tract's ideas.[72] Illiterate Prous, who had lived chastely and in pursuit of humility and poverty for twenty years, whose home was a center of the Beguin community, whose visions occurred as she contemplated the passion of Christ on Good Friday, was as likely a vessel for the Holy Spirit as any. Her Beguin contemporaries, strengthened by the words of authorities like Arnau de Vilanova, would have recognized her as such.

Prous's visions appear to be unique in the fourteenth-century community of Beguins in Languedoc, and this has led many to conclude that she was acting outside the Olivian tradition.[73] That uniqueness did not necessarily divorce her from Olivi, however. Visions were in fact a vital part of Olivi's writings; he attributed visionary authority several times to others, and at least twice to women.[74] One tradition that circulated very widely, as we have seen, even asserts that Olivi claimed a visionary role for himself, saying that he had received all his knowledge directly from Christ in a church in Paris at the third hour.[75] Others of Olivi's disciples and admirers, notably Ubertino

[68] "Encare més, avem oÿt preÿcar que coriosiat de saber coses qui no sien necessàries a mèrit de eternal salut, mena los hòmens a perdició, e que per eytal curiosetat lo diabble engana molt letrats." Ibid., 70–71.

[69] The two chapters of the work most relevant to the present discussion are VII and X. Ibid., 47–48, 68–73.

[70] "Ne volgren aver preeminència o senyoria de doctorat o de dignitat o de prelació per esquivar les ocasions de elació o de arguyl." Ibid., 47.

[71] R. d'Alós, "De la marmessoria d'Arnau de Vilanova," *Miscellania Prat de la Riba* (Barcelona, 1923), 289–306, at 301.

[72] The text of the condemnation of Arnau's works is published in F. Santi, *Arnau de Vilanova: L'obra espiritual* (Valencia, [1987]), 283–289.

[73] Burr, "Olivi, Apocalyptic Expectation, and Visionary Experience," esp. 287–288.

[74] Ibid., 279.

[75] *Manuel* 2:190–193. In his earliest work, Burr dismissed this widely disseminated anecdote, which formed part of the short devotional text celebrating Olivi's death, as

da Casale and Arnau de Vilanova, had also claimed visionary inspiration for their writings, and in 1310 as we have seen, the Conventuals accused the Spirituals of promulgating "dreams and fictitious visions."[76] As Lerner has shown, a recourse to visions as a justification for unorthodox theology, the "ecstasy defense," as he terms it, was an intrinsic part of the Joachite and Olivian tradition and hardly unknown at the beginning of the fourteenth century.[77]

The substance of Prous's visionary program, too, is firmly in the Beguin tradition, with its veneration for both Saint Francis and his conception of the apostolic life and for Olivi. Prous was especially devoted to the latter, referring to him once as "holy father brother Peter,"[78] and saying that "the Lord gave as many graces and as much glory to brother Peter of John as he gave to the Son of God in his person."[79] His writings were not merely worthy, they were "written by the hand of divinity."[80] Just as Jesus did battle with the Devil, just so did Olivi's writings do battle with Antichrist, Pope John XXII.[81] When that pope condemned Peter Olivi's writings, Prous asserted that the sacrament of the altar lost its power.[82] The pope's sin was as great as Adam's sin when he ate the apple.[83] Lastly, like many other Beguins, she called brother Peter "the angel whose face shines like the sun."[84]

The Olivian and Joachite content of Prous's beliefs is manifest on nearly every page of her extraordinary deposition, and it is clear that her personal

---

apocryphal (*Persecution*, 73), but Lerner also notes that Olivi did claim inspiration for his writings elsewhere ("Ecstatic Dissent," 53n72).

[76] See above. Lerner, "Ecstatic Dissent," 42–46, 53n74. *ALKG* 3:102, 119.

[77] Lerner, "Ecstatic Dissent," 33–57.

[78] May, "Confession of Prous Boneta," 18.

[79] "Quod tot gratias et tantam gloriam dedit Dominus fratri Petro Joannis, quot et quantas dedit Filio Dei in personam." Ibid., 22.

[80] "Quae erat scripta per manum divinitatis." Ibid., 14–15.

[81] Ibid., 19.

[82] Ibid., 12, 13, 14–15. Prous dates this event to Christmas, 1323. Presumably, she is referring to the publication of John XXII's bull *Cum inter nonnullos* in November, 1323, which condemned as heretical the idea that Christ and his apostles had owned nothing in private or in common (see chap. 1). She refers directly to this proposition in the next passage: "This pope confessed that Christ was a sinner, since he said that Christ owned things in private and in common." Ibid., 15.

[83] Ibid., 13.

[84] Revelation 10:1. Manselli dates the use of this description of Olivi to 1318 (after the burnings in Marseille), but the cult of Olivi clearly existed considerably before this time. Burr (*Persecution*, 88n48) notes that Olivi was identified with an angel of the apocalypse before the Council of Vienne. Manselli, *Spirituali*, 40–48.

vision has been shaped and formed by her exposure to and belief in Olivi's Joachimism.[85]

> Just as the sin of Adam our first parent was erased and redeemed by Christ's passion, the time of which passion is now finished and complete, so that the sin of this pope, which is as great as the sin of Adam, must be erased and redeemed by the virtue of the Holy Spirit, that is, the Holy Spirit whose beginning is the end of the passion of the Lord Jesus Christ. The new time of the Holy Spirit and the new age of the Church has its beginning in brother Peter of John, and is followed with her who is speaking. Thus, it is now the new age of the Church in which one must believe in the workings of the Holy Spirit.[86]

This classic text is at the very heart of her message. The age of the passion of Jesus Christ, called by Joachim the "age of the Son," is ending; it is time for the new age of the Spirit to begin. Though Joachim always refrained from giving a date for the new age, those who interpreted his works (and those of Olivi) frequently did. Olivi's commentary on the Apocalypse, circulating in an abridged vernacular translation which Prous had surely heard read, would have persuaded his followers in the Midi that the new age was upon them. Though the role Prous took on for herself was unique, and part of her visions intensely personal, the mental world she lived in was common to all the Beguins and the role she claimed was one which her contemporaries would have easily recognized. Eventually, Prous began to proclaim her unique role to a wider audience. The question that remains for us, however, is crucially important: was anyone listening?

At first, Prous told no one of her visions: she kept them secret for a year at God's command, though she felt guilty about not always being able to say the offices correctly (because she fell frequently into ecstasy), and wanted to

---

[85] Papka, "Fictions of Judgment," and Burr, "Na Prous Boneta and Olivi," *Collectanea Franciscana* 67 (1997): 477–500.

[86] "Item dixit et asseruit quod sicut peccatum Adae primi parentis nostri deletum et redemptum fuit per passionem Christi, cuius passionis tempus dicit esse nunc finitum et completum, ita oportet quod peccatum istius papae, quod est ita magnum sicut fuit peccatum Adae, deleatur et redimatur per virtutem Spiritus Sancti, cuius videlicet Sancti Spiritus initium est terminus et finis passionis dicti domini Jesus Christi, asserens quod tempus novum dicti Spiritus Sancti et novus status ecclesiae habuit initium in dicto fratre Petro Joannis, et consequitur in ipsa quae loquitur, sicut dixit; et sic nunc est status ecclesiae novus in quo credere oportet in opere Sancti Spiritus quod superius declaratur." May, "Confession of Prous Boneta," 27.

confess why. Her first listener was a man, probably an unfortunately uniden-tified (and unidentifiable) notary to whom Prous "opened the first seal" of the Book Saint John had seen.[87] According to her, he did not believe her and spoke out against her in public: by doing so, she claimed, he was "crucify-ing the Lord Jesus Christ in spirit publicly." Brother Raimon de Johan, to whom she also revealed her visions, also did not believe her; he was crucify-ing Christ in secret.[88] Nevertheless, he was certainly a frequent visitor to her home (another Beguine mentioned meeting him there), and he may well have been the conduit through which Prous acquired much of her remark-able familiarity with Olivi and the book of Revelation.

Unlike Raimon de Johan, the women of her household believed in Prous's visions and in her special status. Alaraxis, Prous's companion, first told the inquisitor that "she believed the errors she had heard from Na Prous, and she believed that what she had heard from Na Prous was true; she believed that everything would happen just as Na Prous said it would, and that this was the work of God."[89] Though Alaraxis abjured rather quickly, Prous's sister Alisseta was loyal and bold enough to seek to defend her sister to the inquisitors. For nearly three years, Alisseta steadfastly refused to abjure, though frequently so admonished by the inquisitor's representatives. "She would not swear in any way [that her sister was a heretic and heresiarch and that those condemned and burned were heretics] because she did not know God's judgments, nor to what end they would come."[90] Alisseta's stubborn-ness in the face of the demonstrated might of the inquisitors is worthy of Prous's own, and her refusal to acknowledge her sister as a heretic is a cat-egorical refusal to deny the apocalyptic message of Peter Olivi.

Though she had wanted to confess to a friar her inability to pray, Prous was reluctant to tell others of her visions, and it was only at the insistence of God that she did so.[91] She did not wish to be accused of vainglory: "but she had to say and do the will of God."[92] Eventually, compelled, she began to evangelize. On Christ's specific order, she traveled to another town (nearby Mauguio, perhaps, where Peire de Tornamira had lived in a house of poverty?) and she

[87] Ibid., 9, 21, 25. Revelation 5. The only Beguin found in the inquisitorial records who seems to have had notarial training is Peire Trencavel (see below).
[88] May, "Confession of Prous Boneta," 21.
[89] Doat 27, fol. 31v.
[90] "Respondit quod hoc non iuraret aliquo modo quia nescit iudicia Dei qualia sunt, nec ad quem finem poterit deducere supradicta." Doat 27, fol. 29v.
[91] Since she accused the notary to whom she first spoke of "crucifying Christ in pub-lic," it is also likely that he had told others of the content of her visions, which she was then bound to explain.
[92] May, "Confession of Prous Boneta," 27.

preached to an audience of women she knew: "I have nothing to do with your alms or your prayers, but only with two things; that is, that you put your heart and your mind in the work of the Holy Spirit, and that your body be freed to martyrdom if that should be, because the Holy Spirit shall do great things, and give great gifts."[93] Her exhortation was calculated to drive Beguines who were still in hiding to a greater visibility. She encouraged them to be public with their heretical beliefs and to court martyrdom. When her efforts in this first town were unsuccessful, she moved on to another where she preached again, this time in the company of a unidentified male ally, perhaps to a larger and mixed crowd:[94] "I am compelled to speak to you, and unless you believe that which I have said, am saying and shall say, you shall never be saved."[95]

Prous swiftly became the topic of every Beguin conversation. Sibillia Cazelas told the inquisitor that when she visited Montpellier, "from one person she heard that Prous had said that she had received the Holy Spirit, and that she said she was just as holy as the blessed Virgin Mary; from another, she heard that Prous had said that God had transported her soul to Heaven."[96] We can imagine groups of Beguins all talking about the latest news. Pregnant as it was with Olivian ideas and apocalyptic themes, it must have seemed astonishingly bold and yet remarkably familiar. The expectation of imminent dramatic changes in the Church was widespread among the Beguins, and

[93] "Non habem aliquid facere de vestris eleemosinis nec orationibus, sed de duobus causis, scilicet quod ponatis vestrum cor et intellectum in opere Spiritus Sancti, et quod proinde liberetur corpus vestrum ad martirium si opus sit, quia ipse Sanctus Spiritus faciet magna et dabit magna dona." Ibid., 19.

[94] Her mysterious evocation of Brother Guilhem Guiraut, another "apostate friar" never found by the inquisitors, as the first pope of the new age, consecrated by the Holy Spirit, tempts us to conjecture that her companion was he, but the point is unprovable. He was apparently from the convent of Marseille. Ibid., 19–20. Guilhem Guiraut was also Raimon de Johan's teacher in matters apocalyptic, Doat 27, fol. 37r, and was one of the friars summoned to Michel le Moine in 1317. *Bullaire de l'inquisition*, 36.

[95] "Hodie sum compulsa quod vobis dicam, et nisi credatis hoc quod dixi, dico, et dicam, nullo tempore salvabitis vos." May, "Confession of Prous Boneta," 19. Female preachers are, of course, not common in the Middle Ages. It is possible that Prous was influenced in her willingness to preach by the increasing popularity of Mary Magdalen in southern France at this time, particularly in mendicant circles. I am currently preparing an article on this subject. See also Jansen, *The Making of the Magdalen*. For another example of a female Franciscan tertiary preacher in the thirteenth century, see Darleen Pryds, "Proclaiming Sanctity through Proscribed Practices: The Case of Rose of Viterbo," in *Women Preachers and Prophets through Two Millennia of Christianity*, ed. Pamela Walker and Beverly Mayne Kienzle (Berkeley, 1998).

[96] "A quadam persona loqui audivit, qui errores sunt tales videlicet quod dicta naprous dicebat se recepisse Spiritum Sanctum, et asserebat se esse ita sit anctam virginem quam sancta fuerat beata Virgo Maria. Item a quadam persona alia audivit quod dicta naprous dicebat quod Deus transporaverat animam in coelum." Doat 27, fol. 16v–17r.

yet this may have been more than they were prepared to accept. There was considerable controversy within the Beguin community about the validity of Prous's claim.

As we saw in the last chapter, Sibillia's friend Ermessendis Grossa claimed that she was incredulous on hearing the news, but Ermessendis did and said nothing until she was called before the inquisitor in November, 1325, three months after Prous had already confessed. Both Sibillia and Ermessendis said that they had not believed Prous's claims, though as we have seen, Sibillia was reputed to have "confessed badly," that is to say, incompletely.[97] It was certainly to their advantage to deny everything in an attempt to exculpate themselves. It is hard to believe, however, that Sibillia Cazelas, that faithful devotee of Olivi and old friend of Prous, did not at the very least wonder if it all might not be true.

It was in the summer of 1325 that the inquisitor of Carcassonne broke the ring of Beguins in Montpellier. Most of its members were now imprisoned in the Wall of Carcassonne. Henceforth, Prous exercised her authority from within prison.

While the concept of an inquisitorial prison tends to evoke scenes of filth, chains, torture, and what the French so fittingly call "oubliettes," the Wall at Carcassonne was not entirely filled with prisoners chained to the walls in solitary confinement. A commission of two cardinals who examined conditions in the Wall of Carcassonne in 1306 found some prisoners shackled and held "in narrow and very dark prisons,"[98] but a story related by Manenta Rosa Arnaut of Lodève paints a somewhat different picture. This Beguine was able to pass on culpable messages from Jacma Amorosa Lauret, a visitor, to Jacma's imprisoned husband, who was held in a different cell from Manenta.[99] This generally lax attitude does not appear to have made for very tight prison security: several heretics, including Peire Trencavel and his daughter Andrea, escaped from the Wall at Carcassonne.[100] While we

[97] Doat 27, fol. 18v.

[98] Given, *Inquisition*, 65.

[99] Doat 27, fols. 79v–82r. The testimony of Bernard Clergue of Montaillou makes it clear that similarly lax conditions existed in the prison of the Allemans in Pamiers. Clergue was able to wander about at will, continuing to intimidate the inhabitants of his village, and even managed to procure his own set of keys. Men and women do not appear to have been held separately, and could freely move around and speak openly with each other. *Registre* 2:277–290. Another example which makes this relative freedom clear is the testimony of Blanche de Rodès before the inquisitor of Carcassonne in 1308, concerning the inquisitorial prison in Foix: *L'inquisiteur Geoffroy d'Ablis*, 232–233, 236–237. Given also discusses prison conditions and security: *Inquisition*, 63–65.

[100] See below.

cannot say for certain in what conditions any particular prisoner was actually held in the Wall, it appears that a majority were held in rather relaxed circumstances.

Thanks to these relatively relaxed conditions, Prous Boneta continued to act as a leader of the Beguins even in prison, and she affected even those who had not known her on the outside. Guillerma Civile, who with her husband Peire Civile, a weaver of Narbonne (now a fugitive), had been closely associated with Beguin circles for some time, had not known Prous in Montpellier, for example. Prous gave Guillerma the strength to resist interrogation, and it was only after many months in prison that Guillerma confessed to having had heretical beliefs: "She would have told the truth earlier, had it not been for Na Prous Boneta held in the prison near her who restrained her from confessing."[101] Guilhem Ademar, another Narbonnais weaver, who also appears not to have known Prous before his incarceration, told a similar story. Also possibly called because of his acquaintance with the fugitive Peire Civile, Guilhem confessed his beliefs; released, then called and held again, he denied them "against his own sworn testimony."[102] Prous Boneta, held in the prison with him, had persuaded him to deny everything.[103] By September 1325, Prous had already confessed to the inquisitor of Carcassonne, and her beliefs and her visions were no secret to the Beguins imprisoned in the Wall; still, she exerted enough influence on two individuals she had not known before to persuade them to change their testimony. In the early stages of her imprisonment at least, Prous also received visits from Beguins still free: Johan Orlach, the draper of Montpellier, came to the prison to visit "Na Prous Boneta, heresiarch" sometime before November 1325—a point that implies that she had not been completely rejected by the community of Beguin supporters in her own city.[104]

Two other Beguins who were imprisoned with Prous also changed their testimony during their incarceration. When Guilhem Domergue Veyrier of Narbonne, a fugitive of long standing and an old acquaintance of Prous's, was first captured in May 1325, he chose to abjure his heresy, but in October 1325, he declared that he wished to elaborate on the testimony he had given earlier. Here he affirmed that both the burned Franciscans and the burned Beguins were "glorious martyrs," Olivi was an uncanonized saint, and his doctrines were lawful, the Rule of Saint Francis was the same as the Gospel,

---

[101] Doat 28, fols. 226v–228r.
[102] "Contra proprium iuramentum."
[103] Doat 28, fols. 228r–231r. Both Guilhem and Guillelma were sentenced to the Wall.
[104] Doat 27, fols. 24r–26r.

and the poverty of Christ was absolute: if Christ had had property, even in common, then Saint Francis would be more perfect than Christ, which he asserted was absurd. "Asked why he had said that he wished to turn away from these things and to repent, he replied that he had then had something else in his heart than he had now, and that afterwards God had placed this other intention in his heart, in which newer intention he wished to remain and to persevere as long as it would be given to him by God."[105] Guilhem Serallier's turnaround was even more dramatic. Though he abjured shortly after his capture in May 1325, at the General Sermon in Carcassonne on March 1, 1327, having discovered that he was to be burned at the stake as a relapsed heretic, he cried out his allegiance to the writings and doctrine of Peter Olivi, which he said were holy and catholic. "He obstinately persevered in each and every one of the opinions and errors contained in his confession."[106] Like Guilhem Domergue Veyrier, in prison he had found the courage to abjure his abjuration and to declare the faith that, though perhaps vanishing in the world outside, was clearly still alive among the prisoners held in the Wall of Carcassonne. Guilhem Serallier and Guilhem Domergue Veyrier were both handed over to the secular arm that day, and burned. Though we cannot say for sure that either Veyrier or Serallier was directly influenced by contact with the impenitent Prous or by the apocalyptic ideology that she no doubt continued to expound, something or someone had given both of them the courage to refuse to abjure. At the very least, Prous had contributed to the atmosphere of continued Beguin resistance which made these reversals possible.

Prous had mentioned the possibility of martyrdom many times, of course: when she had preached in that nearby town, she called on a group of women to be ready to be martyred for their beliefs.[107] She also said that just as the Jews had crucified the Son of God in person, the "lawyers of the Christians" were crucifying the Holy Spirit in person, in her.[108] Her view of the apocalyptic vision and of the inevitable correlations between the old dispensation

[105] "Interrogatus quare dudum dixerat se velle resilire a predictis et penitere de eisdem, dixi quia tunc habebat aliud in corde quam hunc habeat et quia postea Deus dedit sibi aliud propositum in corde suo, in quo proposito, videlicet moderno, asserit se velle stare et perseverare quamdiu a Domino fuerit sibi datum." Manselli, *Spirituali*, 322–324.

[106] "Perseveravitque in omnibus et singulis opinionibus et erroribus in sua confessione contentis, obstinatus in eisdem." Ibid., 324–326.

[107] May, "Confession of Prous Boneta," 19.

[108] "Ita isti, scilicet legisperiti Christianorum, crucifixerunt Spiritum Sanctum in persona, scilicet in persona ipsius loquentis." Ibid., 21. The "isti" used by the notary appears to describe the scornful or derogatory tone she used toward the lawyers, and, perhaps, a pointed finger.

and the new meant that she expected and welcomed martyrdom. The apocalyptic script required it. Writers such as Arnau de Vilanova had encouraged it by stressing the example that Christ set for his followers: "Afterwards, [Christ] gave the example of having patience in all adversities, for he wished so to suffer that he was mocked, scorned, blasphemed, vituperated, taken and bound, imprisoned, beaten, and put to a cruel death on the cross."[109] Prous's final words to the inquisitor make her position clear: "she persevered [in all her errors and heresies], stating that in them, as in the truth, she wished to live and die."[110]

For three long years, her sister Alisseta held out, too, but three weeks before she was to be sentenced, she finally abjured, apparently of her own volition.[111] We may well wonder why: perhaps her sister was taken away from her and held elsewhere in the prison, or perhaps Prous herself encouraged her to abjure, leaving at least one to spread the message of the new age of the Spirit.[112]

[109] "Aprés donà exemple de haver paciència en totes adversitats, car volc sofferir que fos scarnit, menyspreat, blasfemat, vituperat, pres e ligat, encarcerat, batut, e ocís a cruel mort en la creu": Arnau de Vilanova, "Lliçó de Narbona," *Obres Catalanes* 1:144.

[110] "Perseveravit in eis, asserens in praedictis, tanquam in veritate se velle vivere atque mori." May, "Confession of Prous Boneta," 30.

[111] Her deposition reads: "At length, after she had persisted for a long time in prison, freely and spontaneously, without being asked and without admonition, she said that she repented of each and every statement she had said before, and she abjured in judicial process, stating that she repented" ("tandem vero postquam in dicto carcere longo tempore perstitisset gratis, et sponte absque monitione, et requisitione dixit se poenitere de praedictis, et omnia praedicta, et singula abiuravit in iudicio constituta dicit se poenitere"). Doat 27, fol. 29v.

[112] Alisseta Boneta was initially sentenced to the Wall on November 11, 1328, but was released less than a year later and sentenced to pilgrimages and crosses. Doat 27, 91v–94v, 193v–196v (September 10, 1329). I have found one possible reference to Alisseta or another sister in a will of 1347 (AMM Fonds de la Commune Clôture, EE 1057, armoire H, no. 290; Dainville and Gouron, *Inventaire*, 200). Johanna Raynaudin Ferrier of Montpellier, widow of a Montpellierain merchant (apparently in textiles), elected to be buried in the church of the Friars Minor of Montpellier. She appears to have been relatively wealthy, leaving over £250 worth of enumerated legacies, and establishing a chaplaincy at Notre Dame des Tables, while still leaving her home and all her remaining goods to the Franciscans. Among her many individual legacies was one of 12 d. to a certain "domina Boneta" who lived in the same street as she herself in the faubourg of Las Barcas, located in the King's Part of Montpellier, near the Franciscan convent. The amount is the same as that to be given to four poor widows chosen from among those on her street, to two other female neighbors, and also to each of the recluses of the city; closer friends and family received far greater sums. If Alisseta returned to Montpellier after her release from the Wall of Carcassonne and after she accomplished her pilgrimages (or they were forgotten), it is natural to assume that she would have returned to the same neighborhood where she had lived before (Las Barcas was close to the douve), and surely she would have

We are left with one other clue, but an important one, regarding the reception of Prous's ideas and the nature of her role of leadership within her community. A bull of John XXII of 1327–1328, recommending that "a certain woman named [ ] Boneta" be burned at Carcassonne, and not at Montpellier, suggests that the execution in question was likely to cause trouble in Montpellier.[113] Though the first name of the woman to be sentenced is extremely difficult to read because of water damage on the original register, the likelihood that the name is that of Prous Boneta is great.[114] While the inquisitors may have believed that burning Prous in the town where she had lived for twenty-two years and had many friends and acquaintances would set an example, the pope's advisers in Avignon seem to have felt that it would instead harden the population in error. That Prous's case apparently attracted the attention of the papacy is in itself significant. What is certain is that on November 11, 1328, in Carcassonne, Prous was handed over to the secular arm, and burned.

Especially since a female leader of a resistance movement is such a rare phenomenon, we would like to be able to determine if her social position contributed to Prous's authority as a leader of the Beguin community. She exerted influence on a variety of men: was that because they came from lower social strata than she herself? As we have seen, Prous's family were probably comfortable but not wealthy immigrants from a tiny village; at best, she came from a milieu very similar to that of her followers.[115] Some

---

continued to frequent the Franciscan convent, as did Johanna Ferrier. Mme Ferrier may have considered her a charity case similar to the recluses. Mme Ferrier also had ties to the Cévennes, for she left the sum of 20 s. to a church in Alès, and also several legacies to individuals from that town.

[113] "Quandam mulierem [ ] Boneta," *Bullaire de l'inquisition*, 128–129. This bull comes not from the Collection Doat, but from a register in the Archivio Segreto Vaticano (*Regestum Vaticanum*, vol. 114, n. 1795), and is thus a more reliable source. There is an additional lacuna where the actual date was located, but the regnal year of John XXII is indicated, "anno duodecimo." John XXII was elected pope August 7, 1316.

[114] It is just possible that the bull refers to Alisseta instead; but her case does not seem as likely to have attracted the attention of the papacy as that of Prous. A recent reexamination of the original register on my behalf by Pietro Cajazza and Maria Galante confirms Vidal's lacuna for the date, and suggests several possibilities for the damaged name: "...*pres*," "...*pns*," "...*ores*," and "...*ons*." They also affirm that the final letter of the last name is decidedly *a*, and not *e*. These observations help to confirm the identification with Prous (frequently written *Naprous*, or even *Napros* in the sources) instead of Alisseta. I am deeply grateful to Professor Roberto Rusconi for his assistance in acquiring this information, and to Dr. Cajazza and Professor Galante for securing it. Manselli accepts the identification with Prous Boneta as a given: *Spirituali*, 249.

[115] By translating her title, "Na," as "Dame," or "Lady," Biget implies that Prous Boneta came from a wealthy family, a point that he also makes explicitly (303). He also suggests that Alaraxis, described in the sources as Prous's and Alisseta's "*socia*," was their

of these men are identifiable through the sources: Guilhem Serallier was a locksmith; Guilhem Domergue Veyrier was a candlemaker; Guilhem Ademar was a tailor; and Johan Orlach was a draper (one of Montpellier's most exalted professions) wealthy enough to pay for the celebration of Olivi's feast for a substantial group of Beguins. Peire de Tornamira certainly came from the political and social elite of Montpellier. The mysterious disciple who accompanied Prous on her evangelizing missions to other towns cannot be identified at all. It seems probable that unlike that of Guglielma of Milan, a princess of Bohemia and inspirational leader of a group of Milanese heretics around the year 1300,[116] Prous's influence does not appear to have been enhanced by her position in society, but rather rested entirely on the authority given her by her holy life and especially her visions.

Prous's authority was inspirational in nature, however, not pragmatic. She was able to urge her fellows toward martyrdom and to persuade at least some of the truth of her visions. Though she and her sister and companion might feed or house a fugitive Franciscan like Raimon de Johan, it was not their role to direct the resistance of the Beguins on a practical level. For that we turn to Peire Trencavel.

A "SCARLET PIMPERNEL": PEIRE TRENCAVEL

While Sibillia Cazelas was so successfully secretive about her clandestine actions on behalf of herself and other Beguins that her efforts have remained hidden for nearly 700 years, Peire Trencavel was the Beguins' public face and Olivi's most indefatigable disciple, known to all.[117] He was the most sought after of all the Beguin fugitives and also the most elusive, seen here and there in both Languedoc and Provence, but always a step or two ahead

---

servant: "Culte et rayonnement," 285. I disagree with this interpretation of the evidence. All three women (as well as Stephana Boneta, probably another sister) were immigrants from the same region, and there is no reason to assume that Alaraxis was poorer than her companions. Alaraxis's father, who swore *caslania* to the Crown of France in 1293, may well have been more wealthy and owned more land than Duran Bonet, the father of the Bonet sisters, who was not required to swear. *Cartulaire de Maguelone*, vol. 3, 521–575, no. 887 (see above).

[116] Barbara Newman, *From Virile Woman to WomanChrist: Studies in Medieval Religion and Literature* (Philadelphia, 1995), 237. She notes: "Although Guglielma was reticent about her past, her royalty must have contributed to the mystique of her holiness."

[117] Though Peire Trencavel was twice captured by the inquisitors, any deposition he gave to them has been lost. Thus I have based this account on the testimony of many others, indicated in the notes.

of the inquisitors who sought to detain him. They actually captured him twice—but on both occasions, he managed to escape from their custody. Peire was a kind of Scarlet Pimpernel of the fourteenth century, an elusive mastermind of escape, a "gallant and mysterious leader of the reckless little band, who risked his life daily, who gave it freely and without ostentation, for the sake of humanity," as the Baroness Orczy described her daring character Sir Percy Blakeney in his struggle against the French Revolution.[118] He brought news to those who needed it, helped other fugitives find safe places to hide, and, above all, consistently sought a future for the ideas and writings of Peter Olivi. And yet, the story of Peire Trencavel has its own mysteries, the answers to which have also lain hidden very nearly as long as Sibillia's plotting.

Though Peire himself was from Béziers, he lived for many years in Narbonne, the epicenter of all things Olivi. Since he was a member of the Franciscan Third Order, he probably moved there in solidarity with the friars of the short habits. The only thing we know about his family is that he had a daughter named Andrea. His occupation is unknown to us, but he was quite well educated, able to read and write both in the vernacular and in Latin even though he was not in holy orders. His elegant hand (we have samples of his handwriting) was equally comfortable in a chancery and a notarial style; he may well have trained or practiced as a notary in Narbonne or Béziers.[119]

By the time the troubles began for the Spiritual Franciscan friars of Languedoc in 1316, Peire Trencavel was living in Narbonne, where he welcomed Beguin visitors from afar to his home, especially on occasions like the celebration of the feast of Peter Olivi. Narbonne, like Montpellier, was officially two cities (the City and the Bourg, each with its own consulate), and the Franciscan convent was located not far outside the walls of the City on the route to Béziers.[120] As we might have expected, the Beguin community of Narbonne was very large, numbering well over 40 individuals. If we can judge from their names, many of them were from out of town, like Peire. There were Beguins from as close as Cuxac d'Aude or Quarante, just north of the city, and from as far away as Provence,

---

[118] Baroness Emmuska Orczy, *The Scarlet Pimpernel* (New York, 1905), 87.

[119] Many depositions describe him as being "from Béziers," but others indicate that he lived in Narbonne. See, for example, Alaraxis Biasse (Manselli, *Spirituali*, 320), and Esteve Gramat (Doat 27, fol. 9r). Photographs and discussion of Trencavel's handwriting (which Troncarelli describes as "un'elegantissima bastarda cancelleresca francese" and "una grafia corsiva, decisamente notarile") are in Troncarelli, "Pietro Trencavelli, visconte di Carcassonne," 25–26.

[120] Emery, *Heresy and Inquisition*, 19–54, map on 20.

Elne, Urgel, Gerona, and other places in Catalonia.[121] All of them had come to Narbonne to be closer to the shrine of their patron saint Olivi and closer to the spiritual counsel of the friars of the Franciscan convent. Some of them were very poor, like the two Beguines named Na Dossa and Na Guillelma who appeared in a list of all the poor women of the city in 1305.[122] Others were tradesmen or artisans, like Guilhem Ademar, Peire Civile, and Guilhem Quartier, all weavers, Guilhem Domergue Veyrier, a candlemaker, or Astruga de Rundaria and Berengaria Donas, both seamstresses.[123] There were even a number of wealthy and influential individuals who were supporters of the Spirituals and the Beguins, though they themselves were not members of the Third Order. Imbert Rubei, Bernard Hulard, Johan D'Avinhon, and Blaize Boyer, for example, were all supporters of the Beguins as well as former or future consuls of the Bourg or the City and belonged to some of Narbonne's most prominent families.[124] Whether because of his literacy or simply his personality, Peire Trencavel was one of their indisputed leaders.

It is hardly surprising that a committed Beguin like Peire would have moved to Narbonne from Béziers. Narbonne had always been especially welcoming and supportive of the Spiritual friars. In 1309, officials lodged a protest on behalf of their friars to Pope Clement V, and in 1315, the townspeople participated eagerly in the fighting that led to the expulsion of the Conventual superiors who had attempted to stifle the Spirituals. In 1316, a public protest of the consuls of the Bourg resulted in a dramatic showdown before the papal provost of Maguelone in Montpellier.[125] Angelo Clareno explained the involvement of the townspeople this way: "they held [the Spiritual friars] in great reverence and devotion, both because of their holiness, which they knew to be in them, and because of the virtues and the signs which they could see happening daily at the tomb of the holy man Peter of John, who in his life had illuminated them by the example of his good works

---

[121] Astruga de Rundaria and her sister Maria were both identified as being from Cuxac (Doat 28, fols. 224–226v), and Pons de Sant Gili was from Provence (Doat 28, fols. 235v–237r). The other names are from the Beguins burned February 28, 1322, in Narbonne as listed in the Beguin Martyrology. See also the list in Emery, *Heresy and Inquisition*, 164–165, which provides further names.

[122] Emery, *Heresy and Inquisition*, 131.

[123] Guilhem Ademar (Doat 28, fols. 228r–231r), Guillelma Civile, wife of Peire Civile (Doat 28, fols. 226v–228r), Guilhem Quartier (Doat 28, fols. 205r–207r), Guilhem Domergue Veyrier (MS, 321–324), Astruga de Rundaria (Doat 28, fols. 224–226v), and Berengaria Donas (Doat 28, fols. 219r–222v).

[124] Emery, *Heresy and Inquisition*, 166–169.

[125] *ALKG* 3:18, cap. I; Pou y Marti, *Visionarios*, 87–89; and Doat 51, fols. 464v–470v.

and his doctrine."[126] The consuls of the Bourg described the relationship of the townspeople to the convent as close and friendly:

> Many good men and women of this community go every day to the house or the church of the Friars Minor of Narbonne in order to hear the divine ministries, for openly and publicly they celebrate the divine mysteries daily. And they go to hear masses celebrated and prayers said on behalf of the souls of their relatives, friends and benefactors who are buried in this monastery.[127]

This meant that when the Spiritual friars were summoned to Avignon in May 1317, many townspeople followed them. Even a merely lukewarm supporter of the Beguins like Peire Esperendiu went along to Avignon, and we may assume that the far more committed Peire Trencavel did also.

Certainly, Peire was one of the first to advertise the dreadful news a year later, when three of the city's beloved friars were burned at the stake in Marseille (the fourth friar was from the convent of Béziers). Peire Calvet of Cintegabelle vividly remembered Peire Trencavel's arrival in Eastertide (that is to say, before the feast of Ascension on June 1) and the news he brought, news that confirmed for the Beguins of Cintegabelle that the end times were upon them and Peter Olivi's predictions had been right. Since Trencavel went to Cintegabelle, he may also have visited Beguins in Carcassonne, Montréal, Limoux, and Belpech, for all of these would have been more or less on his way on a trip that might have gone as far as Toulouse, approximately 150 kilometers from Narbonne. This was to be only the beginning of Peire's many long and secretive journeys on behalf of the Spirituals and the Beguins.

Peire was forced to make these journeys in secret because of rapidly increasingly inquisitorial pressure in Narbonne, where the earliest investigations of heresy among the Beguins were carried out by the archbishop.

---

[126] "Homines illarum civitatum in multa eos reverencia et devocione habebant, et propter sanctitatem, quam in eis esse cognoscebant et propter virtutes et signa, que ad sepulcrum viri sancti Petri Johannis, qui in vita eos illuminaverat exemplo bonorum operum et doctrina, videbant cotidie fieri." *ALKG* 2:142.

[127] "Quare cum dictae monitiones et sententiae quam plurimum sint praeiudiciales universitati Burgi Narbonae praedicti, et singulis de eadem, praesertim cum multi viri boni, et mulieres de dicta universitate confluant quotidie pro divinis ministeriis audiendis, ad domum seu ecclesiam minorum Narbonae praedictam, ubi palam, et publice divina misteria quotidie celebrantur, et pro fieri celebrandis, et dicendis missas et orationes propter animas parentum amicorum et benefactorum eorumdem, qui in dicto monasterio sunt sepulti." Doat 51, fols. 467v–468r.

Episcopal inquisitions were not generally known for their efficiency—the fact that had led Pope Gregory IX to establish Dominican inquisitors in the first place—but Narbonne's archbishop, with the cooperation of royal officials, achieved the first condemnation of Beguin heretics in Languedoc in October 1319.[128] He also created Narbonne's first Beguin martyrs when the beloved and apparently obstinate and impenitent "brother Mai" and Peire de Fraxino were burned. The horror and shock of that event, witnessed by many and heard of by more, rippled through Narbonne and Languedoc as a whole. We do not know what led the archbishop to prosecute these two in particular so quickly, but perhaps they had preached an incautious sermon, or otherwise made their sympathies plain and unmistakable.

From this time onward, Peire and his fellows began to organize their resistance to all inquisitions, whether archiepiscopal or Dominican, more systematically. When the Narbonne Beguins were questioned by the archbishop's inquisition, many of them used devious answers in order to allow them to deny their faith publicly while not offending their own consciences. In his inquisitorial manual, Bernard Gui was very clear about the potential for deceit in the testimony of heretics, and provided some examples of the ways Beguins guilefully responded to questions.

There are some malicious and crafty people among the Beguins who, in order to veil the truth, shield their accomplices and prevent their error and falsity from being discovered, respond so ambiguously, obscurely, generally and confusingly to questions that the clear truth cannot be gathered from their replies. Thus, asked what they believe about some statement or statements proposed to them, they reply, "I believe about this what the holy church of God believes," and they do not wish to speak more explicitly or respond in any other way. In this case, to exclude the ruse they use (or rather abuse) in referring in this way to the church of God, they should diligently, subtly and perspicaciously be asked what they mean by "the church of God," whether they mean the church of God as they understand it; for, as is clear from the errors presented above, they use the phrase "church of God" misleadingly. For they say they themselves and their accomplices are the church of God or are of the church of God. But those who believe differently than they and persecute them they do not consider to be the church of God or part of it.[129]

128 See Emery, *Heresy and Inquisition*, 146.
129 This translation is by David Burr, *Manuel*, 188–190. Burr points out a possible example of this in the case of Alaraxis Biasse of Servian: Burr, *Spiritual Franciscans*, 229.

When they knew that they might be arrested and questioned, they talked together about exactly such techniques and also conspired to "fix" certain answers for their questioners. Even before any of them were incarcerated, Amoda Sepian of Limoux, for example, took part in a gathering "with many other Beguines and two Beguins, where the Beguines were instructed how to respond if anyone should interrogate them." At some risk to himself and his oath not to impede the inquisition, Raimon d'Antusan took the precaution of telling the newly captured Peire Arrufat that he had already confessed to seeing the burned body of a Beguine in Arrufat's home.[130] Given his learning and powerful personality, Peire was probably one of those who formulated these deceptive practices and taught them to others.

As a public figure (if he were indeed a notary, as it appears), Peire was surely particularly affected by the loyalty oath demanded of citizens by royal and consular officials in Narbonne early in 1320. Though the inhabitants also swore to uphold the franchises of the town and to "faithfully maintain the rights of their Lords," the bulk of the oath concerned their religious convictions. Inhabitants of the Bourg swore first of all that they were "loyal Christians, and firmly believe the faith of the Catholic Church of Rome," and also swore to reject and avoid "any sects, or any kind of heresy." Curiously, the oath appears to have been recycled from an earlier time. The inhabitants had to swear to reject Waldensianism, for instance, and also that they had not taken part in the death of any inquisitorial officials in Carcassonne or in Avignonet, or in the death of scribes and the burning of inquisitorial registers in Caunes, all events that had taken place in the previous century (the most recent was 1296, but other events dated back to 1242). This early in the Beguin crisis, so different from earlier heretical situations, the authorities would not even have had a concrete name to put on the heresy that was apparently before them. Nonetheless, they sought to protect themselves as best they could.[131]

Such a warning could not have failed to rally the Beguins, and Peire Trencavel immediately took action. As it began to be necessary to conceal certain of their co-believers from the authorities, whether because they were unwilling to lie or because they had already been caught out in their lies, Beguins

---

[130] "Item in quadam congregatione fuit cum multis aliis Begguinabus et duobus Begguinis, ubi fuerunt informatae qualiter responderent si contigeret eas interrogare." (Amoda Sepian) Doat 28, fol. 239r; *Liber sententiarum* 2:1350. Given (*Inquisition*, 126), reports other such cases in the thirteenth century: several entire villages were caught colluding to lie to the inquisitors Bernard de Caux and Jean de Saint-Pierre. We have seen other examples in the story of Prous Boneta and her influence on others.

[131] Doat 52, fols. 45r–46v.

began to organize secret hiding places in Narbonne and the means of getting fugitives out of the city and into safe havens elsewhere. Peire concealed fugitives in the houses of Berengaria Donas, Guilhem Domergue Veyrier and his wife Berengaria, and Peire Arrufat and his wife Raimonda, to name only three locations. When those houses became too dangerous, since the owners were known to the royal officers who did the arresting, the conspirators resorted to more obscure hiding places. Johan d'Almatii, for instance, gave Peire the key to his enclosed garden so that Peire could use it at any time of day or night.[132] Berengaria Donas was even more wily. On one occasion when she had several fugitives in her home, the servants of the inquisitors placed ambushes and guards at all the gates of the city, preventing anyone from leaving unespyed. Her guests did not know how to escape, but she found a ruse, as she put it (when she related it to the inquisitor, she actually seemed quite proud of her cleverness). She led the fugitives to an enclosed field of hers next to the walls of the city where they hid for a day, and the next night they were able to escape by climbing over the walls to safety.[133]

Once fugitives were out of the city, Peire Trencavel and his companion Peire Arrufat led them to more distant hiding places. They took them to Cintegabelle, to Montréal, to Toulouse, and even to out-of-the-way locations like Olargues in the Montagne Noire, where a sympathetic notary named Bernard Fabre and his wife Galharda were accustomed to receiving fugitive Beguins and apostate friars.[134] Peire Trencavel was the coordinator of all these efforts, a point made clear by Alaraxis Biasse of Sauvian near Béziers, Peter Olivi's niece. Quite a number of apostate Franciscan friars made their way to her house in this small village near the Mediterranean, and she knew many of them personally from the convents of Béziers and Narbonne (one was actually her cousin). One day, however, when she had two friars hiding in her attic, two men whom she did not know appeared on her doorstep. They claimed to be from Sicily and wanted to help any apostate friars who wanted to join others of their kind who had already made the

---

[132] "Item cum quadam die servientes inquisitionis eosdem fugitivos, seu eorum aliquo perquirerent, et capere vellent in Narbona, posuissent que insidias, et execubias in singulis exitibus villae Narbonensis iidemque apostatae et fugitivi timentes capi nescirent per quem locum evadere possent, ipsa quae loquitur hoc percepto invenit cautelam, per quam eos liberavit, nam duxit eos ad quandam virideam suam clausam muris qui actingebant campos extra omnes Barras villae Narbonensis, ubi per diem latuerunt, et etiam per aliquam partem notis et postmodum ascendentes supra muros prout eos docuit aufugerunt, et postquam etiam recessissent ipsa quae loquitur sequta fuit eos versus quandam villam extra Narbonam, sed non invenit eosdem." Doat 28, fol. 29r.

[133] Doat 28, fols. 220v–221r.

[134] Doat 28, fols. 122v–126r.

voyage to Sicily. Cautious, she did not commit herself or her secret guests, but sent them away for the moment and traveled herself to Narbonne to see Peire Trencavel. With his approval, she revealed the presence of the fugitives to her visitors, and one dark Saturday evening, they all boarded a ship bound for Majorca along with four other friars whom Peire Trencavel had apparently sent to join the exodus.[135] When Guillerma Berengaria Ty-eura, who sheltered fugitives in both Narbonne and Montagnac and traveled to Gignac on occasion to fetch them, needed a breviary for a fugitive friar who was without, she went to Peire Trencavel to get it.[136] When our friend Raimon d'Antusan of Cintegabelle considered fleeing to Greece or to Jerusalem in this period, he gave Peire the vast sum of 350 gold coins so that Peire might be able to give it back to him once they all arrived safely abroad. He also knew of many others who had given large quantities of money to Peire.[137] Blaize Boyer, a wealthy tailor from Narbonne, took money from Peire, who "specially instructed" him to take four apostate friars from Narbonne to Toulouse and to rent them a house.[138]

In 1320 and 1321, Peire was witness to ever more fiery executions of the Beguins. Capestang, Béziers, Pézenas, Agde, Lunel—all were the sites of autos-da-fé that burned close to 40 more of the individuals whom he had been trying to protect. The burnings in Béziers were probably particularly painful for him personally as this was his hometown, where he had first joined the Third Order of Saint Francis, and where he knew many of the Beguins and also many priests. The deaths of Guilhem Anuli and Peire Brun, both priests of Béziers, must have hit him very hard.[139] If he was present at

---

[135] Doat 28, fols. 217v–218v. Alaraxis identified one of the fugitive friars as her cousin, whose identity is debated. The similarity of names, as well as his evident familiarity with her (he stayed in her home on at least one occasion) makes it seem possible that this cousin was brother Raimon de Johan. Manselli and Biget both accept this scenario as a given (Manselli, *Spirituali*, 226–227, esp. 227; Biget, "Culte et Rayonnement," 304). However, a comparison with the career of Raimon de Johan and the probable timing of this voyage to Majorca and Sicily, make it seem less likely that Raimon de Johan was the cousin involved (see above, and Burr, "Raymond Déjean," 63–66). Still, one of the friars summoned to the papal court in 1317 from Béziers was named Peire "Bayssi," or "Boissini," which makes it possible to surmise instead that this individual, whose only other appearance in the literature was when he agreed to obey *Quorumdam exigit* before Michael of Cesena, is the cousin who fled to Sicily. *BF*, 5:120; Manselli, *Spirituali*, 296.

[136] Doat 28, fol. 207r–v.

[137] *Liber sententiarum* 2:1350.

[138] Doat 27, fols. 84v–85r.

[139] The testimony of Johan Rotgier, who held a benefice in Béziers, reveals Peire's friendship both with himself and with two other priests named Johan Adzorit and R. Amalfredi. Manselli, *Spirituali*, 306–309.

the burning on January 11, 1321, he was undoubtedly moved, like so many others, by the steadfast faith of a young girl of only fifteen, Amegiardis, who "suffered her martyrdom patiently."[140] Since he was the father of a young daughter himself, Andrea, and since he had brought her up in the faith that was now so beleaguered, Amegiardis's death must have been especially chilling. Faith in the sanctity of the burned Beguins was growing, belief in their status as martyrs was widespread, and yet as a father, Peire doubtless wished to avoid such a fate for his own daughter.

When twenty-one members of the Beguin community of Narbonne were burned in the ditch outside the walls of the Bourg in February 1322, it marked another milestone for Peire Trencavel and his fugitive companions. His friend Peire Tort of Montréal, who was captured with two other Beguins just outside of Cintegabelle in April 1322, may have expressed doubts about the sanctity of some of these Beguin "martyrs" later to Bernard Gui, but to the Beguins he encountered in Cintegabelle (Bernarda d'Antusan and Guilhem Ros), Peire Tort and Peire Arrufat simply said that the twenty-one had died "stalwartly and strongly."[141] There was no longer any further doubt that all the Beguins were now targets of inquisitorial wrath and that it was becoming even more difficult to escape prison or martyrdom. For one thing, efforts to capture fugitive Beguins were becoming better coordinated among the various episcopal and Dominican inquisitions of Languedoc. Peire Tort, for instance, was captured initially by a consul of Cintegabelle, sent to Pamiers where Jacques Fournier was the inquisiting bishop, and ultimately found himself before the Dominican inquisitor Bernard Gui in Toulouse. After the General Sermon of July 1322 in Toulouse, he was sent to the Wall of Carcassonne to live out his sentence of perpetual immurement.[142]

Sometime in 1322 or early 1323, Peire Trencavel himself was captured and also brought to the Wall of Carcassonne, though none of our sources are able to tell us exactly when or how he was taken. If he escaped the arrests

[140] "Dicta iuvencula patienter suum martirium sustinuerat." Johan Vascon, Doat 28, fol. 232r–v.

[141] "Valenter et fortiter": *Liber sententiarum* 2:1594. David Burr considers Peire Tort to belong to the "little tent" school of Beguin martyrdom, and it is certainly possible that Bernard Gui's thoughtful questioning was able to bring Tort's doubts to the surface. See Burr, *Spiritual Franciscans*, 221–228; *Liber sententiarum* 2:1406–1409.

[142] Guilhem Ros and Raimon d'Antusan refer to Peire Tort's capture and the fact that he was bound for Pamiers (*Liber sententiarum* 2:1351 and 1592–1595). Peire's deposition and sentence tell us the rest: ibid., 1397–1423. The chronicle of Nicolaus Minorita further informs us that by 1321, the archbishop of Narbonne was no longer operating alone as inquisitor, but was coordinating his efforts with the inquisitor of Carcassonne, Jean de Beaune. *Nicolaus Minorita: Chronica*, 62.

of the spring of 1322 (Guilhem Ros said that he was expecting to see Peire in Cintegabelle around Easter), he may have been rounded up along with two Beguins of Béziers, Johan Conilli and Bernard de Bosc, who were captured in June.[143] Such a notorious fugitive and leader of the Beguins as Peire Trencavel would have surely ended up on the stake on April 24, 1323, when these two others were burned except for one extraordinary fact. He escaped.

If you visit the magnificently medieval city of Carcassonne now, colorful flyers advertising exhibitions of torture instruments and the like will surely come your way, and if you are like the vast majority of visitors to the city, you will assume that prisoners of the inquisitors were held either in the impressive-looking Château or in one of the many towers that regularly interrupt the famous walls. The fact that everyone in Languedoc called the inquisitorial prison "the Wall" simply contributes to this misconception (after all, the walls of Carcassonne are the city's most distinctive feature). The term "Wall," however, simply comes from the word used for any monastic prison.[144] Prisoners of the Dominican inquisition of Carcassonne were actually held in one of two places, neither of them particularly impregnable. Either they were held in a prison in the Bourg of Carcassonne (that is, outside the famous walls), or in a large but otherwise fairly ordinary house and its associated outbuildings just inside the Porte d'Aude of the City.[145] Escape from such a place was not merely not impossible, but it was actually fairly common. The Cathar perfect Guilhem Bélibaste was a notorious escapee from the inquisitorial prison of Carcassonne: he spent many years as a fugitive in Catalonia before his eventual recapture by an inquisitorial spy.[146] Two other Cathar perfects, Jacme Authié and Prades Tavernier, also escaped from the Wall.[147] Even the prisons of Bernard Gui, inquisitor *par*

---

[143] Only Bernard de Bosc is named in the Beguin Martyrology, but Johan Conilli also appears in the accounts for the General Sermon where they burned. Johan Conilli is not specifically labeled as a Beguin, but he and Bernard de Bosc (whom we know from many depositions) were evidently captured at the same time, and had been held in Carcassonne for 305 days before their death. Doat 34, fols. 219–224r.

[144] Given, *Inquisition*, 30; Edward Peters, "Prison before the Prison: The Ancient and Medieval Worlds," in *The Oxford History of the Prison*, ed. Norval Morris and David J. Rothman (New York, 1995), 28–99.

[145] See Antoine Sarraute, *Le Logis de l'Inquisition: Maison historique* (Toulouse, [1914]).

[146] Bélibaste's story is exhaustively related in the deposition of the spy Arnaud Sicre. *Registre* 2:20–81.

[147] Jacme Authié, son of Peire Authié, the leader of the Cathar revival in the Pays de Foix, is certainly known to have escaped. Other sources imply that Prades Tavernier, another *perfectus* who was captured with Jacme, also escaped with him, but the point is not certain. *Registre* 2:57, and 3:145; *L'Inquisiteur Geoffroy d'Ablis*, 77, 342–343. Both Duvernoy and Palès-Gobilliard believe that Prades escaped with Jacme.

excellence, were not invulnerable: eight men escaped from the Wall of Toulouse in 1309–1310, for instance.[148]

Less than a month after his escape, Peire Trencavel was back in Béziers, and it appears to have been at this time that he first articulated what was to become his great mission: saving Olivi's written works from destruction. When Johan Rotgier remembered meeting Peire at this time in Johan Adzorit's home (both Rotgier and Adzorit were priests in Béziers), Peire's arms were full of texts. He gave a copy of an Olivian gloss on the psalter to Rotgier and several more books to Adzorit, including what were almost certainly some of Olivi's *Questions on Evangelical Perfection*, three or four booklets of Olivi's sermons, Olivi's *Treatise on Poor Use*, and a commentary on Daniel by Bartholomeus Sicard, another controversial Franciscan author.[149]

Peire gave some texts to friends like Johan Adzorit and Johan Rotgier for safekeeping, but he also tried simply to take others out of the inquisitors' reach. When Bernard Maury, the priest whose life across the Rhône we followed in chapter 2, came across Peire Trencavel in the summer of 1323, Peire had with him "many books of the doctrine of brother Peter of John, so that these books and this doctrine might not be destroyed nor condemned."[150] Bernard was somewhat vague as to exactly which books Peire had brought to Provence, but one of them was almost certainly Olivi's commentary on the

---

[148] Given, *Inquisition*, 30, 101–102. See British Library Additional Manuscript 4697, fols. 23v, 26r, 28v, and 30r, and *Liber sententiarum* 1:226, 230, 250–252, 278, 280, and 294. Since escapes from the inquisitorial prisons of both Toulouse and Carcassonne were not uncommon, it is unnecessary for us to resort to the explanation proposed by Fabio Troncarelli in order to account for Peire Trencavel's escape. Troncarelli believes that Peire Trencavel was a member of the thirteenth-century "Trencavel family" and thus exerted undue influence over the staff of the prison (Troncarelli refers to Peire as the "visconte di Carcassonne"). Additionally, Troncarelli suggests that a certain Master Bernard Trencavel, a jurist of Pamiers who was named custodian of the Carcassonne prison in 1306, and then Penitentiary of Pope Clement VI in 1309, was a relative of Peire's and also had undue influence over the prison staff some fourteen years after his probable resignation as custodian. There is no evidence, however, that Peire and Bernard were related to one another, and even less evidence that such a thing as a "Trencavel family" of viscounts existed in either the thirteenth or fourteenth century, as modern use of this idea probably dates no further back than the seventeenth century. I am deeply grateful to Fredric Cheyette for his patience with my repeated pestering on the topic of the Trencavels and their name. Troncarelli, "Pietro Trencavelli," esp. 14–26. See also Fredric Cheyette, *Ermengard of Narbonne and the World of the Troubadours* (Ithaca, 2001), esp. 25ff.

[149] Manselli, *Spirituali*, 306–308. For more information about Barthelemy Sicard's commentary on the Book of Daniel, see Sylvain Piron, "La critique de l'Église chez les Spirituels languedociens," *CF* 38 (2003): 77–109.

[150] "Dictus Petrus Trencavelli constituerat se in fugam et recesserat a partibus Narbone et Biterris cum multis libris doctrine fratris Petri Johannis ad hoc ut dicti libri et doctrina non destruerentur nec dampnarentur." Manselli, *Spirituali*, 335.

Apocalypse (or its Occitan translation that also circulated), the book prized above all others in Olivi's oeuvre. Peire also had a pamphlet in the vernacular written by Olivi that spoke of prayer and fasting, and another about the poverty of Christ. Peire was not alone in his desire to keep the works of Olivi in safe hands: Guilhem de Johan of Limoux left a copy of Olivi's *Commentary on the Rule of St. Francis* with Bernard Maury when Guilhem was headed to Rome in 1325.[151]

By July 1323, Peire Trencavel had crossed the Rhône and was living in St. Martin de la Brasque, a small village on the south side of the Grand Lubéron, a wild mountain area then and now. His daughter Andrea was now with him, and she also had a companion, a young woman named Sicilia. Peire often visited a nobleman who lived in the region, a certain Hugolin, knight of the Order of Saint John of Jerusalem who had bought the rents of Ste Catherine, only a league away from St. Martin.[152] Peire and Hugolin spent a great deal of time speaking together in secret, and Hugolin was known to remark that Peire "knew many good things."[153] Everyone who met with him remembered how he spoke about Olivi, about the doctrines of the Spiritual Franciscans, and about the end times that were upon them all. From being the type of resistance leader who coordinated the escapes of others, Peire became an inspirational missionary, armed with Olivi's texts which he frequently read aloud.

Peire and his daughter also visited with other fugitives in Provence. On several occasions, Peire visited Apt, where Berenguier Hulard of Narbonne had found a community of like-minded individuals, and met Bernard Maury and a priest named Huc Rubaud in the inn. His daughter Andrea traveled with Bernard and her companion Sicilia to Avignon, where they visited friends from Narbonne and Catalonia in a house near the Carmelite convent. In the fall, Peire and his household moved to Marseille, where they were able to live more freely. Though Marseille in the 1320s was a commercial city on the decline, it was nonetheless far larger than any other city in Provence except Avignon, with close to 25,000 inhabitants. Among Marseille's "respectable

---

[151] Ibid., 335–336.

[152] It is interesting to note that this area of the Lubéron is notorious in French history for the battles over religion that occurred in the sixteenth century between Waldensians (fairly recent immigrants from the Piedmont) and Catholics. Abandoned Waldensian villages are common. Later still, the Lubéron had a large Protestant population. See Gabriel Audisio, *The Waldensian Dissent: Persecution and Survival, c. 1170–c. 1570*, trans. Claire Davison (Cambridge, England, 1999).

[153] Manselli, *Spirituali*, 333.

laborers, fishermen, and mariners; tradesmen and tradeswomen, retailers, and artisans, physicians, notaries, jurists, and schoolmasters; bankers and moneylenders," not to mention its "impecunious laborers, ruffians, thieves, murderers, prostitutes, lepers and abandoned children," immigrants like Peire Trencavel and his family would have easily been able to find a comfortable and reasonably secure place to live in one of the city's many and diverse neighborhoods.[154] There were other immigrants from Languedoc who had come there for respectable business reasons, like Johan Blaize, nephew of Arnau de Vilanova and a native of Montpellier, a surgeon who preferred business to surgery and who has left accounts of twenty years of mercantile transactions in the archives of Marseille.[155] Though it is probable that Peire and his household avoided the Franciscan convent in the bourg of Syon just outside the market gate on the eastern side of town for fear of being recognized, they no doubt made clandestine trips to pray in the Great Market in front of the Church of Notre Dame des Accoules (only the bell-tower is still standing), where the four Spiritual friars had been burned in 1318.

Though Marseille was probably as safe a refuge as any, by late summer of 1324 Peire Trencavel was back in Languedoc, this time in Montpellier.[156] He seems to have left Andrea and Sicilia in Marseille, as he certainly intended at least to pass through the city on his way elsewhere. In Montpellier, Peire met with what can be said to constitute the most active remnant of the Beguins: Guilhem Domergue Veyrier and his wife Berengaria of Narbonne, old acquaintants of Peire's, Esteve Gramat of Villeneuve-lès-Béziers, brother Raimon de Johan, Peire de Tornamira, the Boneta sisters, and the rest of the Montpellierain Beguins. No doubt after much discussion and argumentation, they collectively sketched out a two-pronged plan for a new life far from Languedoc. Peire de Tornamira rallied support for an exodus to Sicily by sea, and Peire Trencavel and Guilhem Domergue Veyrier were to lead another group on the land route, first to Provence and perhaps beyond.

Tensions were running high among the fugitives by this point, however, and it was not long after their departure that Guilhem Domergue Veyrier and Peire Trencavel began to argue (perhaps over their final destination). Both had been acting in secret and independently for so long that it was no

---

[154] Smail, *Imaginary Cartographies*, 58. A useful map can be found on 46–47.

[155] M. Batllori, "La documentacion de Marsella sobre Arnau de Vilanova y Joan Blasi," *Analecta Sacra Tarraconensia* 21 (1949): 75–119.

[156] The following account of the meeting in Montpellier and the travels to Provence comes from the testimonies of Esteve Gramat (Doat 27, fols. 9r–10v) and Pons de Sant Gili (Doat 28, fols. 235v–237r).

doubt difficult to share authority. When Guilhem wanted to take the group up north to Orange, Peire took off on his own and presumably returned to his daughter in Marseille. Solidarity among the Beguins was too precious to waste for long over petty quarrels, however, and Peire continued his travels around Provence, where he visited Guilhem in Orange and was seen by others in Avignon and elsewhere in addition to Marseille.

From the time that Guilhem Domergue Veyrier and Pons de Sant Gili were captured in Orange in April 1325 to the spring of 1327, we have very few indications of Peire's whereabouts. He was in Marseille late in 1325, where Esteve Gramat saw him as he was on his way back to Languedoc from Provence. It seems most probable that he and Andrea remained in Marseille. Back in Languedoc, however, the testimony of Guilhem Veyrier and Guilhem Serralier, who was captured in May, brought down what was left of the Beguin underground network. Nearly forty Beguins or their sympathizers were captured beginning in the summer of 1325, and their arrest also spelled danger for the Beguins who were still hiding in Provence. A Beguin from Apt (perhaps Berenguier Hulard) was arrested in September 1325, prompting Bernard Maury and the three Beguines with whom he lived in Manosque to change residence to Brignoles. In November, Bernard Maury received a visit from a Beguin of Limoux, clearly fleeing prosecution. At the end of March 1326, Bernard's companions were arrested in Brignoles and Bernard himself fled for Italy, but was captured early in May. After a summer of relentless questioning by the inquisitor of Provence, he was burned in Avignon on November 19. But for a short while at least, Peire Trencavel and his family remained at large, perhaps because they left the place in Marseille where too many had known where to find them, or perhaps because all those who testified declared that they did not know where he was living, as Bernard Maury had. Peire Trencavel had been an indefatigable missionary and protector of others; perhaps those he had helped on so many occasions showed their gratitude by professing ignorance of his whereabouts.

On March 1, 1327, Guilhem Domergue Veyrier and his wife Berengaria, Guilhem Serralier, and three others were handed over to the secular arm and burned in Carcassonne. But at nearly the same moment that these long-time fugitives went to their deaths proudly crying out their allegiance to the faith of Peter Olivi and the burned Beguins, the other most-sought-after fugitive was captured yet again. By the middle of March, Peire Trencavel and his daughter had been captured somewhere in Provence, and Pope John XXII ordered Michel le Moine, the inquisitor of Provence, to send them to Carcassonne for questioning. Because of his previous escape, Peire's fate was already sealed, but Andrea was described simply as being "vehemently suspected" of heresy.[157]

The inquisitors of Languedoc obviously had a strong interest in seeing Peire Trencavel alive, since he might have been a gold mine of information for them had he chosen to speak and to reveal the many places where he had hidden heretics over the years and the many collaborators who had helped him. It was doubtless at their request that John XXII ordered the transfer of Peire and Andrea.

But in one of the enduring mysteries of the Beguin story, Peire Trencavel and his daughter were never seen again by the inquisitors. The Scarlet Pimpernel of Languedoc and Provence simply vanished, and no surviving inquisitorial document has the slightest mention of his fate or his daughter's. They were neither imprisoned nor burned, not sent on pilgrimages nor released to wear yellow crosses on their clothing. Through what combination of guile, force, and corruption we do not know, it appears that they simply escaped from the inquisitors' clutches—and disappeared from the historical record.

The story of Peire Trencavel might have remained simply that, an unresolved and unresolvable mystery, save for the discovery of a fascinating manuscript in the Italian city of Padua by Fabio Troncarelli. At the bottom of a commentary on the *Sentences* of Peter Lombard by the thirteenth-century Franciscan theologian Alexander of Alessandria appear the following words:

> This is the end of the commentary on the fourth part of the Sentences. Good and useful. Thanks be to God, Amen, Amen. In the convent of Padua, Peire Trencavel of Narbonne in the province of Provence.[158]

Through a combination of handwriting analysis and dating of the watermark on the paper used to write the manuscript, Troncarelli has been able to date this no earlier than 1331 or 1332, thus proving that Peire Trencavel himself, at least, made it over the Alps and into Italy. There, it would appear, he was able to take refuge in a sympathetic Franciscan convent and was given access to and some kind of employ in their library. The leopard had

---

[157] March 21, 1327: *Bullaire de l'inquisition*, 123–125.

[158] "Explicit lectura super quartum sententiarum. Bona, utilis. Deo gratias. Amen. Amen. Conventus Padue. Petrus Trinchavelli de Narbona provincia Provinciae." Troncarelli, "Pietro Trencavelli," 26 (illustration on 25). Narbonne was part of the Franciscan province of Provence.

not changed his spots, for some of the other annotations in his hand have a poignant Olivian tone:

I am he who speaks with you says the Lord of Hosts.
  To endure patiently, look at the wounds of the crucifix. The sufferings that He bore are worth a thousand sufferings.[159]

So many of the companions he had helped during his years of clandestine travel on behalf of others died at the stake or were imprisoned, but Peire Trencavel finally made his way into a safe exile in Italy.

With some luck and determined searching, Peire should have been able to make contact with other Languedocian exiles elsewhere in Italy. There were at least a few Beguins in Assisi in the 1330s, for we have a manuscript full of texts useful for and precious to Beguins that was part of the collection of the Carcere, Saint Francis's hermitage retreat not far outside the city that became a haven for radicals.[160] The scribe who wrote down a translation of the Rule of the Third Order and numerous short texts by Olivi was an exile like Peire, who adapted to life in Italy, but never stopped speaking his native Occitan. There were also other groups of sympathizers in Italy, and if Peire had ventured even further south, to Apulia, he could have found a community of friars whom he had known from his years in Narbonne. Brother Bernard d'Alzonne, originally from the convent of Narbonne, was the leader of a group of Spirituals who survived in Apulia until the time of the Black Death, keeping alive faith in Olivi (whom they called "the holy doctor brother Peter John of Narbonne"), and living out Olivi's doctrine of poor use and evangelical poverty.[161] The inquisitors triumphed in Languedoc itself, but pockets of their faith were able to survive in exile.

That the Beguin movement survived the determined assault of the inquisitors at all was due to resolute and strong individuals like Peire Trencavel and

[159] "Ego sum qui loquor tecum dicit Dominus exercituum" (this line is accompanied by a sketch of a substantial head of a man with a tonsure in profile: Peire himself? Peter Lombard? Alexander of Alessandria? A mere doodle?), and "Ut patienter agas crucifixi respice plagas. Est penas mille penae quas pertulit ille." Ibid., 26.
[160] See Marcella Gatti, *Le Carceri di San Francesco del Subasio* (Assisi, 1969), esp. 95–103, but also the 1341 will of Letitia, daughter of Ugolino Lete of Assisi, summarized in Cesare Cenci, *Documentazione di vita assisana, 1300–1530* (Grottaferrata, 1974), 1:83, that clearly indicates the presence of "fraticelli" at the Carceri.
[161] A vernacular chronicle of the second half of the fourteenth century mentions Bernard d'Alzonne, "Bartolomeo di Provenza," a certain brother Raimon, and "many other solemn friars." Tocco, *Studii Francescani*, 520–522. For other groups of "fraticelli di paupere vita," see Douie, *The Nature and Effect of the Heresy of the Fraticelli*, 217–223.

Prous Boneta. Though at the distance of all these centuries, we find their confidence in the immediacy of the end times misplaced, we can nonetheless admire their courage and determination. Neither martyrdom nor exile was easy, and there were no doubt many times when either one might have chosen other than they did.

It is all too easy for us, just as it has been for generations of historians, to dismiss the importance of the Beguin phenomenon. It lasted only a few short decades, after all, and was limited in its geographical range to the south of France (a hot spot for heresies) and a few small pockets outside. But we must not forget that the inquisitors of Languedoc—powerful, effective men like Jacques Fournier and Bernard Gui—did not take the Beguin threat lightly, but devoted their time and considerable resources to its eradication over a fifteen-year period. The conflict over poverty in the Franciscan Order and the heresy of the Beguins was one of the defining preoccupations of John XXII's papacy, and all the events I have described took place in the papal court's backyard, sharpening their impact and increasing the anxiety of John and his advisers. Both Peire Trencavel and Prous Boneta, heresiarchs of the Beguins, were thorns in the side of the entire ecclesiastical hierarchy, leaders of a movement that caused many a papal and inquisitorial migraine.

CONCLUSION

Though the plight of the Beguins of Languedoc has not been of great interest to historians until now, the larger context of the poverty controversy within the Franciscan Order within which we have found ourselves is well enough known that it has even provided the ingenious setting for two modern novels. The best known, of course, is Umberto Eco's *The Name of the Rose*, set in November 1327, though the poverty controversy no doubt seems to many merely a rather lengthy and tedious introduction to the story of the mysterious killer haunting Eco's Alpine abbey and the search for the second book of Aristotle's *Poetics*.[1] Nevertheless, while William of Baskerville and Adso of Melk may be Eco's inventions, Michael of Cesena, Bonagratia of Bergamo, Ubertino da Casale, and Bernard Gui (not to mention the other representa-

---

[1] Eco famously remarked "I began writing in March of 1978, prodded by a seminal idea: I felt like poisoning a monk." He also acknowledges that the choice of November 1327 and the poverty controversy was accidental, a mere consequence of the fact that he "needed an investigator, English if possible (intertextual quotation) with a great gift of observation and a special sensitivity in interpreting evidence. These qualities could be found only among the Franciscans, and only after Roger Bacon; furthermore, we find a developed series of signs only with the Occamites." But as he further observes, "the narrator is the prisoner of his own premises." *Postscript to the Name of the Rose*, trans. William Weaver (San Diego, 1984), 13, 26, 28.

tives of the two sides who meet at the abbey) are historical figures, and the distrust between the two sides depicted in the secret talks to which William of Baskerville was privy was real, though the aborted negotiations are fictional.

While for Eco, the poverty controversy is little more than a setting within which his semiotic syllogisms are able to shine, for another academic-turned-novelist, G. G. Coulton, it is rather more. Coulton's time-travel novel *Friar's Lantern* takes every possible opportunity to bash the modern Roman Catholic Church and its medieval antecedents, and events of the 1320s provide ample grist for his mill.[2] As Coulton's hero, The Reverend Herbert Rashleigh, wends his tragic way from a quiet English village through the highways and byways of fourteenth-century France toward Avignon, he meets with every possible type of medieval churchman: corrupt bishops, incontinent canons, a self-satisfied friar who might as well be named Friar Tuck—and at the very last, when all hope seems lost, a saintly Spiritual Franciscan hermit and a family of warm, welcoming, and clandestine Beguins (though in the end, the enlightened Rashleigh comes to see even their devotion to their cause as fanaticism). In another work, Coulton described the persecution of the Spiritual friars and their lay followers as a prime example of "the cynical frankness with which loyalty to the first traditions of the Order was proclaimed to be heresy,"[3] and in *Friar's Lantern*, he clearly saw in it a delicious means to hoist the Church by its own petard.[4]

Historical fiction, however conscientious, provides a wonderful opportunity for the author to shape events to suit his or her agenda. While no

[2] Coulton (1858–1947), a scholar whose peripatetic academic career was worthy of a gyrovague or a Goliard, was a prolific writer. Though he is now probably best known for his popular *From St. Francis to Dante: A Translation of All That Is of Primary Interest in the Chronicle of the Franciscan Salimbene* (London, 1906) and *Medieval Panorama: The English Scene from Conquest to Reformation* (New York, 1938), both many times reprinted in paperback and widely available in used bookstores, or for his more scholarly four-volume *Five Centuries of Religion* (Cambridge, England, 1923–1950), he was also a pamphleteer and controversialist, an opponent of Belloc and Chesterton, and a bitter enemy of Cardinal Gasquet. Among his publications are many with inflammatory titles such as *Catholic Truth and Historical Truth* (Cairo, [c.1906]), *Inquisition and Liberty* (London, 1938) and *Romanism and Truth* (London, 1930). His self-laudatory autobiography, *Fourscore Years* (Cambridge, 1943), is best supplemented by his daughter's somewhat less than filial recollections: Sarah Campion, *Father: A Portrait of G. G. Coulton at Home* (London, 1948).

[3] Coulton, "The Failure of the Friars," in *Ten Medieval Studies* (Cambridge, 1930), 171n1.

[4] *Romanism and Truth*, 2:116–117. Nor are these two the only works of fiction set in and around the controversies over poverty in southern France, though Suzanne Bernard's *La Beguine* (Paris, 2000) conflates the beguines of Douceline of Digne's foundations in Provence (the so-called ladies of Roubaud) with the followers of Peter Olivi in Languedoc, and mistakenly assumes that the beguines of Provence were the object of papal and inquisitorial prosecution.

historian in our postmodern age would argue that we are free of bias (it continually shapes our enterprise from its concerns all the way to our conclusions), we are nonetheless bound by texts, sources, and the likely limits of the possible. However, some of the dramatic events and memorable characters of the 1320s make novelization seem almost superfluous. Alan Friedlander's evocation of the world of Bernard Délicieux, who died in prison in the aftermath of the infamous audience before Pope John XXII in Avignon in 1317, *The Hammer of the Inquisitors*, is an excellent example of a compelling story eloquently told; David Burr's *The Spiritual Franciscans* is another. As these historians and others have shown, the lessons we learn do not necessarily have to be either apologetic or polemic.

When we look at the stories of the Beguins of Languedoc, we enter into the world of fourteenth-century religious controversy and can draw many conclusions. Peire de Tornamira, Esclarmonda Durban, Raimon and Bernarda d'Antusan, Bernard Maury, Peire Trencavel, Sibillia Cazelas, and Prous Boneta were men and women whose commitment to their cause in the face of ecclesiastical repression led them to subterfuge, bribery, acts of daring, exile, and death—for some, freely chosen as martyrdom.

The first conclusion we must come to is the tremendous success of the "weapons of the truly weak" employed by the Beguins as they evaded and fought against the bishops, inquisitors, and representatives of the papacy who sought to repress their movement. They employed many effective tactics. Beguins like Ramon and Bernarda d'Antusan protected, hid, and fed their fugitive fellows, constituting a veritable underground railway across Languedoc and beyond. They lied as necessary. Like Prous and Alisseta Boneta, Bernard Peyrotas, and Peire Trencavel, they visited each other in prison, providing food and money. They laughed about the inquisitors behind their backs, mocked the pope, and delighted in the clever tricks they played on the inquisitors' minions. Some of them, like Prous Boneta and Esclarmonda Durban, defied the entire ecclesiastical hierarchy by insisting on martyrdom instead of betraying their fellows. Like Peire Trencavel and Bernard Maury, many traveled in disguise, made excuses, and some of them (like Peire) were lucky enough, or resourceful enough, to escape from inquisitorial prisons. Beguins like Sibillia Cazelas even bribed inquisitors, procuring lesser sentences for themselves and their fellows. As a last resort, many of them fled Languedoc entirely, traveling to Provence, like Bernard Maury, Italy, like Peire Trencavel, or Sicily, like Peire de Tornamira. In a fascinating transformation of orthodox piety calculated to arouse the inquisitors' particular ire (as well as to perpetuate their own faith), they venerated their burned brethren as saints, carrying their holy relics from place to place and distributing them to the faithful. The martyrs—their faith, their resolve, their steadfastness in the face of the flames—were an inspiration to all of the Beguins, and the tangible reminder of their sacrifice in the form of the bodily relics that their companions venerated was a sign that victory could even be found in defeat.

These weapons also contributed to the survival of a movement that outlived what we might call its fifteen minutes (or ten years) of fame. Though the public presence of the Spiritual Franciscans and Beguins of Languedoc abated after 1330, they had by no means entirely disappeared. One Languedocian trial of the 1350s provides a tantalizing hint that some of the *fraticelli* in Italy were linked very closely to the Languedocian conflict of the 1320s. In June 1354, two heretics from Italy were consigned to the flames in Avignon after a trial that has provided scholars with vitally important information about the Beguin controversy. The two, a Franciscan priest named Giovanni Godulchi of Castiglione, and a Franciscan *conversus* named Francesco de Arquata, had been captured in the hospital of Saint Bartholomew in Montpellier and taken to Carcassonne, where they spent eight months imprisoned in the Wall.[5] In March 1353, Pope Innocent VI sent for them, and they were conveyed to Avignon,[6] standing trial at the beginning of October. Captured with them was a little book (*libellum*), whose contents were entered into the record *in extenso*.[7] The *libellum* appears to have been in two

---

[5] Though there are two towns called Arquata in Italy, the most likely is Arquata del Tronto in the Marche. Castiglione is an even more common name, but there is a Castiglione del Lago, and a Castiglion Fiorentino, both very close to Assisi. Also in the same prison was John of Rupescissa, who certainly knew them. Two months after their death, Rupescissa was asked if he thought they were glorious martyrs or damned heretics. At first he did not wish to respond, but when pressed, he predicated his response on the precise reason they were condemned: if they were burned because of hatred of evangelical poverty and for their support of *Exiit qui seminat*, then they were glorious martyrs, but if they had mixed in other heresies, then they were indeed heretics. Everything depended on one's answer to that "if." While Rupescissa staunchly upheld his own orthodoxy (and who can blame him?), in his *Liber Ostensor* (dated 1356), he also observed that a total of 113 martyrs had "burned for evangelical poverty." Since that figure matches the number at the bottom of the Beguin martyrology brought to Avignon by Giovanni and Francesco, it seems likely that he shared their views, and conversed with them in prison. Robert E. Lerner, "Historical Introduction," Johannes de Rupescissa, *Liber secretorum eventuum*, ed. Christine Morerod-Fattebert (Fribourg, Switzerland, 1994). Jeanne Bignami-Odier, "Jean de Roquetaillade (de Rupescissa), théologien, polémiste, alchimiste," *Hist. Litt.* 41 (1981): 75–284, at 97–100. Mme Bignami-Odier does not provide a precise citation for Rupescissa's comments on the 113 martyrs.

[6] Several papal letters related to their journey from Carcassonne to Avignon are in *Bullaire de l'inquisition*, 332–335.

[7] This *libellum* is the source for the Wolfenbüttel Martyrology. The existence of this trial has long been known, thanks to Rinaldi, *Annales ecclesiastici* (ann. 1354, 31). The papal

parts. First was a "Confession of some paupers from the time of pope John." The confession is composed of a list of familiar Spiritual and Beguin errors: The pope does not have the power to change the Rule of Saint Francis. The decretal *Quorumdam exigit* is unjust. Peter Olivi is a saint in Paradise. The friars burned in Marseille were "holy and religious martyrs for Jesus Christ who died for the Gospel." This section of the manuscript closes with the observation that "these are the articles for which the holy evangelical Friars Minor were burned in the provinces of Aquitania and Catalonia."[8] Both men on trial insisted on subscribing to all of these errors, which they took for their own, and declared that they wished to persevere in them unto death.

The second half of the *libellum* is the martyrology that has been such an important source for the persecution of the Beguins, listing over a hundred of the Beguins and friars burned, primarily in Languedoc. Careful examination of the burnings listed in the martyrology, however, allows us to speculate that it was removed from Languedoc after approximately 1323. Up until that date, all the burnings of which we are aware are listed; after that, the martyrology is more sporadic and less precise, listing several burnings in distant locations (Naples, Metz, England) without dates in addition to a few autos-da-fé of the late 1320s, but not all of them.[9] At the end, several burnings in 1337 and 1347 round out the martyrology. The very fact that *fraticelli* of Tuscany were caught in a city of Languedoc carrying a list of Languedocian martyrs implies that they may have been seeking to renew ties between sympathetic groups in Italy and the south of France.[10] The two

---

bull of March 31, 1353, is also preserved in Doat 35, fol. 130r. Some of the documents are found in other manuscripts; see Robert Lerner, "New Evidence for the Condemnation of Meister Eckhart," *Speculum* 72 (1997): 347–366, at 352–353. A manuscript in Prague (University Library IV. B. 15, fols. 304a–315a) also contains the martyrology. The manuscript I have used is Wolfenbüttel Helmstedt MS. 1006, fols. 9v–26v.

[8] This confession runs from 11v to 12r.

[9] And some of these entries are inaccurate: we know from records of the inquisitors (Doat 28, fols. 240r–252v) that at least Guilhem Serallier, Peire Espere-en-Diu, and Guilhem Domergue Veyrier died on March 1, 1327, but the martyrology (appendix A, lines 45–48) lists only Guilhem Domergue Veyrier and his wife, and three others not known through the inquisitorial record to have been burned that day (though since the records from this Sermon are incomplete, breaking off in the middle of a sentence, it is certainly possible that they were).

[10] They were certainly connected with such groups in Italy. The testimony of Francesco de Arquata reveals that he was in touch with a number of other friars who held similar views: Jacobus de Floris, Blasius de Cicilia, Nicholaus de Assisio, Pascalis de Narva, Paulus de Torena, Raymundus de Provincia Aquitanie, Nicholaus de Regno Apulie, and Paulus de Tuscia. He had met the last three in Rome, and they attempted to put him in touch with Duke Luigi of Durazzo, who was to be tried for his Spiritual connections in 1362. Douie, *Heresy of the Fraticelli*, 213.

heretical friars were condemned and burned on June 4, 1354. According to the chronicle of Heinrich Rebdorf, they went to the flames proclaiming "Gloria in excelsis Deo," and according to the same chronicler, there were many others in "Gascony" and Italy who defended these same errors.

The contents of the martyrology that they carried confirm this. Five "evangelical paupers" had apparently already been burned in 1347 in Carcassonne, and at least one of them was from Toulouse. Another Beguin or friar was burned in Toulouse, probably in that same year. If these six were caught and burned, whether as relapsed heretics or impenitent ones, we can expect that there were others hidden more effectively, or who were able to persuade the inquisitors that their repentance and abjurations were genuine.

The fate of many of the original Spiritual friars is also unknown. Sixty-one friars from the convents of Narbonne and Béziers were summoned to Avignon in April 1317, and twenty-six were sent on to the inquisitor Michel le Moine in November. Of those twenty-six, we can account for the fates of only seven—and one of these is a friar (Serviatius) who appears to have been living peacefully somewhere in Auvergne.[11] Another (brother Peire Fabre) fled as far as Naples before he was captured and burned.[12] Two other friars (Guilhem Guiraut and Bernard d'Antinhan) are known to have been fugitive in Languedoc in the 1320s, and it does not appear that they were ever caught.[13] Thus, seventeen of the original Spiritual friars tried by the inquisitor of Marseille remain entirely unaccounted for, and may well have remained at large.

Additionally, we know that at least some of the original forty-one friars who submitted to papal authority in the summer or fall of 1317 later regretted that decision, and became fugitives. No doubt many of those who initially agreed to obey *Quorumdam exigit* at first obeyed the orders given to them and went to the obscure Franciscan convents where they were sent. Many of these probably finished their days in conventual prisons, or settled down to an ordinary Franciscan life. At least some of the others, like the two friars who took refuge with Alaraxis Biasse in Sauvian, opened the sealed letters sent with them. When they saw that they were to be imprisoned, they

---

[11] Manselli, *Spirituali*, 307.

[12] Wolfenbüttel martyrology. The date is not mentioned, though it was during the pontificate of John XXII, and thus before 1334.

[13] Guilhem Guiraut was mentioned by Raimon de Johan (Manselli, *Spirituali*, 303) and by Prous Boneta (May, "Confession of Prous Boneta," 20). Bernard de Antinhano was specifically mentioned by Raimon d'Antusan of Cintegabelle in the company of other fugitive apostate friars (*Liber sententiarum* 2:1346). Neither was ever referred to as "combustus," or "immurandus," in any of the inquisitorial material.

apostatized and took flight.[14] Others, like Raimon de Johan, whom we have seen in many contexts, stayed in the convents where they were sent for a certain time (perhaps until the burning in Marseille in May 1318), and then fled.[15] We know for certain that six apostate friars were living together in Toulouse for a while; others may have been living in other cities of the Midi, and many surely fled the area entirely.[16]

Though little trace can be found of such fugitives, some names have come to light. It has long been known that there were many Spiritual friars in various places in Italy in the later years of the fourteenth century.[17] A vernacular chronicle from the second half of the century, certainly written in a Spiritual context (it refers to Peter Olivi as "santo doctore fra Pier Giovanni da Nerbona") informs us that some of these were from Languedoc. The author wrote that the Spirituals "fled into the reign of France, in Greece, in Crete, and in Italy, as I said above, but the greatest part of them...fled to the realm of Apulia." A brother Bernard d'Alzonne from the convent of Narbonne, one of those summoned to Avignon in 1317 who initially agreed to obey *Quorumdam exigit*, was active in Apulia until his death in the plague of 1348. Two other fugitives from Languedoc, "Bartolomeo di Provenza" and a certain Raimon, were also in Apulia in this period.[18] The author of the chronicle even remarked that "with all solicitude, [the friars] went to find the relics of the spirituals and holy men," an indication that not all the relics of Languedoc were seized by the inquisitors.[19] Though only these four were named, the chronicler wrote that along with those, there were "many other solemn brothers" (*molti altri solenni frati*).[20]

---

[14] "Qui fratres dixerunt ipsi loquenti quod sic ibant in habitu seculari quia noluerant ire ad Conventos remotos, ad quos mittebantur per eorum ministro pro eo videlicet quia in litteris clausis quas portabant inspexerant et viderant quod eorum ministri mandabant eos incarcerari in conventibus ipsis ad quos mittebantur." Doat 28, fols. 216v–217r.

[15] Peire Raimon Gontard from the convent of Béziers, who agreed to obey *Quorumdam exigit* in 1317, is another example. In April 1329, he was sentenced to be imprisoned by his brothers. Doat 27, fol. 160r.

[16] The names of the six in Toulouse are never given, though several Beguins mention them. A friar named Raimon Carlat of Alet (summoned to Avignon from Narbonne in 1317) was mentioned by Raimon d'Antusan of Cintegabelle as an apostate, however (*Liber sententiarum* 2:1346).

[17] See Douie, *Heresy of the Fraticelli*, 217–223.

[18] Tocco, *Studii Francescani*, 520. It is difficult to identify either of these with any of the friars certainly present in Avignon in 1317–1318. There was no Bartholomeus among these friars, though Raimon could be any of five untraceable Raimons.

[19] Ibid., 522.

[20] Ibid., 520.

There are also other signs of the enduring quality of Beguin ideology. Sometime after 1331, Beguin sympathizers in Languedoc created a collection of illustrated prophecies regarding the papacy known as the *Ascende calve* prophecies. Since it is always easier to comment trenchantly on events that have already occurred, medieval "prophecies" combine their genuine predictions for the future with a polemical mixture of descriptions of the past and observations about the present known as *ex eventu* prophecy. It should therefore come as no surprise that John XXII is one of the "bad popes" in the *Ascende calve* tradition, where he appears as a persecutor of the "dove" and as a powerful friend of the "crow."[21] This imagery of doves and crows (signifying Franciscans and Dominicans) neatly matches a famous sermon delivered by friar Bernard Délicieux in his struggles against the inquisitors of Carcassonne and refers to John persecuting the Spirituals and the Beguins using Dominican friars.[22] The *Ascende calve* prophecies eventually became part of a larger collection known as the *Vaticinia de summis pontificibus*, which were widely copied and distributed into the modern era. Their predictions make periodic appearances at the time of papal conclaves, faint echoes of far-away heretical concerns.

But my study of the heresy and the resistance of the Beguins has a significance beyond pointing to their mere survival, important as that may have been for the survivors. Heresy has been studied through many lenses, using many kinds of sources. A book I made extensive use of in graduate school (and continue to use in my teaching), Walter Wakefield and Austin P. Evans, *Heresies of the High Middle Ages*, for example, mostly relies on chronicles and theological treatises written both by heretics and their opponents. It is primarily a history of ideas, and only secondarily of people. Le Roy Ladurie's *Montaillou* stands at the opposite end of the spectrum, with a focus on the

---

[21] Orit Schwartz and Robert E. Lerner, "Illuminated Propaganda: The Origins of the 'Ascende calve' Pope Prophecies," *Journal of Medieval History* 20 (1994): 157–191, at 169–170. The title *Ascende calve* comes from the first words of the first panel of the prophecies, "Arise, oh bald one!" For an introduction to the politicized world of medieval pope prophecies see Robert E. Lerner, "Ursprung, Verbreitung und Ausstrahlung der Papstprophetien des Mittelalters," in Lerner and Robert Moynihan, *Weissagungen über die Päbste. Vat. Ross. 374*, 2 vols. (Stuttgart, 1985), 1:11–75, and Lerner, "Recent Work on the Origins of the 'Genus Nequam' Prophecies," *Florensia* 7 (1993), 121–138. Schwartz and Lerner derive the post-1331 date from their observation that in the ninth unit of the prophecies, there is a reference to a "false prophet who will seduce many," and the iconography depicts the "prophet" as wearing a papal tiara. This appears to refer to the brief reign of the anti-pope Nicholas V, Pietro of Corvaro, who was elected May 12, 1328, under the protection of Ludwig IV of Bavaria, but whose surrender to papal authorities in Avignon was negotiated in May 1330, and who finally resigned July 25, 1330.

[22] Friedlander, *Hammer of the Inquisitors*, 132–138.

down-to-earth, even racy details related in inquisitorial depositions. The villagers of Montaillou may have been prosecuted as Cathar heretics, and the early fourteenth-century "Cathar revival" is the frame within which their story is told, but both the author and the reader are more interested in Béatrice de Planissoles's love life than in matters of theology or spirituality.

Throughout this book, I have sought to strike a balance between these two extremes, and I have made wide use of a variety of documentary sources ranging from the lofty to the mundane. Inquisitorial depositions are the indispensable linchpins to any history of medieval heretics, but they cannot be our only source, and they must be used with great caution and care. Though they are often prolix on the subject of heretical activities and suspect beliefs, they are interested more in the "what" than in the "why." We must also seek out sources that help us to understand the religious motivation of these men and women who risked their lives for their beliefs, sources such as the didactic tracts that were written for their edification and for which they risked so much. Moreover, since our heretics were men and women of their time, they occasionally make appearances in more prosaic sources that we must scour in search of them. At times that search can feel like looking for the proverbial needle in a haystack, but the results are worth the effort, for these precious documents help us to understand their communities and the places they held within them. And sometimes, as in the case of Sibillia Cazelas's appearances in Johan Holanie's register, we are rewarded with the discovery of clandestine activity only hinted at in any of our other sources. It is in the careful weaving together of all these threads that the tapestry which depicts medieval heretics as real men and women with complex motivations and many-layered lives can emerge.

Finally, I would like to emphasize the importance of this short-lived religious movement. For Pope John XXII and for the inquisitors of Languedoc in the 1310s and 1320s, the Beguins constituted perhaps the most important threat to the unity of the Church. Bernard Gui, inquisitor par excellence, devoted many more pages in his inquisitorial manual to the Beguins than to Cathars, Waldensians, Pseudo-Apostles, converted Jews, or any other category of heretic.[23] In part this was because they were new and he was describing their beliefs and tactics for the first time, but it is also because he considered

[23] In Mollat's edition and translation of the *Manual*, the section on the Beguins and their errors covers a full 86 pages, while Cathars receive only 24, Waldensians 50, and "the perfidy of the Jews" a mere 13. Though there is a lengthy appendix (54 pages) on the history of the Pseudo-Apostles and attempts to suppress them, the section on the Pseudo-Apostles in the manual itself is only 24 pages.

them to be a substantial and pressing menace to the Church. The efforts of the Church to repress the Beguin movement that I have chronicled in these pages are a further tribute to their perceived importance: inquisitors indefatigably pursued the Beguins from town to town across Languedoc, into Gascony, and even across the Rhône into Provence. They effectively used tools of repression far more devastating than torture—cooperation among inquisitors, good recordkeeping and cross-referencing—to make sure that heretics did not play one inquisitor or bishop against another and did not escape the inquisitorial dragnet for long.

And yet, the resilience of the Beguins surprised all of them, just as it impresses us. Nearly seven hundred years have passed since their "great light" first became such "great smoke." It is time to let the light shine through the clouds once again.

APPENDIX: BURNINGS OF BEGUINS IN LANGUEDOC AND PROVENCE, 1318-1330

May 7, 1318 *Marseille*	Four Franciscan friars: Johan Barran, Guilhem Santon, Deodat Michael (all priests) and Pons Roca (deacon)[1]
October 14, 1319 *Narbonne*	Three Beguins: Mai de Blandisio or de Brandis, Peire de Franchis or de Fraxino of Narbonne, and Bernard Raimon de Monesco of Toulouse[2]
October 18, 1319 *Capestang*	Three Beguins: Johan Barra, Peire Canonici, and one other unknown Beguin[3]
May 25, 1320 *Capestang*	One friar, one priest, and four Beguins: brother Jacme de Rieux (lector in theology), Johan Martin, a priest, Bernard Martin of Montpellier, Johan Durban of Lodève, Bernard Leon of Montréal, and Bernard (or Raimon) Surio of Cailhavel[4]

[1] The feast was the vigil of the revelation of Saint Michael (also the second Sunday after Easter). WM, ll. 1–4. The sentence is in Baluze-Mansi 2:248–251.

[2] The feast of Saint Calixtus, pope, a Sunday. WM, ll. 5–6, and Baluze-Mansi 2:257–258. The Martyrology lists only 2 (Madius de Blandisio and Petrus de Franchis), while the sentence printed in Baluze-Mansi has three names: Magtarellus de Brandis, Petrus sartor de Fraxino, and Bernardus Raymundi de Monesco.

[3] The feast of Saint Luke the Evangelist, a Thursday. There are only two names in WM (ll. 7–8), though the testimony of Bernard Malaura of Lodève (an eyewitness) establishes that three Beguins were burned in total (Manselli, *Spirituali*, 312).

[4] The feast of the translation of Saint Francis (also Trinity Sunday). WM, ll. 9–12. Several of those burned are known from other sources. Jacme de Rieux was not summoned to Avignon, but was nonetheless handed over to Michel le Moine in November 1317 (*Bullaire de l'Inquisition*, 36). Bernard Martin was mentioned by Peire de Tornamira (Germain, "Une consultation inquisitoriale," 336). Bernard Leon is mentioned in many depositions from that town and in the deposition of Raimon de Johan OFM, Doat 28, fols. 191v, 197v,

June 2, 1320 *Béziers*	One priest, and one Beguin: Guilhem Anuli, priest, and Eustache Major of Béziers[5]
January 11, 1321 *Béziers*	One priest, five Beguins, and one Beguine: Peire Brun, priest, Bernard Sers, Johan Holier Essorbon, someone named Bernard, another named Ciracus, another named Peire, and a girl only 15 years of age named Amegiardis[6]
[date unknown] *Agde*	number unknown[7]
September 21, 1321 *Pézenas*	Four Beguins: Raimon Fornier of Florensac, Peire Abani, Johan de Mezea, and Guilhem Bon[8]
October 18, 1321 *Lunel*	One priest, nine Beguins, and seven Beguines: Guilhem Fabre, priest, Raimon Camba, Peire Alfand, men named Peire, Berenguier, Nicholau, Rotgier, Vezian, Guiraut, and Aimeric, Esclarmonda Durban of Lodève, Astruga of Lodève, and other women named Johanna, Biatris, and Ermessendis, and one unnamed woman, possibly Guillelma of Mirepoix[9]
February 28, 1322 *Narbonne*	Sixteen Beguins and five Beguines: Bernardin Anuli, Bernard de Perinhaco [or Peruihaco], Bonhome of Gascony, Peire of Elne, Bernard de Argistris,

and 231v, and Manselli, *Spirituali*, 305. Bernard (or Raimon) Surio is alluded to in a later trial (Coulet, "Un moine accusé," 368).

[5] A Monday. WM, ll. 13–14. Eustache Major is mentioned by Guilhem Serralier (Manselli, *Spirituali*, 325).

[6] The feast of Saint Hyginus, pope (also Epiphany Sunday). WM, ll. 15–18. Amegiardis is mentioned by others (Doat 28, fol. 232 r–v).

[7] Manselli, *Spirituali*, 317. Bernard Peyrotas, an eyewitness, does not provide a precise date, the number of individuals burned (though it was plural), or any names. It appears that the execution took place shortly after the January 11 auto-da-fé in Béziers.

[8] The feast of Saint Matthew the Evangelist (a Monday). WM, ll. 19–21. Bernard Peyrotas (an eyewitness) mentioned Raimon Fornier (Manselli, *Spirituali*, 317).

[9] The feast of Saint Luke the Evangelist (a Sunday). WM, ll. 22–27. An account of this auto-da-fé and the collection of relics after it can be found in Manselli, *Spirituali*, 309–319. Astruga was particularly revered as a saint (314). Guillelma of Mirepoix was mentioned by Alisseta Boneta (Doat 27, fol. 27v).

Guilhem of Urgel, Guilhem Separdi, Castilio of Gerona, Jacme de la Cros, Rotbert of Narbonne, Fornier de Fefensaco, Peire Almardi, and four unnamed men, Deruna Cathalana, Raymunda of Quarante, Sicarda de Corberia and two sisters named Bermonda and Elizabeth of St. Geniès[10]

June 13, 1322 *Carcassonne*	Six Beguins: Bernard Espruassora (or Espinesseria) of Agde, Raimon Lobat of Agde, Johan de Echis, Huc de Onlavis, Peire Arrufat, and a man named Aimeric[11]
September 27, 1322 *Toulouse*	Four Beguins: Peire Guiraut of Gignac, Peire Hospital (or Christian) of Montpellier, Peire Domergue of Hounoux from Narbonne, and Guilhem Ros of Cintegabelle[12]
April 24, 1323 *Carcassonne*	One Franciscan friar and three Beguins: Raimon Maistre of Villemoustaussou, OFM, Bernard de Bosco of Béziers Peire de Johan (or Julian) of Narbonne, and Johan Conilli of Béziers[13]

[10] Quadragesima Sunday. 12 Beguins, 5 Beguines identified in WM (ll. 31–39). According to the Chronicle of Saint Paul, *HGL* 5, cols. 45–46, there were a total of 21: 16 men and 5 women. None of these are known from other sources. WM also mentions a certain Symonis Extraneus, who died in prison, and he is probably the same as the "frater Simone Stranei," from whom a Beguin notary of Gerona, Guillem des Quer, received a copy of a work by Olivi (Questio XVI). Perarnau, "Opere di Fr. Petrus Johannis in processi catalani d'inquisizione della prima metà del XIV secolo," *AFH* 91 (1998): 505–516, at 512n16.

[11] The feast of Saint Antony the Confessor (Anthony of Padua, OFM), a Sunday. WM, ll. 40–43. The martyrology lists 7, but Raimunda Arrufat (Peire's wife) was actually burned in 1329; see below. Bernard Espinesseria was mentioned by Raimunda Arrufat (Doat 28, fol. 210v). Raimon Lobat was mentioned by Raimunda Arrufat, and his goods were reported seized (Doat 34, fol. 196r [£19 5s.], and Doat 28, fol. 210v). Peire Arrufat was a well-known Beguin, mentioned in many depositions (Manselli, *Spirituali*, 315; Doat 28, fol. 123r, fol. 223v). The accounting of the confiscation of his goods is in Doat 34, fols. 195r and 215r. His goods amounted to some £20 6s., 2d.

[12] The feast of Saints Cosmas and Damian, a Monday. WM, ll. 52–53. The testimony of these four can be found in *Liber sententiarum* 2:1593–1635 (the General Sermon of September 12, 1322). Guilhem Ros is missing from all versions of the Beguin Martyrology.

[13] The vigil of the feast of Saint Mark the Evangelist, a Sunday. WM, ll. 47–49. The accounts for this Sermon are in Doat 34, fols. 219–224r. The Beguin martyrology lists only Bernard de Bosco, Raimon Maistre, and one unknown Beguin. Brother Raimon Maistre was summoned to Avignon in April 1317, and was a member of the convent of

[after June 19, 1323]	Four Beguins: Peire Calvet of Cintegabelle, Raimon
Toulouse	de Brachio (or de Buxo) of Belpech, Peire Morier of
	Belpech, Bernard de Na Jacma (or Germain)[14]

[unknown]	Four Franciscan friars: Frances Aribert, Jacme de
[unknown]	Cesteramnicis, Jannet of Clermont, and Johan
	Bauscii[15]

August 10, 1323	One Franciscan friar, one priest, and one Beguin:
Lodève	Esteve Seret, friar and priest, Bernard Peyrotas,
	priest, and Frances Bastier[16]

| November 19, 1326 | One priest: Bernard Maury of Narbonne[17] |
| Avignon | |

March 1, 1327	Six Beguins and one Beguine: Guilhem Domergue
Carcassonne	Veyrier and his wife Berengaria Aliorus de Sesena,
	Peire de Cursaca, Raimon Esteve from Croux in the
	diocese of Alet, Guilhem Serralier of Lodève, and
	Peire Espere-en-Diu[18]

Narbonne (*BF*, 5:119). Bernard de Bosco was mentioned by Berenguier Jaoul and Bernard Peyrotas (Manselli, *Spirituali*, 316–317). The goods confiscated from him appear in the accounts in Doat 34, fol. 216r.

[14] WM, ll. 54–56 (which reads "*diversis postea temporibus*"). The individuals are all known, and testified for Bernard Gui in March 1321. In September 1322, they had been condemned to the Walls of Pamiers and Toulouse. Their depositions are in *Liber sententiarum* 2:1366–1371, 1299–1311, 1314–1341, and their original sentences are at *Liber sententiarum* 2:1416–1423.

[15] Bernard Malaura of Lodève listed five friars who had all later been condemned and burned. Four of them cannot be found in the Wolfenbüttel martyrology or in any other source. The fifth is Esteve Seret, burned at Lodève (Manselli, *Spirituali*, 313).

[16] The feast of Saint Lawrence, a Wednesday. WM, ll. 28–30. Brother Esteve Seret was mentioned by Bernard Malaura (Manselli, *Spirituali*, 313). Bernard Peyrotas testified before the inquisitor first on November 11, 1321, and then again on July 20, 1322. He was sentenced to be defrocked on July 3, 1323 (Doat 28, fols. 36–37v), but the sentence is incomplete, as the Doat scribe noted. He is also mentioned by Peire Massot (Doat 27, fol. 13r), by Berengaria Estorgua (Doat 28, fol. 195v), and by Amada Orlach (Doat 28, fol. 194r).

[17] The feast of Saint Elizabeth of Hungary, a Wednesday. WM, ll. 50–51. The process is found in Doat 35, fol. 19–47v, edited in Manselli, *Spirituali*, 328–345.

[18] Quadragesima Sunday. WM, ll. 44–47. Only 5 names are mentioned in the Beguin Martyrology. The Sermon's records in Doat 28, fols. 177v–252v, are incomplete, though they also provide two more names of Beguins handed over to the secular arm (Guilhem Serralier and Peire Esperendiu). Berengaria Domergue Veyrier was sentenced to solitary

| November 11, 1328
Carcassonne | One Beguine: Prous Boneta[19] |
| September 10, 1329
Carcassonne | One Beguine: Raimunda Arrufat[20] |

Total:	12 Franciscan friars
	6 secular priests
	68 Beguins
	16 Beguines
	102 Total (plus an unidentified number burned at Agde in 1321)

---

confinement on February 24, 1325 (Doat 28, fols. 153v–157v). It is possible that she died in prison. Raimon Esteve was immured in Carcassonne in July 1322 (*Liber sententiarum* 2:1421), and his culpa is in *Liber sententiarum* 2:1382–1389. Nothing further is known of Aliorus de Sesena or Peire de Cursaca.

[19] The feast of Saint Martin, a Friday. Sentence, Doat 27, fols. 95–96v, edited in Lea, *Inquisition* 3:653–654. She is also mentioned by her sister Alisseta (Doat 27, fols. 26r–30r), her companion Alaraxis (Doat 27, fols. 30r–33r), Ermessendis Grossa (Doat 27, fol. 14v), Sibillia Cazelas (Doat 27, fols. 16r–18v), and briefly by two others (Doat 28, fols. 228r and 230v–231r). Prous Boneta does not appear in the Beguin Martyrology.

[20] A Sunday. Raimunda Arrufat. Sentence, Doat 27, fols. 232v–234r. Raimunda appears in the Beguin Martyrology, but under the wrong date (January 17, 1322).

BIBLIOGRAPHY

ARCHIVAL SOURCES

ADH, Notarial Registers

2E 36 1–8	Notaries of Ganges (1280–1325)
2E 368	J. Holanie (July 7, 1327–April 3, 1328)
2E 369	J. Holanie (March 26, 1333–December 20, 1333)
2E 370	J. Holanie (April 16, 1336–September 7, 1336)
2E 371	J. Holanie (March 26, 1342–October 18, 1342)
2E 372	J. Holanie (March 26, 1343–February 24, 1344)
2E 373	G. Delpech (1333)
2E 374	G. Nogaret (October 10, 1337–November 12, 1342)
2E 375	P. Pena (March 31, 1339–November 22, 1339)
2E 376	J. Laurens (1343–1346)
2E 377	E. Dupie (January 17, 1347–June 23, 1348)

AMM, Notarial Registers

BB1	J. Grimaud (September 7, 1293–March 22, 1294)
BB2	J. Grimaud (April 15, 1301–June 23, 1302)
BB3	J. Laurens (March 24, 1342–April 12, 1343)

AMM, fonds de la Commune Clôture, wills
AMM, Petit Thalamus
AMM, Thalamus de la Commune Clôture
Assisi, Chiesa Nuova MS. 9
Barcelona, Biblioteca de Catalunya, MS. 740
BnF. Collection Doat vols. 27, 28, 34, 35, 51, 52
BnF. Lat. MS. 4224
Florence Laurentiana Plut. sin. 3, carta 181
Herzog-August-Bibliothek, Wolfenbüttel, Helmstedt MS. 1006
London, British Library Additional MS. 4697
Prague, University of Prague IV. B. 15
Vatican Borghesiana MS. 46
Vatican Borghesiana MS. 357

Vatican Borghesiana MS. 358
Vatican. Lat. MS. 4986

PRINTED SOURCES

Archiv für Literatur- und Kirchengeschichte des Mittelalters. Ed. Henri Denifle and F. Ehrle. 7 vols. Berlin, 1885–1900. Reprinted Graz, 1955–1956.

Arnau de Vilanova. *L'"Alia Informatio Beguinorum" d'Arnau de Vilanova.* Ed. Josep Perarnau. Barcelona, 1978.

——. *Arnau de Vilanova: L'obra espiritual.* Ed. Francesco Santi. Valencia, [1987].

——. *Obres Catalanes.* Ed. Joaquin Carreras y Artau and Miguel Batllori. Vol. 1. Barcelona, 1947.

——. *Arnaldi de Villanova Opera medica omnia.* Vol. 3. Ed. M. R. McVaugh. Barcelona, 1985.

Arthur, Ingrid. "*Lo Cavalier armat*, version provençal du *Miles armatus* attribué à Pierre de Jean Olivi." *Studia neophilologica* 31 (1959): 43–64.

Baluze, Étienne. *Vitae Paparum Avenionensium.* Ed. G. Mollat. Paris, 1921.

Benjamin of Tudela. *The Itinerary of Benjamin of Tudela: Travels in the Middle Ages.* Trans. Marcus Nathan Adler. Introductions by Michael A. Signer, Marcus Nathan Adler, A. Asher. [Malibu, CA], 1983.

Bianchi De Vecchi, Paola. "Un opuscolo inedito in lingua d'oc: *Ayssi son las collatios de XII. santz payres ermitas.*" In *Miscellanea di studi romanzi offerta a Giuliano Gasca Queirazza*, 1:23–47. Alessandria, 1988.

——. *Testi ascetici in antico provenzale.* Perugia, 1984.

Bihl, Michael. "Aventures du messager envoyé par les Spirituels de Narbonne et de Béziers au Chapitre Général de Naples en mai 1316." *AFH* 5 (1912): 777–779.

——. "Elenchi Bononienses Fratrum de Poenitentia, 1252–1288." *AFH* 7 (1914): 226–233.

Blanc, A. "Le Livre de comptes de Jacme Olivier." In *Bulletin de la commission archéologique de Narbonne*, vols. 3–8 (1895–1902).

Bonaventure, Saint. *Miracles que Dieus ha mostratz per sant Frances apres la sua fi: Version occitane de la Legenda Maior Sancti Francisci, Miracula de saint Bonaventure.* Ed. Ingrid Arthur. Uppsala, 1992.

——. *Opera Omnia.* 10 vols. Ed. Collegium Sancti Bonaventurae. Quaracchi, 1882–1901.

——. *La Vida del Glorios Sant Frances: Version provençale de la Legenda Maior Sancti Francisci de Saint Bonaventure.* Ed. Ingrid Arthur. Uppsala, 1955.

——. *The Works of Bonaventure.* 5 vols. Trans. José de Vinck. Paterson, NJ, 1966.

Boneta, Prous. "Na Prous Boneta." Trans. David Burr. http://www.history.vt.edu/ Burr/heresy/beguins/Prous.html

Botineau, P., ed. "Les tribulations de Raimond Barrau, O.P. (1295–1338)." *Mélanges d'Archéologie et d'Histoire, École Française de Rome* 76 (1965): 475–528.

Bullaire de l'inquisition française au XIVe siècle et jusqu'à la fin du Grand Schisme. Ed. J.-M. Vidal. Paris, 1913.

Bullarii Franciscani Epitome. Ed. Conrad Eubel. Quaracchi, 1908.

Bullarium Franciscanum, vols. 5–6. Ed. Conrad Eubel. Rome, 1898–1904.

Cartagegia, Oriana, and J. Perarnau. "El Text Sencer de *L'Epistola ad Gerentes Zonam Pelliceam* d'Arnau de Vilanova." *Arxiu de textos catalans antics* 12 (1993): 7–42.

Cartulaire de l'Université de Montpellier. Ed. Alexandre Germain. 2 vols. Montpellier, 1890.

Cartulaire de Maguelone. Ed. J. Rouquette and A. Villemagne. 6 vols. numbered 1–5, 7. Montpellier, 1912–1925.

Cartulaire et archives des communes de l'ancien diocèse et de l'arrondissement administratif de Carcassonne. 6 vols. Ed. M. Mahul. Paris, 1857–1882.

Cenci, Cesare. *Documentazione di vita assisana, 1300–1530*. Grottaferrata, 1974.

Chabás, R. "Inventario de los libros, ropas y demás efectos de Arnaldo de Villa- neuva." *Revista de archivos* II Epoca 9 (1903): 189–203.

Chartularium universitatis parisiensis. Vol. 2. Ed. Henri Denifle. Paris, 1891.

Clareno, Angelo. *Angeli Clareni Opera*, bk. I, *Epistole*. Ed. Lydia Von Auw. Rome, 1980.

———. *A Chronicle or History of the Seven Tribulations of the Order of Brothers Minor*. Trans. David Burr and E. Randolph Daniel. St. Bonaventure, NY, 2005.

———. *The Chronicle or History of the Seven Tribulations of the Order of Friars Minor*. Ed. Mary Bartholomew McDonald and Fr. George Marcil. St. Bonaventure, NY, 1983.

Comptes royaux (1314–1328), vol. 1. Ed. François Maillard. Paris, 1953.

Corpus Iuris Canonici. Ed. Emil Friedberg. 2 vols. Leipzig, 1879–1881.

Coulon, Auguste. *Lettres secrètes et curiales du Pape Jean XXII (1316) relatives à la France*. Paris, 1900.

Dainville, Maurice de, and Marcel Gouron, eds. *Inventaire. Série EE: Fonds de la Commune Clôture, et Affaires Militaires*. Montpellier, 1974.

Delorme, F. M. "Constitutiones provinciae Provinciae." *AFH* 14 (1921): 432–433.

———. "Frère Mathieu de Bouzigues, Confessio Fidei." *Études Franciscaines* 49 (1937): 224–239.

Devic, Claude, and Joseph Vaissète. *Histoire générale de Languedoc*, ed. Auguste Mo- linier. 16 vols. Toulouse, 1872–1904.

Döllinger, Johann Joseph Ignaz von, ed. *Beiträge zur Sektengeschichte des Mittelalters*. 2 vols. Munich, 1890.

Dossat, Yves. "Le plus ancien manuel de l'inquisition méridionale: Le *processus inquisitionis* (1248–1249)." *Bulletin philologique et historique du Comité des travaux historiques et scientifiques* (1948–1949): 33–37.

Douais, Célestin. *La procédure inquisitoriale en Languedoc au quatorzième siècle d'après un procès inédit de l'année 1337*. Paris, 1900.

———. *Documents pour servir à l'histoire de l'inquisition dans le Languedoc*. 2 vols. Paris, 1900.

Durieux, Fidèle. "La Règle des Frères Mineurs et le Testament de saint François d'Assise en langue d'oc du XIVe siècle." *Études Franciscaines*, n.s. 9 (1959): 204–227.

——. "Les Propos du frère Gilles d'Assise en occitan du XIVe siècle." *Annales de l'Institut d'Études Occitanes*, numéro spécial (1965): 58–87.

Duvernoy, Jean. *Registre de Bernard de Caux, Pamiers (1246–47)*. Foix, 1990.

Extrauagantes Iohannis XXII, Monumenta Iuris Canonici, ser. B: *Corpus Collectionum*, vol. 6. Ed. Jacqueline Tarrant. Vatican City, 1983.

Eymerich, Nicholas. *Directorium inquisitorium*. 3 vols. Rome, 1578.

Francis of Assisi: Early Documents 2. Trans. Regis J. Armstrong et al. New York, 2000.

Germain, Alexandre. "Une consultation inquisitoriale au XIVe siècle." *Publications de la Société Archéologique de Montpellier* 4 (1857): 309–344.

——. "Inventaire inédit concernant les archives de l'inquisition de Carcassonne." *Mémoires de la société archéologique de Montpellier* 4, 1st ser. (1855): 287–294, 332–344.

Gratien, R. P. "Instrumentum publicum de quodam nuntio conventus ordinis minorum Narbone ad Capitulum generale congretatum Neapoli in ecclesia St. Laurentii vulnerato." *Études Franciscaines* 27 (1912): 422–426.

Gregory the Great. *Dialogues*. Ed. Adalbert de Vogüé. Vol 3. Paris, 1980.

Gui, Bernard. "Bernard Gui: Inquisitor's Manual." Trans. David Burr http://www.history.vt.edu/Burr/heresy/beguins/Gui_beguins.html

——. *Le livre des sentences de l'inquisiteur Bernard Gui (1308–1323)*. 2 vols. Ed. and trans. Annette Palès-Gobilliard. Paris, 2002.

——. *Manuel de l'Inquisiteur*. Ed. and trans. G. Mollat. 2 vols. Paris, 1926–27.

Harris, M. Roy. *The Occitan Translations of John XII and XIII–XVII from a Fourteenth-Century Franciscan Codex (Assisi, Chiesa Nuova MS. 9)*. Philadelphia, 1985.

L'inquisiteur Geoffroy d'Ablis et les cathares du comté de Foix (1308–1309). Ed. and trans. Annette Palès-Gobilliard. Paris, 1984.

Lewis, Warren. "Peter John Olivi: Prophet of the Year 2000." Ph.D. diss., Tübingen University, 1972.

Liber instrumentorum memorialium: Cartulaire des Guillems de Montpellier. Ed. la Société Archéologique de Montpellier. Montpellier, 1884–1886.

The Life of Saint Douceline, Beguine of Provence. Trans. Kathleen Garay and Madeleine Jeay. Cambridge, 2001.

Limborch, Philipp van. *Historia inquisitionis, cui subjungitur Liber sententiarum inquisitionis Tholosanae ab anno Christi MCCCVI ad annum MCCCXXIII*. Amsterdam, 1692.

Mansi, Giovanni. *Stephani Baluzii Tutelensis Miscellanea*. 4 vols. Paris, 1761–1764.

Martène, E., and U. Durand, eds. *Thesaurus novus anecdotorum*. 5 vols. Paris, 1717.

May, W. H. "The Confession of Prous Boneta, Heretic and Heresiarch." In *Essays in Medieval Life and Thought*, ed. A. P. Evans, 3–30. New York, 1955.

Meerseman, G. G. *Dossier de l'ordre de la pénitence au XIIIe siècle*, 2nd edition. Fribourg, Switzerland, 1982.

Michael Monachus. "Inquisitoris sententia contra combustos in Massilia." *Oliviana* 2 (2006). http://www.oliviana.org/document36.html.

Oliger, Livarius. "*Fr. Bertrandi de Turre processus contra spirituales Aquitaniae* (1315) *et Card. Iacobi de Columna litterae defensoriae spiritualium Provinciae* (1316)." *AFH* 16 (1923): 323–355.

Olivi, Peter. *Peter Olivi's Rule Commentary.* Ed. David Flood. Wiesbaden, 1972.

———. *Pietro di Giovanni Olivi: Scritti scelti.* Ed. Paolo Vian. Rome, 1989.

Nicolaus Minorita: Chronica. Ed. Gedéon Gál and David Flood. St. Bonaventure, NY, 1996.

Perarnau, Josep. "L'*Ars catholicae philosophiae* (primera redacció de la *philosophia catholica et divina*) d'Arnau de Vilanova." *Arxiu de textos catalans antics* 10 (1991): 7–223.

———. "Documents de tema inquisitorial del bisbe de Barcelona, Fra Ferrer d'Abella (1334–1344)." *Revista Catalana de Teologia* 5 (1980): 443–478.

Processus Bernardi Delitiosi: The Trial of Fr. Bernard Délicieux, 3 September–8 December 1319. Ed. Alan Friedlander. Philadelphia, 1996.

Pryor, John. *Business Contracts of Medieval Provence: Selected Notulae from the Cartulary of Giraud Amalric of Marseilles, 1248.* Toronto, 1981.

Puig i Oliver, Jaume de. "Notes sobre el manuscript del Directorium Inquisitorum de Nicolau Eimeric conservat a la Biblioteca de l'Éscorial (ms. N. I. 18)," *Arxiu de textos catalans antics* 19 (2000): 538–539.

Le Registre d'inquisition de Jacques Fournier (1318–1325). 3 vols. Ed. Jean Duvernoy. Toulouse, 1965.

Renart, Jean. *L'Escoufle: Roman d'aventure.* Ed. Franklin Sweetser. Geneva, 1974.

Rinaldi, Odorico. *Annales ecclesiastici.* 37 vols. Bar-le-Duc, 1864–1883.

Roqueta, J. "Las Admonicios de St. Francés, text occitan del segle XIV, trach del manuscrit de la Chiesa Nuova d'Assis." *Revue des langues romanes* 77 (1967): 85–123.

Salimbene de Adam. *The Chronicle of Salimbene de Adam.* Trans. Joseph L. Baird et al. Binghamton, NY, 1986.

Société Archéologique de Montpellier, ed. *Thalamus parvus: Le petit thalamus de Montpellier.* Ed. la Montpellier, 1840.

Tardif, A. "Document pour l'histoire du *processus per inquisitionem* et de *l'inquisitio heretice pravitatis.*" *Nouvelle revue historique de droit francais et étranger* 7 (1883): 669–78.

Terré, Gui. *Summa de haeresibus.* Paris, 1528.

Terré, Gui, Bertrand de la Tour, Guillaume de Laudun, Nicolas de Saint-Just, Laurentius Anglicus, Simon Anglicus, Arnaud Royard et Pierre de la Palud. "Littera magistrorum." *Oliviana* 2 (2006). http://www.oliviana.org/document179.html

Tocco, Felice. *Studii Francescani.* Naples, 1909.

Vidal, J.-M. "Procès d'inquisition contre Adhémar de Mosset, noble roussillonais, inculpé de béguinisme (1332–1334)." *Revue d'histoire de l'église de France* 1 (1910): 555–589, 682–699, 711–724.

Wadding, L. *Annales minorum seu trium ordinum a S. Francisco institutorum.*
Ed. J. M. Fonseca. Vol. 6. Quaracchi, 1931.

Wakefield, Walter, and Austin P. Evans. *Heresies of the High Middle Ages.* New York,
1991.

Wolfkiel, Kathryn Betts. "*The Life of the Blessed Saint Doucelina* (d. 1274): An Edition and Translation with Commentary." Ph.D. diss., Northwestern University,
1993.

Zorzi, Diego. "Testi inediti francescani in lingua provenzale." *Miscellanea del Centro
di Studi Medievali* 58 (Milan, 1956): 249–324.

SECONDARY SOURCES

Abels R., and E. Harrison. "The Participation of Women in Languedocian Catharism." *Mediaeval Studies* 41 (1979): 215–251.

Aguiló i Fuster, Marian. *Diccionari Aguiló.* Ed. Pompeu Fabra and Manuel de Montoliu. Barcelona, 1915.

Alor-Treboutte, Josiane, and Alexis Lucchesi. *Randonnées dans le Massif de la Saint
Baume.* Aix-en-Provence, 1997.

Ames, Christine Caldwell. "Does Inquisition Belong to Religious History?" *American Historical Review* 110 (2005): 11–37.

Anderson, Wendy Love. "Free Spirits, Presumptuous Women, and False Prophets:
The Discernment of Spirits in the Late Middle Ages." Ph.D. diss., University of
Chicago, 2002.

Arnold, John. "The Historian as Inquisitor: The Ethics of Interrogating Subaltern
Voices." *Rethinking History* 2 (1998): 379–386.

———. *Inquisition and Power: Catharism and the Confessing Subject in Medieval
Languedoc.* Philadelphia, 2001.

———. "Inquisition, Catharism, and the Confessing Subject; The Discourse of Heresy in Languedoc, c. 1200–c.1330." Ph.D. diss., University of York, 1996.

———. "Inquisition, Texts, and Discourse." In *Texts and the Repression of Medieval
Heresy*, ed. Caterina Bruschi and Peter Biller, 63–80. York, 2003.

Audisio, Gabriel. *The Waldensian Dissent: Persecution and Survival, c. 1170–1570.*
Trans. Claire Davison. Cambridge, England, 1999.

Avril, J. T. *Dictionnaire Provençal-Français.* Apt, 1839.

Backman, Clifford. "Arnau de Vilanova and the Franciscan Spirituals in Sicily."
Franciscan Studies 50 (1990): 3–29.

Baedeker, Karl. *Southern France including Corsica*, sixth edition. Leipzig, 1914.

Barber, Malcolm. *The Cathars: Dualist Heretics in Languedoc in the High Middle Ages.*
Harrow, England, 2001.

Batllori, M. "La documentacion de Marsella sobre Arnau de Vilanova y Joan Blasi."
Analecta Sacra Tarraconensia 21 (1949): 75–119.

Baumel, Jean. *Histoire d'une seigneurie du Midi de la France*. 3 vols. Montpellier, 1969–1973.

Bazan, Bernardo, et al. *Les questions disputées et les questions quodlibétiques dans les facultés de théologie, de droit et de médecine*. Turnhout, Belgium, 1985.

Benad, Matthias. *Domus und Religion in Montaillou*. Tübingen, 1990.

Berlioz, Jacques. *'Tuez-les tous, Dieu reconnaîtra les siens': La croisade contre les Albigeois vue par Césaire de Heisterbach*. Portet-sur-Garonne, 1994.

Bernard, Suzanne. *La Beguine*. Paris, 2000.

Bigaroni, M. "Catalogo dei manoscritti della Biblioteca storico-francescana di Chiesa Nuova di Assisi." *Atti dell'Accademia Properziana del Subasio*, ser. 6, n. 1 (Assisi, 1978): 9–43.

Biget, Jean-Louis. "Autour de Bernard Délicieux: Franciscanisme et société en Languedoc entre 1295 et 1330." *Revue d'histoire de l'église de France* 70 (1984): 75–93.

——. "Culte et rayonnement de Pierre Déjean-Olieu en Languedoc au début du XIVe siècle." In *PdJO*, 276–308. Paris, 1999.

Bignami-Odier, Jeanne. "Jean de Roquetaillade (de Rupescissa), théologien, polémiste, alchimiste." *Hist. Litt.* 41 (1981): 75–284.

Boureau, Alain, and Sylvain Piron, eds. *Pierre de Jean Olivi (1248–1298): Pensée scolastique, dissidence spirituelle et société*. Paris, 1999.

Boyle, Leonard E. "Montaillou Revisited: Mentalité and Methodology." In *Pathways to Medieval Peasants*, ed. J. A. Raftis, 119–140. Papers in Mediaeval Studies 2. Toronto, 1981.

Brenon, Anne. *Les femmes cathares*. Paris, 1992.

——. *Le vrai visage du catharisme*. Loubatières, [1989].

Bruschi, Caterina. "'Magna diligentia est habenda per inquisitorem': Precautions before Reading Doat 21–26." In *Texts and the Repression of Medieval Heresy*, ed. Caterina Bruschi and Peter Biller, 81–110. York, 2003.

Burnham, Louisa A. "Les Franciscains Spirituels et les Béguins du Midi." In *Le pays cathare: Les religions médiévales et leurs expressions méridionales*, ed. Jacques Berlioz, 147–160. Paris, 2000.

——. "A Prosopography of the Beguins and Spiritual Friars of Languedoc." *Oliviana* 2 (2006). http://www.oliviana.org/document37.html

——. "Reliques et résistance chez les Béguins de Languedoc." *Annales du Midi* 108 (2006): 352–368.

——. "So Great a Light, So Great a Smoke: The Heresy and Resistance of the Beguins of Languedoc (1318–1330)." Ph.D. diss., Northwestern University, 2000.

——. "The Visionary Authority of Na Prous Boneta." In *PdJO*, 319–339. Paris, 1999.

Burr, David. "Did the Beguins Understand Olivi?" In *PdJO*, 309–318. Paris, 1999 .

——. "Na Prous Boneta and Olivi." *Collectanea Franciscana* 67 (1997): 477–500.

———. *Olivi and Franciscan Poverty: The Origins of the Usus Pauper Controversy.* Philadelphia, 1989.

———. "Olivi, Apocalyptic Expectation, and Visionary Experience." *Traditio* 41 (1985): 273–288.

———. *Olivi's Peaceable Kingdom.* Philadelphia, 1993.

———. "Olivi, Prous and the Separation of Apocalypse from Eschatology." In *That Others May Know and Love: Essays in Honor of Zachary Hayes, OFM; Franciscan, Educator, Scholar,* ed. M. Cusato and F. E. Coughlin, 285–304. St. Bonaventure, NY, 1997.

———. *The Persecution of Peter Olivi.* Philadelphia, 1976.

———. "Raymond Déjean, Franciscan Renegade." *Franciscan Studies* 57 (1999): 57–78.

———. *The Spiritual Franciscans: From Protest to Persecution in the Century after Saint Francis.* University Park, PA, 2003.

Bylina, Stanislaw. "*Martires Gloriosi:* Le martyre et la souffrance chez les contesteurs franciscains en Languedoc au XIVe siècle." *Les Cahiers de Varsovie* 14 (1988): 73–84.

Bynum, Caroline Walker. *Holy Feast, Holy Fast: The Religious Significance of Food to Medieval Women.* Berkeley, 1987.

———. *Jesus as Mother: Studies in the Spirituality of the High Middle Ages.* Berkeley, 1982.

Caciola, Nancy. *Discerning Spirits: Divine and Demonic Possession in the Middle Ages.* Ithaca, 2003.

Caille, Jacqueline. "L'élan urbain en Languedoc du XIe au XIVe siècle: L'exemple de Narbonne et de Montpellier." *Archéologie du midi médiéval* 13 (1995): 79–90.

———. *Hôpitaux et charité publique à Narbonne au Moyen Age.* Toulouse, 1978.

Campion, Sarah. *Father: A Portrait of G. G. Coulton at Home.* London, 1948.

Cazenave, Annie. "Joachinisme et pauvreté chez les béguins du Languedoc." In *Conformité et déviances au moyen âge.* Les cahiers du CRISIMA 2, 77–98. Montpellier, 1995.

Cheyette, Fredric. *Ermengard of Narbonne and the World of the Troubadours.* Ithaca, 2001.

Cohn, Norman. *Europe's Inner Demons: An Enquiry Inspired by the Great Witch-Hunt.* New York, 1975.

Coulet, Noël. "Un moine languedocien accusé de béguinisme." *CF* 19 (1984): 365–389.

Coulton, G. G. *Catholic Truth and Historical Truth.* Cairo, [ca. 1906].

———. "The Failure of the Friars." In *Ten Medieval Studies,* 166–188. Cambridge, 1930.

———. *Five Centuries of Religion.* Cambridge, 1923–1950.

———. *From St. Francis to Dante: A Translation of All That Is of Primary Interest in the Chronicle of the Franciscan Salimbene.* London, 1906.

———. *Inquisition and Liberty.* London, 1938.

———. *Medieval Panorama: The English Scene from Conquest to Reformation.* New York, 1938.

———. *Romanism and Truth.* 2 vols. London, 1930.

d'Alatri, M., ed. *I Frati Penitenti di san Francesco nella società del Due e Trecento.* Rome, 1977.

———, ed. *Il movimento francescano della Penitenza nella società medioevale.* Rome, 1980.

———. "Penitenti francescani di Romagna." *Aetas poenitentialis: L'antico Ordine francescano della penitenza.* Rome, 1993. First published in *Il movimento francescano della penitenza nella società medioevale (Atti del 30 convegno di studi francescani. Padova, 25–26–27 settembre 1979),* ed. M. d'Alatri, 323–362. Rome, 1980.

d'Alós, R. "De la marmessoria d'Arnau de Vilanova." In *Miscellania Prat de la Riba,* 289–306. Barcelona, 1923.

d'Alverny, Marie-Thérèse. "Un adversaire de Saint Thomas: Petrus Iohannis Olivi." In *St. Thomas Aquinas 1274–1974: Commemorative Studies 2,* 179–218. Toronto, 1974.

Desbonnets, Théophile. "La lettre à tous les fidèles de François d'Assise." In *I Frati Minori e il Terzo ordine, problemi e discussioni storiografiche, Convegni del centro di studi sulla spiritualità medievale (17–20 ottobre 1982),* 51–76. Todi, 1985.

Dictionnaire des lettres françaises: Le môyen âge. Paris, 1992.

Doehaerd, Renée. *Les relations commerciales entre Gênes, la Belgique et l'Outremont d'après les archives notariales génoises aux XIIIe et XIVe siècles.* 3 vols. Brussels, 1941.

Dondaine, Antoine. "Le Manuel de l'Inquisiteur (1230–1330)." Archivum Fratrum Praedicatorum 17 (1947): 85–194.

Dossat, Yves. *Les crises de l'inquisition toulousaine au XIIIe siècle (1233–1273).* Bordeaux, 1959.

Douie, Decima. *The Nature and Effect of the Heresy of the Fraticelli.* Manchester, England, 1932.

Duffy, Eamon. "The Parish, Piety, and Patronage in Late Medieval East Anglia: The Evidence of Rood Screens." In *The Parish in English Life, 1400–1600,* ed. Katherine L. French, Gary G. Gibbs, and Beat A. Kümin, 133–162. Manchester, 1997.

Dulieu, Louis. *La médecine à Montpellier.* Vol. 1. Avignon, 1975.

Durieux, Fidèle. "Un manuscrit occitan des spirituels de Narbonne au début du XIVe siècle: Essai d'interprétation franciscaine." *CF* 10 (1975): 231–242.

Duvernoy, Jean. "Une hérésie en Bas-Languedoc: L'affaire des Béguins (1299–1329." *Études sur l'Hérault* 4, 2nd ser. (1988): 85–90.

Eco, Umberto. *The Name of the Rose.* Trans. William Weaver. New York, 1983.

———. *Postscript to the Name of the Rose.* Trans. William Weaver. San Diego, 1984.

Elliott, Dyan. *Proving Woman: Female Spirituality and Inquisitional Culture in the Later Middle Ages.* Princeton, 2004.

Emery, Richard W. *The Friars in Medieval France: A Catalogue of French Mendicant Convents, 1200–1550.* New York, 1962.

———. *Heresy and Inquisition in Narbonne.* New York, 1941.

Eubel, Conrad, ed. *Hierarchia catholica medii aevi*, vol. 1. Regensburg, 1913.

Fabre de Morlhon, Jacques. *Le Montpellier des Guilhem et des rois d'Aragon*. Montpellier, 1967.

——. "Le Montpellier médiéval." Map drawn by Lucien Albaret (n.d.).

Fabre, Ghislaine, and Thierry Lochard. *Montpellier: La ville médiévale*. Paris, 1992.

Favier, Jean. *Philippe le Bel*. Paris, 1978.

Fliche, Augustin. "La vie religieuse à Montpellier sous le pontificat d'Innocent III (1198–1216)." In *Mélanges d'Histoire du Moyen Âge dédiés à la mémoire de Louis Halphen*, 217–224. Paris, 1951.

Flood, David. "Poverty as Virtue, Poverty as Warning, and Peter of John Olivi." In *PdJO*, 157–172. Paris, 1999

Foy, Danièle. *Le verre médiéval et son artisanat en France méditerranéenne*. Paris, 1988.

Friedlander, Alan. *The Hammer of the Inquisitors: Brother Bernard Délicieux and the Struggle against the Inquisition in Fourteenth-Century France*. Leiden, 2000.

Gatti, Marcella. *Le Carceri di San Francesco del Subasio*. Assisi, 1969.

Geary, Patrick. *Furta Sacra: Thefts of Relics in the Central Middle Ages*. Rev. ed. Princeton, 1990.

Germer-Durand, M. E. *Dictionnaire topographique du département du Gard*. Paris, 1868.

Ginzburg, Carlo. "The Inquisitor as Anthropologist." In his *Clues, Myths, and the Historical Method*, trans. John and Anne C. Tedeschi, 156–164. Baltimore, 1989.

Giono, Jean. *The Horseman on the Roof*. Trans. Jonathan Griffin. San Francisco, 1982.

Given, James. "The Béguins in Bernard Gui's *Liber sententiarum*." In *Texts and the Repression of Medieval Heresy*, ed. Caterina Bruschi and Peter Biller, 147–162. York, 2003.

——. "Les inquisiteurs de Languedoc et leurs ennemis." Paper given at the École des Hautes Études en Sciences Sociales, Paris, March 1998.

——. *Inquisition and Medieval Society: Power, Discipline, and Resistance in Languedoc*. Ithaca, 1997.

——. "The Inquisitors of Languedoc and the Medieval Technology of Power." *American Historical Review* 94 (1989): 336–359.

Godefroy, Frédéric. *Lexique de l'Ancien Français*. New ed. Paris, 1994.

Golubovich, Girolamo. *Biblioteca bio-bibliografica della Terra Santa e dell'Oriente francescano*. Ser. 1, vol. 2. Quaracchi, 1913.

Gouron, André. *La réglementation des métiers en Languedoc au Moyen Age*. Geneva, 1958.

Grasset-Morel. *Montpellier, ses sixains, ses îles et ses rues*. Montpellier, 1908. Reprinted Montpellier, 1989.

Gratien de Paris. *Histoire de la fondation et de l'évolution de l'Ordre des Frères Mineurs au XIIIe siècle*. Paris, 1928.

Gray, Patience. *Honey from a Weed.* New York, 1986.

Grundmann, Herbert. *Religious Movements of the Middle Ages: The Historical Links between Heresy, the Mendicant Orders, and the Women's Religious Movement in the Twelfth and Thirteenth Century, with the Historical Foundations of German Mysticism.* Trans. Steven Rowan. Notre Dame, IN, 1995.

Guenée, Bernard. *Between Church and State: The Lives of Four French Prelates in the Late Middle Ages.* Trans. Arthur Goldhammer. Chicago, 1991.

Guide Bleu. *Midi-Pyrénées.* Paris, 1989.

Guiraud, Louise. "Recherches topographiques sur Montpellier au Moyen Âge." *Mémoires de la Société Archéologique de Montpellier* 1, 2nd ser. (1899).

Head, Thomas. "Saints, Heretics, and Fire: Finding Meaning through the Ordeal." In *Monks and Nuns, Saints and Outcasts: Religious Expression and Social Meaning in the Middle Ages,* ed. Barbara Rosenwein and Sharon Farmer, 220–238. Ithaca, 2000.

Heinemann, Otto Von. *Kataloge der Herzog-August Bibliothek Wolfenbüttel, Die Helmstedter Handschriften,* vol. 3. Frankfurt am Main, 1965.

Herrmann-Mascard, Nicole. *Les reliques des saints: Formation coutumière d'un droit.* Paris, 1975.

Heysse. "Descriptio codicis bibliothecae Laurentianae Florentinae, S. Crucis, plut. 31 sin. cod. 3." *AFH* 11 (1918): 251–269.

Hilaire, Jean. *Le régime des biens entre époux dans la région de Montpellier du début du XIIIe siècle à la fin du XVIe siècle.* Montpellier, 1957.

Hollywood, Amy. *The Soul as Virgin Wife: Mechtild of Magdeburg, Marguerite Porete, and Meister Eckhart.* Notre Dame, IN, 1995.

Iancu, Carol, ed. *Les juifs à Montpellier et dans le Languedoc à l'époque médiévale.* Montpellier, 1988.

Iancu-Agou, Danièle. "Topographie des quartiers juifs en Provence médiévale." *Revue des études juives* 133 (1974): 11–156.

Jansen, Katherine Ludwig. *The Making of the Magdalen: Preaching and Popular Devotion in the Later Middle Ages.* Princeton, 2000.

Jantzen, Grace. *Power, Gender, and Christian Mysticism.* Cambridge, 1995.

Kelly, Samantha. *The New Solomon: Robert of Naples (1309–1343) and Fourteenth-Century Kingship.* Leiden, 2003.

——. "Robert of Naples (1309–1343) and the Spiritual Franciscans." *Cristianesimo nella storia* 20 (1999): 41–80.

——. "A Second Solomon: The Theory and Practice of Kingship at the Court of Robert of Naples (1309–1343)." Ph.D. diss., Northwestern University, 1998.

Kieckhefer, Richard. "The Office of Inquisition and Medieval Heresy: The Transition from Personal to Institutional Jurisdiction." *Journal of Ecclesiastical History* 46 (1995): 36–61.

——. *The Repression of Heresy in Medieval Germany.* Philadelphia, 1979.

Kleinberg, Aviad. *Prophets in Their Own Country.* Chicago, 1992.

——. "Proving Sanctity: Selection and Authentication of Saints in the Later Middle Ages." *Viator* 20 (1989): 183–205.

Lambert, Malcolm. *The Cathars.* Oxford, 1998.

——. "The Franciscan Crisis under John XXII." *Franciscan Studies* 32 (1972): 123–143.

——. *Franciscan Poverty.* London, 1961.

——. *Medieval Heresy: Popular Movements from the Gregorian Reform to the Reformation.* 2nd ed. Oxford, 1992.

Lambert, Nicole. "La Seube: Témoin de l'art du verre en France méridionale du bas-empire à la fin du moyen-âge." *Journal of Glass Studies* 14 (1972): 77–116.

Lansing, Carol. *Power and Purity: Cathar Heresy in Medieval Italy.* New York, 1998.

Larguier, Gilbert. "Autour de Pierre de Jean Olivi. Narbonne et le Narbonnais, fin XIIIe–début XIVe siècle." In *PdJO*, 254–276. Paris, 1999.

Lea, Henry Charles. *A History of the Inquisition of the Middle Ages.* 3 vols. New York, 1887.

Leff, Gordon. *Heresy in the Later Middle Ages: The Relation of Heterodoxy to Dissent, c. 1250–c. 1450.* 2 vols. Manchester, 1967. Reprinted in 1 vol., 1999.

Lerner, Robert E. "An 'Angel of Philadelphia' in the Reign of Philip the Fair: The Case of Guiard of Cressonessart." In *Order and Innovation in the Middle Ages: Essays in Honor of Joseph R. Strayer,* ed. William C. Jordan et al., 343–364. Princeton, 1976.

——. "Ecstatic Dissent." *Speculum* 67 (1992): 33–57.

——. *The Feast of Saint Abraham: Medieval Millenarians and the Jews.* Philadelphia, 2001.

——. *The Heresy of the Free Spirit in the Later Middle Ages.* Berkeley, 1972.

——. "Historical Introduction." In Johannes de Rupescissa, *Liber secretorum eventuum,* ed. Christine Morerod-Fattebert, 13–85. Fribourg, Switzerland, 1994.

——. "New Evidence for the Condemnation of Meister Eckhart." *Speculum* 72 (1997): 347–366.

——. "On the Origins of the Earliest Latin Pope Prophecies: A Reconsideration." In *Fälschungen im Mittelalter.* Monumenta Germaniae historica, Schriften, 33, vol. 5, 611–635. Hannover, 1988.

——. "The Pope and the Doctor." *Yale Review* 78 (1988–1989): 62–79.

——. "Recent Work on the Origins of the 'Genus Nequam' Prophecies." *Florensia* 7 (1993): 121–138.

——. "Ursprung, Verbreitung und Ausstrahlung der Pabstprophetien des Mittelalters." In Robert Lerner and Robert Moynihan, *Weissagungen über die Päbste. Vat. Ross. 374,* 2 vols., 1:11–75. Stuttgart, 1985.

——. "Writing and Resistance among Beguins of Languedoc and Catalonia." In *Heresy and Literacy (1000–1530),* ed. Peter Biller and Anne Hudson, 186–204. Cambridge, England, 1994.

Lerner, Robert E., Sylvain Piron, and Gian Luca Potestà. "Notes bibliographiques (2002–2003)." *Oliviana* 1 (2003). http://www.oliviana.org/document23.html.

Le Roy Ladurie, Emmanuel. *Montaillou: The Promised Land of Error.* Trans. and abridged by Barbara Bray. New York, 1978.

———. *Montaillou: Village occitan de 1294–1324.* Paris, 1975.

Lewis, Archibald. "The Development of Town Government." *Speculum* 22 (1947): 51–67.

Lewis, Warren. "Peter John Olivi, Author of the *Lectura super Apocalipsim:* Was He Heretical?" In *PdJO*, 135–156. Paris, 1999.

Maier, Anneliese. "Annotazioni autografe di Giovanni XXII in codici Vaticani." *Rivista di storia della chiesa in Italia* 6 (1952): 317–332.

Manselli, Raoul. "Opuscules spirituels de Pierre Jean Olivi et la piété des béguins de langue d'oc." *CF* 11 (1976): 187–201.

———. *Spirituali e beghini in Provenza.* Rome, 1959.

———. *Spirituels et béguins du Midi.* Trans. Jean Duvernoy. Toulouse, 1989.

Martin, John. *Venice's Hidden Enemies: Italian Heretics in a Renaissance City.* Berkeley, 1993.

McVaugh, Michael. *Medicine before the Plague: Practitioners and Their Patients in the Crown of Aragon, 1285–1345.* Cambridge, 1993.

Mollat, G. "L'élection du pape Jean XXII." *Revue d'histoire de l'église de France* 1 (1910): 34–49, 147–166.

———. *The Popes at Avignon (1305–1378).* Edinburgh, 1963.

Moorman, John. *A History of the Franciscan Order from Its Origins to the Year 1517.* Oxford, 1968.

———. *The Sources for the Life of S. Francis.* Manchester, 1940.

Mosheim, Johann Lorenz. *De Beghardis et Beguinabus Commentarius.* Leipzig, 1790.

Muir, Edward, and Guido Ruggiero, eds. *History from Crime.* Trans. Corrada Biazzo Curry, Margaret A. Gallucci, and Mary M. Gallucci. Baltimore, 1994.

Müller, Daniela. "Les Béguines." *Hérésis* 13–14 (1989): 351–389.

Mundy, John. *Men and Women at Toulouse in the Age of the Cathars.* Toronto, 1990.

Newman, Barbara. *From Virile Woman to WomanChrist: Studies in Medieval Religion and Literature.* Philadelphia, 1995.

Nickson, M. A. E. "Locke and the Inquisition of Toulouse." *British Museum Quarterly* 36 (1971–1972): 83–92.

Nougaret, Jean. "La verrerie à Montpellier (XIVe–XVIe siècle): Etat de la question." *Hommage à Jean Combes (1903–1989), Etudes languedociennes, Mémoires de la Société Archéologique de Montpellier* 19, 2nd ser. (1991): 144–154.

Orczy, Baroness Emmuska. *The Scarlet Pimpernel.* New York, 1905.

O'Shea, Stephen. *The Perfect Heresy: The Revolutionary Life and Death of the Medieval Cathars.* New York, 2000.

Otis, Leah Lydia, *Prostitution in Medieval Society: The History of an Urban Institution in Languedoc.* Chicago, 1985.

Papka, Claudia Rattazzi. "Fictions of Judgment: The Apocalyptic 'I' in the Fourteenth Century." Ph.D. diss., Columbia University, 1996.

Pasztor, Edith, "La '*Supra montem*' e la cancelleria pontificia al tempo di Niccolò IV." In *La "Supra montem" di Niccolo IV (1289): Genesi e diffusione di una regola*, ed. Raffaele Pazzelli and L. Temperini, 65–83, appendix, 84–90. Rome, 1988.

Patschovsky, Alexander. "Heresy and Society: On the Political Function of Heresy in the Medieval World." In *Texts and the Repression of Medieval Heresy*, ed. Caterina Bruschi and Peter Biller, 23–44. York, 2003.

——. "Strassburger Beginenverfolgungen im 14. Jahrhundert." *Deutsches Archiv für Erforschung des Mittelalters* 30 (1974): 56–198.

——. "Zwei Rechtsgutachten zum Inquisitionsprozeß gegen den Brünner Goldschmied Heynuß Lugner." In *Quellen zur Böhmischen Inquisition im 14. Jahrhundert*, 87–110. Weimar, 1979.

Pazzelli, Raffaele. *Saint Francis and the Third Order: The Franciscan and pre-Franciscan Penitential Movement.* Trans. from the Italian. Chicago, 1989.

Pazzelli, Raffaele, and L. Temperini, eds. *Prime manifestazioni di vita comunitaria maschile e femminiles nel movimento francescano della Penitenza (1215–1447).* Rome, 1982.

——, eds. *La 'Supra montem' di Niccolò IV (1289): Genesi e diffusione di una regola.* Rome, 1988.

Péano, Pierre. "Les béguins du Languedoc ou la crise du T.O.F. dans la France méridionale (XIII–XIVe siècles)." In *I Frati penitenti di San Francesco nella società del due e trecento*, ed. M. d'Alatri, 139–159. Rome, 1977.

——. "Manifestations de la vie en commun parmi les tertiaires franciscains de la France méridionale." In *Prime manifestazioni di vita comunitaria maschile e femminile nel movimento francescano della Penitenza (1215–1447)*, ed. R. Pazzelli and L. Temperini, 113–131. Rome, 1982.

——. "Ministres provinciaux de Provence et les Spirituels." *CF* 10 (1975): 41–65.

——. "Les 'Pauvres frères de la penitence' ou du 'tiers-ordre du bienheureux François' en France Méridionale au XIIIe siècle." In *L'Ordine della penitenza di San Francesco d'Assisi nel secolo XIII*, ed. O. Schmucki, 211–217. Rome, 1973.

——. "Le tiers-ordre franciscain séculier en France." In *Il Movimento francescano della Penitenza nella società medioevale*, ed. M. d'Alatri, 145–158. Rome, 1980.

Pegg, Mark Gregory. *The Corruption of Angels: The Great Inquisition of 1245–1246.* Princeton, 2001.

——. "The Corruption of Angels: Inquisitors and Heretics in Thirteenth-Century Europe." Ph.D. diss., Princeton University, 1997.

——. "Questions about Questions: Toulouse 609 and the Great Inquisition of 1245–6." In *Texts and the Repression of Medieval Heresy*, ed. Caterina Bruschi and Peter Biller, 111–126. York, 2003.

Perarnau, Josep. "Aportació al tema de les traduccions bíbliques catalanes medievals." *Revista Catalana de Teologia* 3 (1978): 17–98.

Peters, Edward. "Prison before the Prison: The Ancient and Medieval Worlds." In *The Oxford History of the Prison*, ed. Norval Morris and David J. Rothman, 28–99. New York, 1995.

Petroff, Elizabeth Avilda. *Medieval Women's Visionary Literature*. New York, 1986.

Piron, Sylvain. "Un cahier de travail de l'inquisiteur Jean de Beaune." *Oliviana* 2 (2006). http://www.oliviana.org/document26.html

——. "La critique de l'Église chez les Spirituels languedociens." *CF* 38 (2003): 77–109.

——. "Marchands et confesseurs. Le *Traité des contrats* d'Olivi dans son contexte (Narbonne, fin XIIIe–début XIVe siècle)." In Congrès des médiévistes de l'enseignement supérieur, *L'argent au Moyen Âge*, 289–308. Paris, 1998.

——. "Michael Monachus. Inquisitoris sententia contra combustos in Massilia." *Oliviana* 2 (2006). http://www.oliviana.org/document33.html

——. "Parcours d'un intellectuel franciscain. D'une théologie vers une pensée sociale: L'oeuvre de Pierre de Jean Olivi (ca. 1248–1298) et son traité *De contractibus*." Ph.D. diss., L'École des hautes études en sciences sociales, Paris, 1999.

Porter, Roy, and G. S. Rousseau. *Gout: The Patrician Malady*. New Haven, 1998.

Potestà, Gian Luca. *Angelo Clareno dai poveri eremiti ai fraticelli*. Rome, 1990.

——. *Storia ed escatologia in Ubertino da Casale*. Milan, 1980.

Pou y Marti, José M. *Visionarios, Beguinos y Fraticelos Catalanes (Siglos XIII–XV)*. Rev. ed. Madrid, 1991.

Pryds, Darleen. "Proclaiming Sanctity through Proscribed Practices: The Case of Rose of Viterbo." In *Women Preachers and Prophets through Two Millennia of Christianity*, ed. Pamela Walker and Beverly Mayne Kienzle, 159–172. Berkeley, 1998.

Rashdall, Hastings. *The Universities of Europe in the Middle Ages*. New ed. 2 vols. Ed. F. M. Powicke and A. B. Embden. London, 1964.

Ratzinger, Joseph. *The Theology of History in St. Bonaventure*. Trans. from the German by Zachary Hayes. Chicago, 1971.

Reeves, Marjorie. *The Influence of Prophecy in the Later Middle Ages: A Study in Joachimism*. Rev. ed. South Bend, IN, 1993.

Reinmann, Gerald Joseph. *The Third Order Secular of St. Francis*. Washington, DC, 1928.

Reyerson, Kathryn. "The Adolescent Apprentice/Worker in Medieval Montpellier." *Journal of Family History* 17 (1992): 353–370.

——. *Business, Banking, and Finance in Medieval Montpellier*. Toronto, 1985.

——. "Changes in Testamentary Practice at Montpellier on the Eve of the Black Death." *Church History* 47 (1978): 253–269.

——. "Commerce and Society in Montpellier: 1250–1350." 2 vols. Ph.D. diss., Yale University, 1974.

——. "Land, Houses, and Real Estate Investment in Montpellier: A Study of the Notarial Property Transactions, 1293–1348." *Studies in Medieval and Renaissance History* 6 (1983): 39–112.

———. "Lucchese in Montpellier in the Era of Castruccio Castracani: The Mintmasters' Penetration of Languedocian Commerce and Finance." *Actum Luce, Rivista di Studi Lucchesi* 13–14 (1984–1985): 203–215.

———. "Medieval Silks in Montpellier: The Silk Market, ca. 1250–ca. 1350." *Journal of European Economic History* 11 (1982): 117–140.

———. "Patterns of Population Attraction and Mobility: The Case of Montpellier, 1293–1348." *Viator* 10 (1979): 257–281.

———. "Prostitution in Medieval Montpellier: The Ladies of Campus Polverel." *Medieval Prosopography* 18 (1997): 209–228.

———. "Le rôle de Montpellier dans le commerce des draps de laine avant 1350." *Annales du Midi* 94 (1982): 17–24.

———. *Society, Law, and Trade in Medieval Montpellier.* Aldershot, England, 1995.

Rogozinski, Jan. *Power, Caste, and Law: Social Conflict in Fourteenth-Century Montpellier.* Cambridge, MA, 1982.

Romano, David. "La transmission des sciences arabes par les Juifs en Languedoc." *CF* 12 (1977): 363–386.

Rosaldo, Renato. "From the Door of His Tent: The Fieldworker and the Inquisitor." In *Writing Culture: The Poetics and Politics of Ethnography*, ed. James Clifford and George E. Marcus, 77–97. Berkeley, 1986.

Russell, J. C. "L'évolution démographique de Montpellier au moyen âge." *Annales du Midi* 74 (1962): 345–360.

Saint-Quirin [Arthur de Cazenove]. *Les verriers de Languedoc.* Montpellier, 1904.

Sarraute, Antoine. *Le Logis de l'Inquisition: Maison historique.* Toulouse, 1914.

Schmucki, O., ed. *L'Ordine della Penitenza di san Francesco d'Assisi nel sec. XIII.* Rome, 1973.

Schwartz, Orit, and Robert E. Lerner. "Illuminated Propaganda: The Origins of the 'Ascende calve' Pope Prophecies." *Journal of Medieval History* 20 (1994): 157–191.

Scott, James C. *Domination and the Arts of Resistance: Hidden Transcripts.* New Haven, 1990.

———. *Weapons of the Weak: Everyday Forms of Peasant Resistance.* New Haven, 1985.

Sensi, Mario. *Storie di bizzoche tra Umbria e Marche.* Rome, 1995.

Shatzmiller, Joseph. "Contacts et échanges entre savants juifs et chrétiens à Montpellier vers 1300." *CF* 12 (1977): 337–344.

———. "In Search of the 'Book of Figures': Medicine and Astrology in Montpellier at the Turn of the Fourteenth Century." *Association for Jewish Studies Review* 7/8 (1982/1983): 383–407.

Simons, Walter. *Cities of Ladies: Beguine Communities in the Medieval Low Countries, 1200–1565.* Philadelphia, 2001.

Siraisi, Nancy. *Medieval and Early Renaissance Medicine: An Introduction to Knowledge and Practice.* Chicago, 1990.

Smail, Daniel Lord. *Imaginary Cartographies: Possession and Identity in Late Medieval Marseille.* Ithaca, 1999.

Smith, Lacey Baldwin. *Fools, Martyrs, Traitors: The Story of Martyrdom in the Western World.* New York, 1997.

Sournia, Bernard, and Jean-Louis Vayssettes. *Montpellier: La demeure médiévale.* Paris, 1991.

Stewart, Robert M. *"De illis qui faciunt penitentiam." The Rule of the Secular Franciscan Order: Origins, Development, Interpretation.* Rome, 1991.

Strayer, Joseph R. *The Albigensian Crusades.* New York, 1971. New ed. with an epilogue by Carol Lansing. Ann Arbor, 1992.

——. "Consent to Taxation under Philip the Fair." In *Studies in Early French Taxation,* ed. Joseph R. Strayer and Charles H. Taylor, 3–105. Cambridge, MA, 1939.

——. *Les gens du justice du Languedoc sous Philippe le Bel.* Toulouse, 1970.

——. *The Reign of Philip the Fair.* Princeton, 1980.

Tabarroni, Andrea. *Paupertas Christi et Apostolorum: L'ideale francescano in discussione (1322–1324).* Rome, 1990.

Thomas, L.-J. "La population du Bas-Languedoc à la fin du XIIIe siècle et au commencement du XIVe." *Annales du Midi* 20 (1908): 469–487.

Thomson, John A. F. *The Later Lollards, 1414–1520.* Oxford, 1965.

Tissier, J. "Les sources de l'histoire de Languedoc d'après les inventaires des archives narbonnaises." *Bulletin de la Commission archéologique de Narbonne* 11 (1911): 25–26.

Troncarelli, Fabio. "Pietro Trencavelli, visconte di Carcassonne." *Quaderni medievali* 47 (1999): 14–40.

Truhlár, Joseph. *Catalogus Codicum Manuscriptorum Latinorum.* Prague, 1905.

Turley, Thomas. "John XXII and the Franciscans: A Reappraisal." In *Popes, Teachers, and Canon Law in the Middle Ages,* ed. James Ross Sweeney and Stanley Chodorow, 74–88. Ithaca, 1989.

Valois, Noël. "Jacques Duèse, pape sous le nom de Jean XXII." *Hist. Litt.* 34 (1914): 391–630.

Vauchez, André. *La sainteté en occident aux derniers siècles du moyen âge,* 2nd ed. Rome, 1988.

Vidal, J.-M. "Un ascète de sang royal, Philippe de Majorque." *Revue des questions historiques* 88 (1910): 360–403.

——. "Menet de Robécourt, commissaire de l'Inquisition de Carcassonne (1320–1340)." *Le Moyen Âge* 16 (1903): 425–449.

Villemagne, L'abbé A. *Histoire de Teyran.* Montpellier, 1913. Reprinted Paris, 1990.

Von Auw, Lydia. "Angelo Clareno et les Spirituels." *CF* 10 (1975): 243–262.

——. *Angelo Clareno et les spirituels italiens.* Rome, 1979.

Wakefield, Walter. *Heresy, Crusade, and Inquisition.* London, 1974.

Wallis, Faith. "Chronology and Systems of Dating." In *Medieval Latin: An Introduction and Bibliographical Guide,* ed. F. A. C. Mantello and A. G. Rigg, 383–387. Washington, DC, 1996.

Weinstein, Donald, and Rudolph M. Bell. *Saints and Society: The Two Worlds of Western Christendom, 1000–1700.* Chicago, 1982.

Weis, René. *The Yellow Cross: The Story of the Last Cathars' Rebellion against the Inquisition (1290–1329).* New York, 2002.

Zerner, Monique, ed. *Inventer l'hérésie? Discours polémiques et pouvoirs avant l'inquisition. Collection du Centre d'Études Médiévales de Nice,* vol. 2. Nice, 1998.

INDEX

Alaraxis (companion of Prous Boneta),
    143–44, 154
Alaraxis Biasse, 167–68
Albigensian Crusade, 25–27, 53
Alexander of Alessandria, 40, 175
Alisseta Boneta, 143–44, 154, 159
Ames, Christine Caldwell, 56–57
Amoda Sepian, 166
Andrea Trencavel, 90, 172–76
angel: Olivi as, 149–52
Angelo Clareno, 7–8, 24, 36n104,
    42–45, 163
apocalypticism: of Beguins, 2–3, 34–40,
    50, 63–64, 80–81, 104–5, 150–51; and
    Francis, 19; of Franciscans, 12, 39–40;
    of Olivi, 17–20, 36–40, 50, 62–64; and
    poverty, 18–19, 34
Arnaud Amaury, 26
Arnau de Vilanova, 36, 138, 150–51, 159
Arnold, John, 58–59
Ascende calve prophecies, 186
Astruga, 77–78, 85
Avignon: Beguins in, 88–89, 164

Bartholomeu Adalbert, 125
Beguines, 2, 33
Beguin Martyrology, 6, 66n41, 82–84,
    138n12
Beguins: apocalypticism of, 2–3, 34–40, 50,
    63–64, 80–81, 104–5, 150–51; burnings
    of, 71, 74–75, 77–85, 168–69; clothing
    of, 35, 66, 73; communities of, 59–60,
    67–70, 72–73, 113, 131–33; and Francis,
    38; and Franciscans, 3, 9, 32–33, 66–67,
    127–28, 132–33, 136–37; as fugitives,
    88–90, 166–68, 173–75; as heretics,
    2–3, 34–37, 48–50, 65, 134–35, 187–88;
    and inquisitors, 53, 56, 64–67, 73–74,
    115–16, 164–65, 176–77, 187–88; and
    John XXII, 49–50; leaders of, 135–36,
    160–61; martyrology of (*see* Beguin
    Martyrology); as martyrs, 51, 63–66, 71,

74–75, 78–85, 141–42, 158–59, 169,
    182–83; meetings of, 61–63, 67–69;
    and Olivi, 20–24, 34–35, 61–62; and
    penitence, 30–31, 34; pilgrimages of,
    89–91, 124–25; and poverty, 3–4, 38–39,
    73, 103–4; and priests, 86–88; relics of,
    64–65, 78–79, 181–82; prophecies of,
    186; resistance by, 51–52, 67–69, 131–32,
    158, 165–67, 181–82; terminology for,
    2, 30, 33–34; as visionaries, 149–53;
    women as, 34n97, 138–39. *See also names
    of individual Beguins*
Bell, Rudolph, 145n31
Benedict XII, Pope, 56, 60, 125
Berengaria Donas, 167
Berengaria Veyrier, 174–75
Berenguier Hulard, 90
Berenguier Jaoul, 74–75, 77
Berenguier Rocha, 79
Bernard, Suzanne, 180n4
Bernarda d'Antusan, 59–61, 64–66, 69–70
Bernard Aspa, 48
Bernard Baron, 65
Bernard Castillon, 103–4, 107–8
Bernard Clergue, 125, 156n99
Bernard d'Alzonne, 185
Bernard de Bordelas, 128–30
Bernard de Bosc, 170
Bernard Délicieux: and inquisitors, 9n6, 30,
    43–44, 181, 186
Bernard de Na Jacma, 66–69
Bernard Durban, 74, 78
Bernard Gui: on Beguins, 35–40, 60–61,
    81, 165, 187–88; as inquisitor, 29–30,
    55–57, 69, 134; on Olivi, 21n47, 23–24
Bernard Malaura, 75, 78–79
Bernard Maury, 85–87, 90–92, 171–74
Bernard Peyrotas, 75, 79, 81, 87, 106
Béziers: Beguins in, 9, 91; siege of, 26–27
Biget, Jean-Louis, 23n50
Bonaventure, Saint, 12–13, 19, 32
Boneta, Prous. *See* Prous Boneta

Bruschi, Caterina, 58
burning: of Beguins, 71, 74–75, 77–85,
    168–69, 183; as spectacle, 76–77,
    80–81
Burr, David, 12n12, 17–18, 39, 115, 136,
    151n75, 169n141, 181
Bylina, Stanislaw, 85
Bynum, Caroline Walker, 145n31, 148n47

Carcassonne: prison in, 156–57, 170–71
Cathars: and inquisition, 27–28, 53, 78, 98;
    in Languedoc, 24–27, 170
Cazelas, Sibillia. See Sibillia Cazelas
Celestine V, Pope, 8
Charles II, King of Naples, 34–35
Charles of Anjou, 88
Church: Beguins on, 68, 80–81, 115–16;
    Olivi on, 19–20, 37, 39
Christ: poverty of, 13, 73; in visions,
    147–48, 151–52
Cintegabelle: Beguins in, 59–60, 67–70,
    164
Clement V, Pope, 15n25, 40, 163
Clement VI, Pope, 117
Clermont l'Hérault: Beguins in, 72–73
clothing: of Beguins, 35, 66, 73; of
    Franciscans, 14–15, 38, 41, 46, 73, 87
confessions. See documentation
Conventuals. See Franciscans
Coulton, G. G., 180
Crescentius of Iesi, 15n23
Cum inter nonnullos, 10n9, 38, 152n82

Délicieux, Bernard. See Bernard Délicieux
Denifle, Henri, 47n136
Deodat Miquel, 48
documentation: and historiography, 56–59,
    99–100; by inquisitors, 28, 54–56, 187;
    of martyrs, 81–85
Dominic, Saint, 27
Dominicans: as inquisitors, 27–29, 165
Duran Bonet, 143
Durban, Esclarmonda. See Esclarmonda
    Durban

Eco, Umberto, 56, 179–80
Ermessendis Grossa, 121–24, 156
Esclarmonda Durban, 71, 77–79, 85,
    134–35
Esteve Gramat, 91, 110, 174
Esteve Trucha, 117–18
Evans, Austin P., 186
Exiit qui seminat, 13–14, 38
Exivi de Paradiso, 8

Favier, Jean, 29–30
Fidei catholicae fundamento, 8n5
Flood, David, 17
Francesco de Arquata, 182–83
Frances Sans, 44
Francis, Saint: and apocalypticism, 19,
    26–27; and Beguins, 152; on penitence,
    31; poverty of, 10–15, 19; sanctity of, 23
Franciscans: apocalypticism of, 12, 39–40;
    and Beguins, 3, 9, 32–33, 66–67, 87–88,
    127–28, 132–33, 136–37, 152; behavior
    of, 137–38; communities of, 16n27;
    factions among, 8; 12–14, 39–42, 91;
    habits of, 14–15, 38, 41, 46, 73, 87; as
    heretics, 47–49; imprisonment of, 45–46,
    184; and inquisitors, 47–48, 132, 184–86;
    and John XXII, 34, 41–47, 49, 128; and
    Olivi, 16–17, 137–38; and penitence,
    30–32; and poverty, 10–15, 38, 46–48, 73,
    128; resistance by, 51–53, 184–86; and
    Rule of 1289, 31–33, 52; Third Order of
    (see Beguins); as visionaries, 152–53
Friedlander, Alan, 27n71, 181

Gaucelina, Lady, 130
General Sermons: as spectacle, 76–77,
    80–81
Geoffroi de Cournon, 44
Gignac: Beguins in, 121–22
Giono, Jean, 90
Giovanni Godulchi, 182–83
Given, James, 25n25, 51–54, 76, 80
Greene, Graham, 136
Gregory IX, Pope, 11, 27
Grundmann, Herbert, 147n42
Gui, Bernard. See Bernard Gui
Guiard de Cressonessart, 149–50
Guilhem Ademar, 157, 161
Guilhem Agasse, 56
Guilhem Astre, 91–92, 127
Guilhem Bélibaste, 170
Guilhem de Johan, 53n6, 172
Guilhem de Saint Amans, 44, 86, 91
Guilhem de Salvella, 132
Guilhem Domergue Veyrier, 84, 109,
    157–58, 161, 173–75
Guilhem Guiraut, 155n94
Guilhem Ros, 67–68, 70
Guilhem Santon, 48
Guilhem Serallier, 80, 84, 109–10, 158,
    161, 174
Guillerma Berengaria Tyeura, 168
Guillerma Civile, 157
Gui Terré, 18, 47n136

Na Prous Boneta. *See* Prous Boneta
Narbonne: Beguins in, 7–8, 86–88,
    162–65
Newman, Barbara, 161n116
Nicholas III, Pope, 13–14
Nicholas IV, Pope, 31–32, 52
Nicholas V, Pope, 186n21
Nicolau Eymeric, 24

Occitan: in confessions, 55
Olivi, Petrus Johannis. *See* Peter Olivi
Ordinem vestrum, 11

papal bulls. *See under individual titles*
Papka, Claudia Rattazzi, 80n88
Pazzelli, R., 31n87
Pegg, Mark, 57–58
Peire Arrufat, 69–70, 77, 79, 166–69
Peire Calvet, 63, 65, 164
Peire Civile, 157
Peire de Na Bruna, 52n2, 136
Peire de Tornamira, 100–104, 111–12,
    117–18, 154, 161; and inquisitors,
    105–6, 112–17
Peire Domergue, 81–82
Peire Esperendiu, 87
Peire Gastaud, 83
Peire Guiraut, 82, 121, 134
Peire Julian, 45n128, 132
Peire Tort, 69–70, 169
Peire Trencavel, 69, 89–91, 110, 139; as
    fugitive, 169–76; as leader, 161–69, 177;
    and Olivi, 171–72
penitence: and Franciscans, 30–31
Peter Olivi: as angel, 149–52; apoca-
    lypticism of, 2–3, 17–20, 36–40, 50,
    62–64, 80–81, 150; career of, 16–17;
    cult of (*see* Beguins); death of, 20–21;
    feast of, 7–8, 23, 112, 144; and heresy, 41,
    135–46; and inquisitors, 23–24; name of,
    16; popularity of, 2, 7–9; on poverty, 14,
    18–19, 33–35, 38; sanctity of, 2, 21–24,
    49, 62–63, 105, 145; on siege of Béziers,
    26–27; as visionary, 149–52; writings of,
    21n47, 60–62, 67–68, 76, 112, 137–38,
    153, 171–72, 176
Philip IV, King of France ("the Fair"),
    29–30
Philip of Majorca, 103
Pierre Scarrier, 34
Piron, Sylvain, 16n26, 48n138
Pons Bautugat, 45–46
Pons Roca, 48
Potesta, Gian Luca, 43n122

poverty: and apocalypticism, 18–19, 34;
    of Christ, 10–11, 13; and Franciscans,
    10–15, 38, 46–48, 73; John XXII on, 46;
    Olivi on, 14, 18–19, 34–35, 38
Prades Tavernier, 170
prisons: conditions in, 156–57
propaganda: burning as, 80–81
prophecy, 186
Prous Boneta, 3, 23, 84, 122–23, 127;
    family of, 143–44, 160–61; incarceration
    of, 156–57; as leader, 145–47, 154–57,
    160–61, 176–77; as martyr, 140–42,
    158–59; as visionary, 147–54
Provence: Beguins in, 88–89

Quanto studiosius, 11
Quia sapientia, 97n8
Quo elongati, 11, 27
Quorumdam exigit, 38, 46–47, 73, 105,
    183–85

Raimon Amiel, 104n30
Raimon Barrau, 8–9
Raimon Cambos, 107
Raimon d'Antusan, 59–61, 64–66, 69–70,
    79–80, 166, 168
Raimon de Bordelas, 128–29
Raimon de Buxo, 66–67, 85
Raimon de Johan, 110–11, 116, 136, 154,
    168n135
Raimond de Fronsac, 44n126
Raimon Durban, 78–79
Raimon Rouvier, 127
Rashdall, Hastings, 97n8
Reeves, Marjorie, 142n20
registers. *See* documentation
relics: of Beguin martyrs, 64–65, 78–81;
    and sanctity, 22n48
resistance: to inquisitors, 51–53, 67–69,
    158, 165–67, 183–84
Revelation: Olivi on, 19–20, 26–27, 64,
    150; and visionaries, 149–50
Reyerson, Kathryn, 100, 107
Ruggiero, Guido, 59

Sancta romana, 49, 104
sanctity: and Beguins, 64–66, 80–85,
    168–69; of Olivi, 2, 22–23; of women,
    145n31
Schwartz, Orit, 186n21
Scott, James C., 53
Sibillia Cazelas, 121–24, 126–27, 146,
    155–56
Smith, Lacey Baldwin, 84

Spirituals. *See* Franciscans
stake. *See* burning
Strayer, Joseph, 29
Supra montem, 31–32, 52

testimony. *See* documentation
Third Order of Franciscans. *See* Beguins
Thomas of Celano, 10
Tornamira, Peire de. *See* Peire de Tornamira
Tornamira family, 101–2, 117–18
torture: by inquisitors, 56
Trencavel, Peire. *See* Peire Trencavel
Troncarelli, Fabio, 171n148, 175

Ubertino da Casale, 151–52

Vidal, Jean-Marie, 125
violence: and belief, 55–56; and resistance, 52–53
visionaries: Beguins as, 137–39, 149–52; women as, 149
von Auw, Lydia, 46n132

Wakefield, Walter, 186
Weinstein, Donald, 145n31
Wolfenbüttel Martyrology. *See* Beguin Martyrology
women: as Beguins, 34n97, 138–39; as leaders, 160–61; as martyrs, 158–59; sanctity of, 145n31; as visionaries, 149–52. *See also names of individuals*